HOW TO DO THINGS
WITH LOGIC

HOW TO DO THINGS
WITH LOGIC

C. Grant Luckhardt
William Bechtel
Georgia State University

 LAWRENCE ERLBAUM ASSOCIATES, PUBLISHERS
1994   Hillsdale, New Jersey   Hove, UK

Lawrence Erlbaum Associates, Inc., Publishers
365 Broadway
Hillsdale, New Jersey 07642

Cover design by Kate Dusza

Library of Congress Cataloging-in-Publication Data

Luckhardt, C. Grant, 1943-
    How to do things with logic / C. Grant Luckhardt and William
Bechtel.
        p.   cm.
    Includes bibliographical references and index.
    ISBN 0-8058-0075-1 (alk. paper). — ISBN 0-8058-0076-X
(pbk. : alk. paper)
    1. Reasoning. 2. Logic. I. Title.
    BC177.L83 1994
    160—dc20   93-34138
                                                         CIP

Books published by Lawrence Erlbaum Associates are printed on
acid-free paper, and their bindings are chosen for strength and dura-
bility.

Printed in the United States of America
10 9 8 7 6 5 4 3 2 1

Contents

Preface

The title, *How to Do Things with Logic*, encapsulates the conception of logic developed in this book. Our emphasis is on teaching students how they can use logic as a tool to accomplish their ends. This requires that they learn some formal logic. That is, they must understand the concept of *validity* and learn some valid forms of reasoning. These are developed in chapters 2 and 3. In this respect, chapter 3 is the core of the book. Instructors need to spend considerably more time on it than on other chapters. (In our experience, 3 weeks is minimal.) But students do not need to be taught the proof procedures of deductive logic. Instead, we teach students to link simple arguments together in diagrams so as to establish their conclusion. This technique is developed in chapter 6 and is used in subsequent chapters focusing on specialized forms of arguments. We do not recommend trying to cover the entire book in a term, especially if your institution is on the quarter system. Rather, instructors should choose those chapters later in the book that they find most interesting or most relevant for their students.

In the past 15 years a host of critical thinking books have appeared. This book is not in that tradition. In the critical thinking tradition, students learn to find flaws in the arguments of others. A major component of that activity is learning to detect a number of informal fallacies. Having taught such courses in the past we discovered that whereas students would learn to become vicious critics, they continued to commit the very mistakes they criticized in others. As a result, we have adopted the approach of teaching the construction of good arguments first and then introducing criticism as a secondary skill. Moreover, although we do cover informal fallacies in chapter 8, our emphasis is not on learning to name fallacies, but on being able to identify weaknesses in an argument so as to be able to construct an effective critique of that argument.

In our experience with students, we have found it useful to make a couple of simplifications that are not formally correct but allow students more readily to use logic. We have incorporated these into this book. First, to avoid teaching induction as a separate form of reasoning and then teaching students to assess the inductive warrant of an argument, we have adopted the strategy of making all inductive arguments formally valid. Thus, we add the necessary conditional premise to make an inductive argument into an instance of *modus ponens*, and then focus attention on the truth of the conditional premise. Second, to avoid developing a separate apparatus for evaluating categorical arguments, we (a) ignore *I* and *O* statements and (b) provide a procedure for translating *A* and *E* statements into conditional statements and then evaluating the categorical arguments employing them in terms of their corresponding sentential arguments. In order to handle arguments involving categorical claims and claims about individuals (e.g., *all successful people are industrious*, which we translate as *if someone is successful, then that person is industrious*, and *Cathy is successful*), we permit a violation of the principle that the second premise of a modus ponens argument must exactly match the antecedent. Thus, we permit *Cathy* to be substituted for *someone* without violating the fallacy of three terms. Third, we do not explicitly discuss subjunctive or other modal conditional statements, restricting ourselves to the material conditional. In developing their own writing or in choosing an essay to critique, students sometimes will introduce or encounter modal conditionals. Generally the logic of the material conditional suffices for analyzing their use of these statements, but very occasionally cases will arise for which the logic of the material conditional is insufficient. Instructors need to be aware of this potential, and be prepared to guide students around this possible problem.

From our experience, one of the most important crucial factors determining whether students succeed with the material of this text is practice. Logical reasoning is a tool that needs to become automatic for the students, not an object of conscious awareness. This can only be achieved by extensive practice. This is particularly true of the sentential argument forms developed in chapter 3. In the end it is far less important that the students remember such names as *modus ponens* and *affirming the consequent* than that they know how to construct arguments of the first form and know how to demonstrate the error of arguments of the second form. For students who have not had experiences requiring them to pay careful attention to formal structure, extensive practice is needed. The *Exercise Book to Accompany How to Do Things with Logic* provides numerous exercises to help students acquire the material. These exercises, however, need to be supplemented by additional exercises introduced by the instructor in class. Sometimes it may help to pass out answer sheets for selected exercises. Moreover, we have found it useful to employ computer-aided instruction in teaching some of the basic material such as the valid and invalid argument forms.

C. Grant Luckhardt
William Bechtel

Acknowledgments

Many people and institutions have helped us in the development of this book. We are extremely grateful to Georgia State University for its research and writing support. We also thank the many colleagues and instructors who have provided us with suggestions, sometimes on the basis of using preliminary versions of this book in their courses. Among those who have provided important feedback and suggestions are Adele Abrahamsen, Linda Bell, John Beversluis, David Blumenfeld, Frank Ryan, Douglas Seanor, and Milton Snoeyenbos. Additionally, two chapters borrowed material written by Abrahamsen (chapter 1) and Snoeyenbos (chapter 6) when they taught *Logic and Critical Thinking* at Georgia State University. Last, but not least, we thank the many students in that course who used various manuscript versions of the text and exercise book. Their difficulties and successes continuously challenged us to find better ways to teach logic. We hope we have succeeded.

1

Logic as a Tool

THE USES OF LOGIC

One of the most natural questions that occurs to students beginning a logic course is, "Why should I be logical?" Often this question is accompanied by the feeling that being logical is something that others *require* of one—they are trying to force you to think in certain ways. A natural reaction is to resist this force, or at least to question it. Unfortunately, when asked in this way, the question "Why should I be logical?" is also often answered as if force, or compulsion, *were* the real issue: "The reason you *must* be logical is that. . . ."

This book looks at logic in a quite different way. The fundamental question is not, "Why must I be logical?", but "What can I achieve by using logic?" The focus is not on forcing you to do anything, but in providing you with some tools for achieving what you already want to do but want to do well. Aristotle, the founder of logic, wrote several books on the topic that were later collected and called *The Organon. Organon* is the Greek word for tool, and it is the purpose of this book to provide you with these tools. Hence the book's title.

"Tools for what?" The answer is complex, for logic can be put to many uses. But we can start with an example. Perhaps one day at work you hear that your company is starting a new division to produce a new product. You have a great deal of experience with that product and you also have a number of ideas about how to manufacture it in an efficient way that insures high quality. Moreover, you have been looking for an opportunity for a promotion, and the possibility of becoming the manager of the division that will be responsible for producing the new product is very attractive to you. You feel confident that you have sufficient background and the abilities required to perform well in that position.

How should you go after that position? One strategy would be simply to wait and see if you are chosen. But you realize that good people are often passed over for positions because those making the appointment are not aware of their abilities. You decide you must be assertive. You happen to run into your company president as you are leaving work. Feeling bold, you tell the president you have heard of the

1

expansion plans, that you have experience with the product and ideas about producing it, and so you think you are the person to head up the new division.

The president seems impressed with your self-confidence, but doesn't offer you the position on the spot. Instead the president tells you the company is actively searching for the right candidate, and requests that you present the reasons to hire you in a memo.

Your boldness has given you an entrance, but now you must make the case—in writing—that the company should hire you. Here is one context in which you can use logic. You need to convince the president that you are the best qualified. That is, you must offer convincing *reasons*. In logic, we refer to this as making an *argument*. We call the reasons you put forward the *premises* of the argument. The claim you are trying to convince someone to believe is referred to as the *conclusion*. Your conclusion is obvious. You must argue that:

> I should be hired as the manager of the new division responsible for the production of the new product.

The question is, what kind of premises will provide the most effective argument for this conclusion? In this book we examine the process of developing such arguments.

Logic alone won't qualify you for the job you seek. You may not have the abilities to handle the job, or others may perceive flaws in what you think are good ideas about how to manufacture the product. Moreover, the president may find other candidates who are better qualified, or may have already reserved the position for a nephew. Logic cannot help with these matters. What it can do is enable you to present the best possible case for yourself. That is, it can help you present your abilities and your ideas in the memo the president has requested in the most compelling manner. Moreover, this task is an extremely important one. You may be the best candidate for the position. But if you do not present your case effectively, your qualifications and good ideas may count for nothing.

Presenting your case for a goal, such as being promoted, is not the only use of logic. Consider the position the president will be in after receiving your memo. The president will probably have identified other possible candidates, or have received other applications for managing the new division. Assuming a decision has not been made to bestow the position on a nephew, the president must now decide whom to select. The president can analyze the position and what skills will be needed to succeed in it. The president can also analyze the plans different candidates put forward for managing the division. In the process, the president needs to rely on logic. The president must determine what abilities and what plans are most suitable for the position, and then determine who comes closest to satisfying these conditions.

As president, this person may not need to justify the decision regarding who is hired to anyone else. But the president may decide to turn the preparation for the decision over to someone else, perhaps the vice president for manufacturing. Because the new manager will have to report to this vice president, the president asks the vice president to make a recommendation. The president, however, reserves the right to make the final decision. Now the vice president has a need for logic. The vice president must use logic not only to decide whom to recommend, but also to justify the recommendation to the president. In a sense, the vice president is in a position comparable to your own. The vice president does not stand to benefit directly by getting the position, but must rely on logic to ensure the proper person is hired as manager. Moreover, the vice president's reputation as an executive is partly dependent on the ability to succeed in tasks like these. Only if the vice president is able to use logic effectively and make the case for the recommendations will those in higher positions listen to and accept any advice. And only if these recommendations are heard and accepted will the vice president accomplish the sorts of things as vice president that will justify retaining this position or acquiring another one.

The two uses of logic we have focused on here—coming to a conclusion about what to do, and arguing on behalf of a conclusion so as to convince others—are frequently useful. Because we have started with business life, let us consider some other common circumstances people confront regularly in their business pursuits. Your company may need to buy new equipment, and you are asked to develop a recommendation. You analyze the needs of the company, the strengths and weaknesses of the competing brands, and determine which model your company should buy. Here you use logic to make a decision. But now you must convince your supervisors that you have made the best decision. Sometimes you aren't asked to make an evaluation, but you identify a problem, consider possible solutions, and arrive at what you think is the best one. The problem might have to do with inefficiency in company management, or failure to market your products as well as they should be. You have arrived at a recommendation, and now you must convince your superiors. Your superiors are only likely to adopt your recommendation and also note your talents if you can argue effectively on behalf of your proposal.

These same skills carry over to our personal lives as well. Consider three common situations. First, you want to go to a movie and, after reviewing what is playing, decide which best suits your interest. You also want your friend to go with you, so now you need to present reasons to convince that person to go. Second, you have been given a traffic ticket that you think is unjust (the stop sign was covered by shrubbery and so was not visible). After considering whether it is worth fighting the ticket, you elect to go to court to contest it. But not wanting to pay a lawyer, you decide to present your case to the judge yourself. You must now argue the case, giving the reasons why the ticket was unjust and you should not be convicted. Third, you go shopping for a new television. You look at various models and select one that has the features you want. The salesperson tells you that the only one the store has is the display model. You still want it, but you feel you shouldn't have to pay full price. You must now offer an argument to the salesperson, or perhaps to the sales supervisor, explaining why you should pay a lower price. People who can argue effectively in these sorts of circumstances are more likely to achieve their ends than someone whose command of logical argument is weak.

Our civic life is also built on the use of argument. Some societies have been governed exclusively by power. Those who hold power subjugate the others and impose their wishes on the subjects. But such forms of government appear unstable and are, arguably, unjust. We enjoy a different form of government—one in which the power of persuasion is important. Although political persuasion often depends on such other factors as charisma, physical appearance, and even well-modulated speech, in many cases it is the quality of the arguments that carries the day. Thus, to achieve ends that you think are right or just, you need to be able to make arguments. Some of these arguments occur in the great deliberative bodies of government where most of us have only very remote influence. But a great many of the governmental decisions that affect us are made at much lower levels, ones at which the ordinary citizen can have influence. This influence may involve a personal appearance before a city or county council, or it may take the form of a letter to the editor of a local paper. Some people use these occasions just to state their opinions. Whereas this may influence lawmakers, especially if it is apparent that a large number of citizens hold the same opinion, mere statements of opinion are hardly as effective as those with well-developed reasons supporting them. Such arguments (reasons supporting a conclusion) have the potential of influencing others, especially those currently undecided on the issue, to share your opinion.

AN EXAMPLE ARGUMENT

To get more of the flavor of argument, and to introduce some of the important strategies of argument, consider an example of argument used in civic life. The following is an example that might have been written for the opinion page of a local newspaper, or presented as a letter to the person's representative on the city council, or prepared simply as a project in a class such as the one you are now taking. It is the sort of argument this book will teach you to construct.

Mytown Needs Voluntary Curbside Recycling

Our nation's landfills are quickly running out of space. We read stories in the newspapers about the impending catastrophe that we face in disposing of garbage. But we also are discovering a solution that works: More and more people are sorting out glass bottles, plastic jugs, and newspaper and preparing these for recycling. These efforts must be encouraged and expanded. What is needed now is a citywide program of voluntary curbside recycling for glass, plastic, and newspaper. There is legislation currently pending in the city council for this program. I argue that because it will not only help solve a civic problem, but will achieve high levels of citizen participation and can be done for very little cost, the program of voluntary curbside recycling ought to be implemented in Mytown. I also examine some of the objections that might be made to my argument and show how these can be answered.

One should always be cautious in advocating new government-sponsored programs. Budgets are tight, and we know of many programs that simply have not worked. But there are circumstances in which it makes sense for the government to implement new programs. Essentially a new program should be undertaken when three conditions are met. First, the program addresses a civic problem. A civic problem is one that affects the safety, public health, and basic welfare of citizens generally. Other problems are properly left to individual initiatives, but it is to deal with problems of this character that we have governments. Second, the program is one with which the citizens will cooperate. It is futile to set up programs that citizens will reject or obstruct; when, on the other hand, programs are designed with which they will cooperate, then civic problems can be solved. Finally, the program is cost efficient. Our government simply does not have much money and so is obliged to insist that new programs require very little new public money. Consequently, in arguing for a new program of curbside recycling, three things must be shown: that it will help solve a civic problem, that citizens will participate in it, and that it can be accomplished for very little cost. If we can establish that it meets each of these requirements, the program should be approved. I show how it satisfies each of these in turn.

First, there can be little doubt that human garbage constitutes a civic problem and recycling can be a significant help in solving that problem. Garbage pick-up and disposal has been a long-standing activity of local governments. The reasons are linked to public health. Leaving the disposal of garbage to individual citizens is likely to lead to improper disposal and the potential for increased transmission of disease. But traditional means of disposing of garbage are now creating public health problems of their own. Burning garbage generates harmful gases that can both generate health problems, such as cancer, and damage the environment. Dumping of garbage in landfills requires the availability of sites in which the garbage won't end up contaminating the environment by, for example, leaking into the water supply. Good landfill sites are difficult to come by and those now in use are rapidly filling up. The director of our city's department of waste management estimates that a present rates, our landfill will reach maximum capacity within 4 years. So we face a major civic problem. Recycling of glass, plastics, and newspaper can help significantly in dealing with this problem. A major part of our landfill space is consumed by disposing of these products. So, with them removed, we can extend the useful life of our current landfill by several years.

The second requirement is that citizens be willing to cooperate with the program. If a significant number of people are already participating in recycling, and if surveys indicate that more than half of the citizens would participate voluntarily if they did not have to seek out a recycling center on their own, then we can infer that citizens are willing to cooperate with this program. A number of citizens are already engaging in recycling. They collect bottles, plastic jugs, and newspapers, and transport them to recycling centers on their own. Although the number participating is significant, it still is not large. That, however, is not surprising given the effort it now takes to participate. Citizens must identify a recycling center, which may be several miles from their home, save up the materials for recycling, and then drive them to the site. Their participation reveals a basic willingness of people to do what is necessary to solve the garbage disposal problem. But more revealing for our purposes are the responses of citizens of Mytown to a recent survey. The survey was included with the last city tax bill with an envelope to be mailed in separately and anonymously, and better than 60% of taxpayers responded. That is an extremely high response rate to any survey.

Of those responding, 62% indicate they would be willing to participate in a voluntary program of separating glass, plastic, and newspaper, and putting these at the curbside each week for pick-up. Thus, we can reasonably expect a majority of the citizens to participate in this program.

Finally, the program can be accomplished for minimal cost. Costs will be very low if two conditions are satisfied: If there is a market for recycled materials, and collecting and transporting the additional materials will not significantly increase pick-up times. Both of these conditions are met. There is now a sizeable and expanding market for recycled glass, plastic, and newspaper. Manufacturers have discovered that people are quite willing to buy products made of recycled materials. As a result, a number of companies have been created to perform the recycling. They need a constant supply of used glass, plastic, and newspaper, and are willing to pay communities who will contract to supply these to them. Second, there are private companies willing to do the collection of glass, plastic, and newspaper from curbsides. One company, Waste Material Collection Company, will agree to a contract stipulating that if they are able to collect sufficient amounts of the products, they will not charge the city, but settle for whatever they can sell the materials for. Only if collections fall below these levels is there a charge to the city. But given the citizens' response to the survey, collections should not fall below their minimums. Other contractors may even be willing to split profits from the sale of the recyclable material. There will always be slight overhead costs in supervising these contracts, but the city will save money it now spends on disposing these materials in landfills. Thus, the program can be accomplished for minimal costs, and probably can be carried out for less money than is currently expended on disposing of this material in our landfill.

I have shown that all the conditions for setting up a new city program are met. Opponents of recycling, however, are likely to raise some objections to this argument. They are likely to question both the claim that citizens will participate, and that the program can be carried out at little or no new cost to the city. With respect to the first point, they will argue that surveys indicating that people will participate in recycling are meaningless. They will contend that it is easy for people to say they will participate when in fact they never will. In fact they argue that there is pressure for people to say they will participate, for saying *no* may make people appear unpatriotic. Moreover, they will point to examples like Thattown, which started a recycling program 8 years ago, but abandoned it for lack of participation. Second, they will argue that opportunities for selling collected glass, plastic, and newspaper are exaggerated. Othercity, for example, started a recycling program, but later had to dispose of the glass and newspaper it collected in its regular landfill because it was unable to find anyone who would take it. In addition, critics will claim that contracts with private recyclers are always more expensive than they seem. Compliance with the contract will have to be monitored to insure that the contractor does not actually collect more material than it says it does.

These criticisms, however, are easily answered. Although many times people may report one thing on surveys and do something else, there are reasons to believe that this survey, if anything, underestimates the response rate. Cities that have conducted such surveys before starting recycling have found that within a few months of the beginning of the program more people participate than indicated they would. Many citizens seem to be inspired by the fact that their neighbors are acting responsibly, and so they join in. The fear of appearing unpatriotic actually seems to have more effect in increasing participation rates once recycling has begun. The example of Thattown is really quite misleading. They started their program 8 years ago, before consciousness about the need for recycling was raised. Moreover, Thattown imposed a mandatory recycling program, which aroused antagonism from the beginning. A voluntary recycling program will not generate the antipathy of the citizens. The criticisms of my analysis of cost are equally unfounded. In the early days of recycling it is true that there was little market for the materials collected. Today, however, there are companies advertising to buy glass, plastic, and newspaper. Moreover, the anticipated problems concerning contracts with private recyclers are unlikely to be realized. Waste Material Collection Company, for example, has contracts with many other cities like ours, including Nexttown. I have contacted the responsible city agents in Nexttown and several of the other cities, and they have had no problem with this company. The company has never charged any of them for failure to collect sufficient materials and they have never imposed additional charges beyond that in the original contract.

The case for Mytown beginning a voluntary program for curbside recycling of glass, plastic, and newspaper is therefore very strong. The program meets the conditions for starting a new city program: There is a major civic need, the people will participate, and the cost will be minimal. Moreover, I have answered the most likely objections of the critics. The city council should approve such a program and initiate it.

DEMONSTRATION, CRITIQUE, AND DEFENSE

There is occasion to discuss many of the argumentative strategies employed in the previous essay in subsequent chapters. But there are some basic styles of argumentation exhibited in this example that we should distinguish and label at this point, for they provide the structure for our subsequent treatment. Much of the essay was directed to establishing the conclusion that Mytown should begin a program of curbside recycling. It did this by first establishing three conditions under which a new public program should be undertaken, and then showing that these conditions were met for the case of curbside recycling. Such arguments directed to establishing a conclusion we call *demonstrations*. In demonstrations, reasons or premises are advanced to show that a conclusion is true. Sometimes, however, you will find yourself in a situation in which you are given an argument that you do not find compelling. Then you will need to construct what we call a *critique*. A critique is an argument that shows that another argument is flawed. It does not do this by arguing against the conclusion (you can actually agree with the conclusion even when you critique the argument), but by arguing that the premises do not support the conclusion. In our example, the author considered how others might critique the argument. Specifically, the author considered objections directed toward the premise that citizens would participate and toward the premise that the program would result in few additional costs. The author then responded to these possible objections by employing what we call a *defense*. In a defense one shows that a critique directed against a demonstration is itself flawed. Thus, it shows that the original demonstration is still acceptable.

In practical uses of logic we frequently employ all three types of argumentative strategies. For example, suppose you are a sales representative for Glitch Computers, and your company has just one competitor, Crash Computers. Suppose also that in order to decide which computer to buy, the Cheery Cola Company invites both you and the sales representative for your competitor to make your sales presentations at a joint session.

First, a coin flip determines that you give the initial presentation. Your audience is the purchasing director, her assistant, and your competitor. There are so many reasons to buy a Glitch computer that you must select just a few of the strongest ones, and present them quite convincingly. Here you are making a demonstration that a Glitch computer is a good one. To cover all the bases, you also select from the multitude of reasons not to buy a Crash computer the most damaging ones, and present them politely but persuasively. You are here making a second demonstration, but now your conclusion is that Crash is not a good computer. You might also make some complimentary comments about Cheery Cola and incorporate a couple of good jokes; these nonlogical aspects of your presentation enhance its effectiveness, but your main tools of persuasion are your arguments.

Your presentation completed, you sit down and listen to your competitor give a demonstration that the Crash computer is a good one, as well as a demonstration that your Glitch computer is not good. The purchasing director now has a dilemma: Both of you have argued for opposing conclusions, and the decision will have to be made conerning which of you has made the better argument. That is, the director has to conclude that the right computer to buy is Glitch and not Crash, or else that it is Crash and not Glitch. (We suppose for the sake of argument that the director has decided against the alternatives of not buying either computer, and of buying a third brand.) You and your competitor both made some fairly convincing arguments, so the director requests that the two of you go another round.

Now you have to think fast. You could use your second turn to present additional premises in support of the conclusion that Cheery Cola should buy a Glitch computer or that it should not buy a Crash computer (that is, you could expand your demonstration), but you have already used your best direct arguments. Moreover, in doing this you will leave your competitor's demonstration unchallenged. A far better strategy would be to present a critique. This might involve arguing against the premises of your competitor's arguments (or as is discussed later, you might choose instead to focus on inadequacies in the form of the argument). For example, if one of the premises in your competitor's demonstration was that Crash computers are highly reliable, you might note that their previous model had an unusual number of dead-on-arrival (DOA) deliveries, rendering their reliability dubious. As another example, if one of the premises in the Crash computer demonstration was that Glitch computers use unsatisfactory technology (specifically, drives that use unreliable floppy disks) you might counter by noting that these old drives have been replaced in current models with the finest of hard drives, and this puts Glitch computers on the cutting edge of technology.

Suppose you construct a convincing critique using these and other arguments against your competitor's premises, and (unfortunately) your competitor does likewise against the premises of your demonstration. The purchasing director may now decide to permit yet one more round. But this time you are given very specific directions. You are not to present any more new arguments for buying your computer or for not buying your competitor's (that is, no more demonstrations), nor are you to challenge any additional arguments in your competitor's demonstration (that is, no more critiques). Rather, you are permitted simply to rebut any critiques your competitor has made of your initial demonstrations. That is, you are now permitted to offer a defense against your competitor's critique. Suppose that in the critique of your demonstration the Crash representative disputed your claim that Glitch computers have the most ergonomic mouse and the sharpest resolution monitors. In your defense you can now present evidence to show that this critique was flawed, and thus that your initial premises are still true. Your competitor could do likewise by noting that the hard drives you alluded to in your critique result in the loss of data, and that your critique is therefore flawed.

After this round is completed, the purchasing director will probably be anxious to end the session. Later the director will reflect on the various arguments and decide which conclusion has been best supported.

In differentiating these different types of arguments, one thing we should emphasize is that a critique is *an attack on an argument.* When you were trying to show that the Crash computer was bad, you were criticizing it, but you were not yet making a logical critique. That only happened when you argued against the premises that the Crash representative put forward. Notice also that when you have succeeded in critiquing an argument, you have only shown that the particular premises put forward by the arguer are not good reasons for accepting the conclusion. Whether the conclusion itself is true or false is still up for grabs. For example, suppose that your dentist is filling one of your cavities and asserts that Richard Nixon is the best president of the 20th century because he was responsible for getting the Civil Rights Act of 1964 passed. You are astonished at this very poor demonstration and grunt until the dentist takes the drill out of your mouth. You can then deliver your critique. Specifically, you challenge the premise of the demonstration by observing that it was Lyndon Johnson, not Richard Nixon, who helped pass the Civil Rights Act. This jogs a memory and your dentist admits that your critique is correct. But the dentist's original conclusion, that Richard Nixon is the best president of the 20th century, is still up for grabs. Your dentist may still want to argue for it and now offers the evidence that he opened up trade with China. In doing this the dentist is offering a new demonstration, not defending the earlier one. Your dentist has abandoned that argument.

This time you accept the premise and hence have no critique to offer. Instead, you go back to the starting point and present a demonstration that uses a new, unrelated premise to argue for the opposite conclusion: Because Nixon engaged in a coverup of the "dirty tricks" at Watergate, he is not the best president of the 20th century. To keep the conversation going, your dentist could either come back with a critique of your demonstration or offer a new demonstration.

The point of this example is not that it is futile to argue with a dentist, but rather to illustrate that a critique is not the same as a demonstration of the opposite conclusion. A successful critique shows only that a *premise* is false or does not adequately support the conclusion, whereas a successful demonstration of the opposite conclusion shows that the original *conclusion* is false. The critique removes some particular support for a conclusion (namely, that which was origi- nally offered), but it does not show that the conclusion itself is false. People often get confused about this. For example, a theist might offer a demonstration designed to show that there is a God. An atheist may successfully critique the demonstration, and then claim that this shows that there is no God. But the atheist's critique has done no such thing; it has merely shown that the original argument does not show that there is a God, but that leaves open the question of whether there is a God. If atheists wish to show that there is no God, they will have to present a separate line of argument—a demonstration—to support that conclusion.

In the remaining chapters you will learn how to construct simple arguments (chapters 2 and 3). These are the tools to be used in the more complicated forms of argument discussed in later chapters. In chapters 4, 5, and 6 you learn how to combine several arguments into longer, well-constructed demonstrations that are presented in English prose. In chapters 7, 8, and 9 you learn how to use a second round of argument to achieve an effective critique, and in chapter 10 you learn how to mount a well-supported defense. The final three chapters deal with special skills in argumentation: using authorities, arguing for explanations, and arguing from analogy.

2

The Nature of Arguments

In discussing the uses of logic in the last chapter we noted that argumentation is one of the areas in which logic can be useful. Subsequent chapters are devoted to the various forms of argumentation. But before we explore these different varieties, we need to look at the general nature of arguments, that is, what they are and what they are not, what their parts are and what it means to evaluate an argument.

Statements are the basic building blocks of arguments. A statement is a sentence (or part of a sentence) that is true or false. (We will speak of *true* and *false* as the *truth values* a statement might take.) A sentence may have a truth value, and hence be a statement even if we do not know whether it is true or false. For example, "Jupiter has rings" is a statement that is true, although we did not know this until the Voyager transmitted data during its recent fly-by. As a general rule of thumb, declarative sentences such as the following are statements:

> The moon is a bright yellow disc.

Questions, commands, and exclamations are not. Thus, the following are not statements:

> Will you help me study for my exam tonight?
> Get out of my way!
> Ah, for the good old days!

(There are some tough cases and exceptions that need not concern us; for example, does "No new taxes!" have a truth value and therefore qualify as a statement?) Some logicians define statements in terms of the meaning behind a sentence rather than the sentence itself; by that definition, "Es gibt eine Deutschland" is a German sentence expressing the same statement as the English sentence "There is one Germany" (which was true prior to 1945, then false, then true again as of October 3, 1990).

Note that a complex declarative sentence may include more than one statement. If two or more parts of a sentence each has its own truth value and are asserted, then there will be two or more statements. So, for example, there are three statements in "We should have a lottery, because there are too many idle dollars and too few idle people in this state." In recognizing component statements, however, you must insure that the parts are each being asserted. In the following sentence there is only one statement, the one about the meteorologist's belief:

The meteorologist believes it will snow tonight.

The words *it will snow tonight* were not asserted by the person making the statement. She, in fact, may think the meteorologist is wrong.

Compare these three sets of statements:

A. The picnic will be ruined.
B. It is going to rain. Therefore the picnic will be ruined.
C. If it rains, the picnic will be ruined. It is going to rain. Therefore, the picnic will be ruined.

Statement A is an assertion; someone who simply says "The picnic will be ruined" is claiming that it is true that the picnic will be ruined, but is providing no reason why you should accept that claim. It might seem to you that the claim is obviously true, but regardless of whether it is, it is merely an assertion. Set B makes the same claim, but here it is the conclusion of an argument that includes a premise as well. The premise ("It is going to rain.") is offered as a reason for accepting the conclusion ("The picnic will be ruined."). When joined with this premise, "The picnic will be ruined" is not a mere assertion but is the conclusion of an argument. However, with just these two statements as the building blocks, the argument lacks what we will call *validity*. Set C includes an additional premise that makes the argument logically valid. (We explore the notion of validity later in this chapter.)

ASSERTIONS: WHAT ARGUMENTS ARE NOT

The distinction between asserting a claim (as in A) and arguing for a claim (as in B and C) seems obvious enough, but in practice it is easy to forget. Often writers and speakers will pile assertion upon assertion, adding perhaps a few rhetorical appeals such as "as we all know to be true," or "and as anyone can see," and the effect can be that the audience actually feels it has been persuaded by a series of logically cogent arguments. Hitler was a master at this, using not only many of the rhetorical appeals at his disposal, but also the dramatic effects of lighting, music, candles, costumes, uniforms, and so on, to persuade his audience that what he was saying was true, all the while avoiding any semblance of argument. This practice of asserting without argument in fact has a long history. Socrates, the ancient Greek philosopher, spent his life challenging those who were unwilling to defend their beliefs with arguments. Similarly, St. Peter objected to religious believers who indulge in the practice of simply asserting their beliefs without benefit of argument, and he warned Christians in particular to be prepared to back up their beliefs with reasons in support of them—to be "ready always to give an answer to every man that asketh you a reason of the hope that is in you, with meekness and reverence" (I Peter 3:15).

We have defined an argument as a particular way of combining statements: One or more statements (the premises) are cited as logical reasons to accept the truth of another statement (the conclusion). Henceforth when the word *argument* is used in this book, it should always be understood in this logical sense alone. There are other more familiar senses of *argument* that are not intended here. When one has an argument with one's neighbor, for example, reasons may or may not be presented, the truth of a statement may or may not be at issue (one party to such arguments not wanting to establish anything as true, but just wanting to voice a complaint, or air a grievance, or announce some feelings, perhaps), and at least one of the parties is usually angry. Logical arguments, however, do not necessarily involve any anger or feelings of any kind. Indeed the feeling of anger in particular is often thought to cloud logical arguments, so that "Let's be logical about it" is sometimes said as a means of ridding the discussion of hostility.

Another detail of the definition of *argument* that should be noted is that an argument need not be a good one. We have said that in an argument premises are presented that are intended to support the truth of a conclusion. But we have not required that they do so, nor have we said how well they must do so in order to qualify as an argument. This of course opens the doors quite wide—not so wide as to allow assertions and threats to qualify as arguments, but wide enough to allow the following: "They had a bad winter in Alaska last year because the *zampogna* is an Italian bagpipe." This is, to be sure, an extreme example of what might be allowed under our definition of argument, because it is virtually impossible to imagine how a fact about bagpipes could have anything at all to do with Alaska's recent weather, much less be intended to support the claim that it was bad. But it is best at this point to err on the side of inclusiveness, and to count as an argument any set of statements in which the truth of one statement is *intended* to be supported by the other statement (or statements). We can leave aside for now the question of how strong or convincing the intended support actually is.

ARGUMENTS AND INDICATOR WORDS

How do we know whether one statement is being cited in support of another? Speakers and writers typically use indicator words. These make it clear that statements have been combined into a logical argument by marking the role of one or more of the statements. Because there are two different roles that statements can play in an argument, there are two types of indicator words. Premise indicator words tell you that the statement to which they are attached is a premise; for example, "*Because* Melinda sold the most mutual fund shares this year, she will get the promotion to vice president." The indicator word "because" explicitly marks "Melinda sold the most mutual fund shares this year" as the premise of an argument; from that you can infer that "she will get the promotion to vice president" (the only other statement) is the conclusion that the premise supports. Conclusion indicator words offer an alternative way to assign roles; for example, the same argument could be conveyed by "Melinda sold the most mutual fund shares this year; *thus* she will get the promotion to vice president." Occasionally both kinds of indicator words are used together to mark explicitly both the premise and conclusion: "*Inasmuch as* Melinda sold the most mutual fund shares this year, *one must conclude that* she will get the promotion to vice president." This approach may sound pedantic, and cannot even be used with most indicator words. (For example, you cannot say "Because Melinda sold the most mutual fund shares this year, thus she will get the promotion to vice president.")

The use of indicator words is an option that helps avoid ambiguity; it is not a requirement. The following sentence would most likely be properly understood as a premise followed by a conclusion even though there are no indicator words: "Melinda sold the most mutual fund shares this year; she will get the promotion to vice president." Most people hearing this sentence would know that top sales performance tends to be rewarded by a promotion, and would apply that knowledge to arrive at the most plausible interpretation. When a more surprising argument is being made, or listeners lack the necessary background knowledge, indicator words are more important. Observe what happens when we omit the word *because* from the example given earlier: "They had a bad winter in Alaska last year; the *zampogna* is an Italian bagpipe." This sounds like a recital of trivial facts, not an argument. When the word "because" is included (in place of the semicolon) we are forced to regard the sentence as an argument despite the difficulty of surmising the connection between Alaskan weather and Italian bagpipes: "They had a bad winter in Alaska last year *because* the *zampogna* is an Italian bagpipe."

The bagpipe sentence also illustrates that the premise need not precede the conclusion when we write out arguments in English. Most premise indicator words can be used with either way of ordering the argument. Returning to the Melinda example in which we marked the premise, it is perfectly correct to put the premise second: "Melinda will get the promotion to vice president, *because* she sold the most mutual fund shares this year." This puts the premise indicator word (*because*) in the middle of the sentence, and hence shifts the focus from the reason giving to the conclusion. It is more difficult to vary the order when you use a conclusion indicator word. With few exceptions, conclusion indicator words sound correct only when they follow a premise. Notice how odd it sounds if we reverse our previous example to get: "Thus Melinda will get the promotion to vice president; she sold the most mutual fund shares."

You can improve your argumentative writing by putting some thought into how you order your statements (and then choosing your indicator words from those that are appropriate for the order chosen). Either order of premise and conclusion is logically correct; however, each order creates a different impression on your audience, and you can use this to your advantage. In writing an argumentative essay, it is generally advisable to use the conclusion–premise order in your introductory paragraph, and the premise–conclusion order in your concluding paragraph. The conclusion–premise order is an attention getter, which you may want to open with: "I shall demonstrate that mood-altering drugs should be legalized, based upon the social and economic effects of controlling access to these substances." The prem-ise–conclusion order can provide an effective close, because the conclusion of the argument can serve as the conclusion of the paper: "Given the evidence I have presented that legal control of mood-altering drugs has produced a variety of negative effects in the social and economic domains, it follows that legalization should be implemented without delay." (Note that approximately the same state-ments regarding social and economic effects are conveyed by a noun phrase in the opener and a clause in the close.)

Words and phrases typically used to indicate that a premise is being presented are listed here. The two words marked with an asterisk (*) at the bottom are the only ones that cannot be used with either order of premise and conclusion. (If a premise is indicated by *whereas* it must precede the conclusion; if it is indicated by *for* it must follow the conclusion.)

PREMISE INDICATOR WORDS

because (of)	given that
granted that	as
assuming that	as is implied by
supposing that	seeing that
as is shown by	based on (the fact that)
inasmuch as	owing to (the fact that)
is clear from	in light of the fact that
follows from	by virtue of the fact that
as we know from	due to (the fact that)
as we can see from	(for) the reason that
insofar as	*whereas
*for	

Words and phrases typically used to indicate that a conclusion is being stated are listed next. The two words marked with an asterisk (*) at the bottom are the only ones that can be used with either order of premise and conclusion. All of the other words require that the conclusion follow the premise.

CONCLUSION INDICATOR WORDS

thus	for this (these) reason(s)
therefore	so we see that
so	implies that
hence	means that
as a result	shows that
consequently	proves that
as a consequence	suggests that
it follows that	demonstrates that
leads to the conclusion that	is evidence that
*one must conclude that	*it may be inferred that

These lists are by no means complete. English is a rich language that offers many other ways of indicating the roles of premises and conclusions. Neither is it the case that every time one of these words appears between two statements, an argument necessarily occurs there. *Thus* is an often-used conclusion indicator, for example, but in the sentence, "Georgia has many fine whitewater rivers; thus the Chattooga, Cartecay, Toccoa, Chestatee, and Tesnatee all flow within its boundaries," *thus* functions to introduce some illustrations of what has been claimed, not to conclude anything on the basis of what has been claimed.

Some of the words and phrases in the previous lists may sound quite stilted to you, and you may feel uncomfortable using them to construct arguments. You will have to judge from the context of the situation in which you are presenting an argument which words (if any) to use to mark premises and conclusions. "From the considerations given above, we can see that it necessarily follows that. . ." might be entirely appropriate for a college essay in which you argue that the causes of the Crimean War were of a certain kind, but will sound absurd when you are trying to convince a classmate to accompany you to a movie.

STANDARD FORM

As we have just seen, when arguments are written out in ordinary English sentences, the premises can either precede or follow the conclusion. The order chosen will place some limitations on which indicator words can be used, but this is not an onerous constraint, and the order can be varied to focus the reader's attention appropriately. For some purposes, however, it is better to have one precise format in which any argument can be displayed; this makes it easier for you to compare and analyze different arguments. Arguments arranged in this way are said to be put in standard form. To put an argument in standard form we must satisfy the following requirements:

1. Write each of the premises and the conclusion on a separate line, listing the premise(s) first and the conclusion last.
2. Omit the premise and conclusion indicators.
3. Omit words that do not contribute to the content of the premises or conclusion, such as "in my opinion," and so forth.
4. Fill in each statement so that it stands on its own as a separate, complete sentence; for example, replace third-person pronouns with noun phrases to make reference clear.
5. Draw a horizontal line to separate the conclusion from the premise(s).
6. Write a triangle of dots ($\therefore$) in front of the conclusion, which is understood as meaning *therefore*.

Thus, Argument C near the beginning of this chapter would be represented in standard form as:

If it rains, the picnic will be ruined.
It is going to rain.
∴ The picnic will be ruined.

In this example there are two premises and one conclusion. Every argument has exactly one conclusion, but it is quite possible to have less than or more than two premises per argument. Here is an argument with one premise:

No turtles can fly.
∴ None of the things that can fly are turtles.

Here is an argument with four premises:

If birds are flying and fish are swimming and trees are swaying, then the ozone layer must still be OK.
Birds are flying.
Fish are swimming.
Trees are swaying.
∴ The ozone layer is still OK.

GOOD AND BAD ARGUMENTS

So far we have seen how arguments differ from mere assertions, how arguments can be divided into their parts (one or more premises and a conclusion), and how the parts can be displayed in standard form. We have suggested that some arguments are better than others, but have not yet developed the tools needed to evaluate arguments—that is, to rank or grade them in terms of how good or bad they are. In this section we begin to acquire those tools.

On what basis can we grade arguments? The grounds that we adopt are to assess arguments by asking how good they are at doing what they're intended to do. You will recall from our definition of *argument* that arguments are intended to provide reasons that support the truth of statements. Our standard for assessing arguments, then, will be how well the reasons (or premises) they present actually do support the truth of their conclusions.

This is very different from asking how *persuasive* arguments may be. The question "how well do the premises support the conclusion?" is a logical question, whereas the question about how persuasive an argument may be is a psychological one. Psychology is not part of the subject of this book, so when we assess arguments we do not take into account their persuasiveness. If we were interested in persuasion and persuasive techniques, we would want to ask, for example, whether the most persuasive way of presenting several arguments in an essay is to present the strongest first, ending with the weakest, or vice versa. And we would want, perhaps, to ask whether it is more persuasive to say "As I have shown" or "As we have seen," and whether an argument that relies on or appeals to numbers—"Everybody's doing it. Shouldn't you be?", for example—is more persuasive when directed at middle or lower-income audiences. All of these are matters that do and should interest the social psychologist who is interested in what makes people believe the things they do and act the ways they do. But as interesting as these matters might be, they are not part of the subject of logic.

Good arguments are not necessarily persuasive ones, then, and persuasive ones need not be good ones. But although persuasion cannot be the sole aim of logic, it is not totally irrelevant either. Finding the most effective means of presenting arguments that are logically good is certainly a worthwhile task, and there are textbooks that will give you advice on how to argue persuasively—when to use figures of speech in your arguments, how to establish credibility as an arguer, whether to state your conclusion first or last, and so on. These persuasive techniques should be used, however, only with arguments that have already been determined to be logically good. To this extent, logic and the art of persuasion should be seen as complementary, the study of logic leading one to the study of persuasion, but neither of them being sufficient by itself.

Let's turn, then, to see what goes into making arguments logically good or bad. We may begin by comparing two arguments that have been written in standard form (notice how much that helps in comparing them):

D.   All lapwings have crests.
     The bird in the bush doesn't have a crest.
     ∴ The bird in the bush can't be a lapwing.

E.   All lapwings have crests.
     The bird in my hand has a crest.
     ∴ The bird in my hand is a lapwing.

In Argument D the bird in the bush can't be a lapwing (as the conclusion states) if the premises are true. But the bird in Argument E might, for all we know from the evidence given in the premises, have a crest and still not be what the conclusion says it must be, a lapwing. The reason is that there may be other birds with crests, for all we know from the premises, and the bird in my hand may be one of them. What this means is that if you had to place a bet, the conclusion in D would be a much better bet than that in E, given the truth of the premises of both. (In fact, if the premises really are true, it is not just a good bet, but a sure bet.) If the premises in D are true, the conclusion *must also be true*, whereas the premises in E might be true and the conclusion *could* still be false. If the conclusion is true (That bird in my hand is a lapwing), it is for some reason other than the premises supplied in E. The criterion we have just introduced marks the critical logical distinction between *valid* and *invalid* arguments: Valid arguments are arguments in which, if the premises are true, the conclusion must be true. Thus, D is valid whereas E is invalid. (Suggestion: Write "Valid" next to Argument D and "Invalid" next to Argument E to remind yourself of this difference.)

Returning to Argument D, we note that determining that its form is valid is only part of deciding whether it is a good argument. If you had (foolishly) bet your life on the conclusion of D, you would want to do more than ask just whether *if the premises of D were true*, would its conclusion also be true. Before you bet that the bird in the bush was not a lapwing you would no doubt want to find out whether it really was true that all lapwings have crests. If this weren't true, then the argument would not offer a sufficient reason to conclude that the bird was not a lapwing. If you could be absolutely sure of this fact about lapwings, however, and absolutely sure that the bird in the bush didn't have a crest, then the bet would be quite safe.

The distinction we have just been using, between what the argument would or would not show, *if* the premises were true, and whether the premises are in fact true, is one of the most important distinctions in logic. (Unfortunately, it is also a slippery one to grasp, so do not be discouraged if you must work through it more than once to get the distinction firmly fixed in your mind.) Based on this distinction, every argument can be evaluated in two different ways. When we ask whether the premises of an argument are true we have, so to speak, to look "outside" the argument to find the answer. In examples D and E we should have to ask whether it's true that the bird in the bush does not have a crest, whether the bird in my hand does have a crest, and whether it's a fact that lapwings all have crests. These are all claims made *in* the argument, about the world that is outside and independent of the argument. "Is the world the way the premises state that it is?" is the appropriate question to ask when we are evaluating the truth of the premises of an argument.

On the other hand, when we examine validity we *freeze* the truth of the premises of an argument, and ask whether, if those premises were true, it would show what it claims to show. We are now looking *inside* the argument, to see not how the world is, but how *it* is. We are then looking at what logicians call the *logical form* of the argument to see, regardless of what the premises are about and regardless of whether they are true, whether the relation they bear to each other and to the conclusion is or is not such that, if they were true, the conclusion would be guaranteed to be true. That is, there are certain forms of argument for which, if the premises were true, the conclusion would also have to be true. If an argument displays this kind of logical form, it is a valid argument. If it does not, we say that the argument is invalid. Whether or not the premises are actually true does not enter into determining validity; validity has to do with the form of the argument, not the argument's specific content or the match between the content and the world.

Hence, there are two conditions that an argument must satisfy if it is to be evaluated as a good argument: (a) all of its premises must be true (we might call this the condition of *truthfulness*); and (b) its form must be valid. Logicians call an argument that satisfies both of these conditions a *sound argument*. More informally, we can say that an argument is good if both its content and form are good. Logicians are more interested in form than in content, referring to a valid argument when the form is such that if the premises are true, then the conclusion must also be, regardless of whether the premises are actually true.

In fact, evaluating arguments on the basis of both truth and validity yields four different categories of arguments; any particular argument will fall into exactly one of these categories. An argument may be (a) valid with true premises; (b) valid with at least one false premise; (c) invalid with true premises; or (d) invalid with at least one false premise. Category a corresponds to *sound* arguments; categories a and b together are the *valid* arguments; categories c and d together are the *invalid* arguments; and categories b, c, and d together are the *unsound* arguments. There are no special names for any other categories or combinations of categories. Here are examples of each of these kinds of arguments:

1. If Atlanta is the capital of Georgia,   Valid form
    then Georgia's governor has an office in Atlanta.   True premises
    Atlanta is the capital of Georgia.
    ∴ Georgia's governor has an office in Atlanta.

2. If Birmingham is the capital of Georgia, then   Valid form
    Georgia's governor has an office in Birmingham.   At least one
    Birmingham is the capital of Georgia.   false premise
    ∴ Georgia's governor has an office in Birmingham.

3. If Atlanta is the capital of Georgia,   Invalid form
    then Georgia's governor has an office in Atlanta.   True premises
    Georgia's governor has an office in Atlanta.
    ∴ Atlanta is the capital of Georgia.

4. If Birmingham is the capital of Georgia, then   Invalid form
    Georgia's governor has an office in Birmingham.   At least one
    Georgia's governor has an office in Birmingham.   false premise
    ∴ Birmingham is the capital of Georgia.

Only Argument 1 has both true premises and a valid form. As already noted, it is the only one of the four that we shall call a *sound* argument. All of the others we shall call *unsound*. Argument 2 fails the truthfulness condition, Argument 3 fails the validity condition, and Argument 4 fails both.

The reason Arguments 3 and 4 fail the validity condition is not obvious, and is explained in the next chapter. It is easier to see how Arguments 2 and 4 fail the truthfulness condition. The second premise of each of these arguments was clearly false, because these premises stated facts that could be shown to be incorrect. By consulting reference books, you could find that Birmingham is not the capital of Georgia and that Georgia's governor does not have an office in Birmingham. As for the first premise, it happens to be the same for both arguments and also happens to be true. This does not help, however: The truthfulness condition is satisfied only if all of the premises of an argument are true. If any premise is false, then the truthfulness condition has been violated and the argument is thereby unsound. This is not to say that people who use an argument in which both premises are false should not have more logical *fault* found with their argument than someone who uses an argument in which only one premise is false but the other(s) true. When you begin to criticize the arguments of others, you will want to ask whether each of the premises of the argument you are considering is true. An argument in which two premises are false is a "worse" argument than one in which only one is, and

ENTHYMEMES 21

one that is invalid and both of whose premises are false is worse than one that is valid and has false premises.

In considering what it takes for an argument to be sound, we have spoken so far of valid or invalid arguments, and of those with true or false premises, but as yet we have not mentioned conclusions, and the possibility that they may be true or false. Surely, you may feel, we have to require that an argument have a true conclusion before we count it as sound! We do not need to impose this as a separate requirement. Sound arguments will always have true conclusions, but this is a consequence of being valid and having true premises. The definition of *valid* told us that whenever all the premises were true, then the conclusion would also have to be true. Given that a sound argument is valid, and also has true premises, then it follows that its conclusion must be true! We can have valid arguments with false conclusions, invalid arguments with false conclusions, arguments with true premises but false conclusions, and arguments with false premises and false conclusions. But the one thing that never can occur is an argument that is sound—that is, has true premises and a valid form—that also has a false conclusion. The combination of true premises and valid form guarantees that the conclusion of such an argument will be true, and so it goes without saying that sound arguments have true conclusions.

ENTHYMEMES

Consider again Argument B near the beginning of this chapter. Just one premise is explicitly stated, so the standard form would seem to be:

> It is going to rain.
> ∴ The picnic will be ruined.

As we noted earlier, this meets the minimum requirements for an argument, but it is not a valid argument. Valid arguments have a logical form in which, if the premise(s) are true, the conclusion must also be true. But this is not true here. The first assertion might be true even when the second is false. Generally we get a valid form by using a *logical operator* such as "if A, then B" or "either A or B" in one of the premises. Typically this is followed by a second premise that includes the appropriate part of the first premise (here, A), and then a conclusion that includes the other part of the first premise (here, B). In the next chapter we examine many such valid forms, but what we need to note now is that sometimes when arguments are stated, they won't contain all of the premises required to make them valid. At other times it will be the conclusion that is omitted. Arguments in which one (or more) of the premises or the conclusion is not explicitly stated are called *enthymemes* (pronounced en-thi-meems).

Often we can look at an enthymeme and see what missing premise or conclusion needs to be added in order to make it valid. When we can infer what premise or conclusion must be added to make an enthymeme into a valid argument, we can include it in our representation of the argument in standard form as long as we place what we add in parentheses to make clear that it was inferred rather than explicitly stated. Hence, an alternative rendition of Argument B in standard form looks very similar to that of Argument C; the only difference is the parentheses:

> (If it is going to rain, the picnic will be ruined.)
> It is going to rain.
> ∴ The picnic will be ruined.

As you will learn in the next chapter, this form, like C but unlike B, is valid. There is, of course, a danger here that the original arguer did not intend the inferred premise; perhaps the arguer meant exactly what was said, and no more. In ordinary life, however, you are usually on firm ground if you fill in a missing premise to make an enthymeme into a valid argument. For example, the various forms of the Melinda argument presented earlier could all be represented by the following standard form:

> Melinda sold the most mutual fund shares this year.
> ∴ Melinda will get the promotion to vice president.

To make this enthymeme into a valid argument with the same form as we used before, we could add a premise such as the following:

> (If Melinda sold the most mutual fund shares this year, then Melinda will get the promotion to vice president.)
> Melinda sold the most mutual fund shares this year.
> ∴ Melinda will get the promotion to vice president.

One reason people omit premises is that it is often easier in English prose to produce or understand an incomplete argument than a complete, valid one! An argumentative essay in which every premise and conclusion is spelled out in every detail is very tedious to read. Another reason people omit premises is to be polite. Suppose you ask to use the telephone in a small shop. A polite way for the manager to deny your request is to state a reason for denial, leaving the denial itself implicit: "Oh, this is not a public phone." It is only because you are able to carry out the appropriate logical inference that this amounts to a "No." This seems effortless and instantaneous, but writing the complete, valid argument in standard form makes it clear how much logical work goes on in being polite:

> Members of the public may not use this phone.
> (You are a member of the public.)
> (∴ You may not use this phone.)

(Notice that both a premise and conclusion must be inferred here.)

We study enthymemes in more detail in the next chapter, noting now only that whereas it is important that you be able to spot them in other people's arguments, there are hazards as well as benefits in using them in your own writing and speaking. The greatest hazard is that you will fail to be understood, or that the conclusion of your argument will not be grasped by your audience. Because there is always something missing in an enthymeme, when you use one you risk having someone not supply the missing part, thereby undercutting the whole purpose of your argument. On the other hand, an advantage of enthymemes that unscrupulous arguers sometimes employ is that they can be used to *hide* weak premises. Often people use them just so they won't have to state a weak premise, with the hope that their audience will infer it implicitly without thinking about it, and not notice how weak it is. Another advantage of enthymemes is psychological—the level of conviction about the conclusion of an argument is often raised when one's audience has to "work through" the argument itself. Working through an argument can lead, so to speak, to making it one's own, so that listeners who draw the conclusion out of an enthymeme may feel that they are *adopting* the conclusion, rather than having it forced on them by someone else. They may feel that the argument is more *theirs* and less *yours*.

Now that we have seen what it is for an argument to be valid or invalid, to have false or true premises, and to be sound or unsound, it is time to turn to a consideration of the various kinds of argument forms that are valid and invalid. This is the subject of the next chapter.

3

Valid Argument Forms

At the end of the previous chapter we said that if an argument is to be sound, it must satisfy two conditions: It must have true premises and a valid logical form. Truth, we saw, is an extralogical matter in that it lies beyond the scope of the logician to determine which premises are true and which false. Validity, on the other hand, is very much a logical matter, and it is to this aspect of arguments that we now turn.

More specifically, we turn to valid *logical forms*, for once we have learned which logical forms are valid and which are not, we can substitute into the bare forms sentences that actually interest us. If the form we are using is valid, then the argument that uses those sentences will be valid. Another way of putting this is to say that validity is so completely independent of truth that even arguments using nonsense words can be valid, although no one could ever know what the premises or conclusion meant, much less whether they were true. Thus, the following argument, although complete nonsense, is valid:

> If gribbeldyspark is grue, then librat is fecht.
> Gribbeldyspark is grue.
> ∴ Librat is fecht.

Its logical form is the same as the following two arguments:

> If Lincoln is president, then this is the 19th century.
> Lincoln is president.
> ∴ This is the 19th century.

> If 7 is greater than 3, then 70 is greater than 300.
> 7 is greater than 3.
> ∴ 70 is greater than 300.

Notice that in none of these examples are both premises true: Lincoln is not president; it is false that if 7 is greater than 3, then 70 is greater than 300; and the first example has meaningless premises. Nevertheless, these three arguments all

24

exhibit the same logical form. To represent this form, we henceforth use letters near the beginning of the alphabet to stand for sentences. Letting A stand for either "Gribbeldyspark is grue," "Lincoln is president," or "7 is greater than 3," and letting B stand for either "Librat is fecht," "This is the 19th century," or "70 is greater than 300" we can represent the common logical form of all these examples as:

If A, then B.
A
∴ B

We study this form in some detail shortly, and learn its name, but for now it is important only that you recognize that the three examples of arguments we have given have the same form as the barebones argument form that uses A's and B's.

In this chapter we focus on only a few forms of valid arguments, namely, those that are most frequently used by speakers and writers in ordinary contexts. There are more exotic forms, but we ignore them, in the belief that the ordinary user of English can live without most of them, however interesting they may be to formal logicians. The forms on which we focus all have invalid counterparts, which we also learn in order to be sure we avoid using them. The first forms we learn come from an area of logic known as *sentential* or *propositional* logic. Having learned how to use these forms to construct valid arguments, we then look at some forms of *class*, or *category*, logic.

SENTENTIAL OR PROPOSITIONAL LOGIC

Propositional logic is distinctive because it takes propositions or statements as basic units and examines how these units can be put together to produce valid arguments. As we use the terms here, a *proposition* or *statement* is any sentence that is capable of being true or false. Thus, sentences such as "The car is red," "This course is easy," "Kaposi's syndrome is a horribly disfiguring disease," and "This property costs $12,500 per acre" are all statements or propositions. Note that a proposition may consist of a statement of fact, a statement of opinion, or a value statement, and each of these may be true or false. "Meryl Streep is the current president of the United States" is a proposition, even though it is false. Because a proposition is a sentence that is capable of being true or false, the following sentences are not propositions: "Help!", "What time is it?", "Clean up your bedroom!", and "Would you please pass the sugar?" Requests, commands, and questions are just not the sort of thing that anyone would ever respond "That's true" or "That's false" to. If someone asks you what astrological sign you fall under, and you respond "Yes, that's true," the questioner will not regard your response as coherent, and will probably assume that you misunderstood. Neither can commands be regarded as true or false. No recruit could ever meaningfully respond to "Do 25 pushups" with "True."

Logical Operators (or Connectives)

The examples of propositions we have given previously are all simple, in the sense that there is only one proposition in each sentence. We use simple propositions in the arguments we construct, but we also use propositions in which *logical operators* are used to construct new, compound, propositions out of simple propositions. Thus, "The car is red" is a simple proposition, but we can use the logical operator *not* on this proposition to generate the new proposition, "It is not true that the car is red," or "The car is not red." Similarly, we can use the logical operator *and* on the two propositions, "The car is red" and "The car has only 18,000 miles on it" to generate the new proposition, "The car is red and it has only 18,000 miles on it."

All the operators we examine have the notable characteristic that they are *truth-functional*. This means that the truth (or falsity) of any compound proposition that uses any of these operators is entirely dependent on the truth of the simple propositions that the logical operators were applied to. Let's look at each of these operators, to see what rules we can learn about their truth-functionality.

Not.   The easiest operator to understand is *not*. Consider the proposition, "Today is Sunday." Applying the operator *not* to this proposition generates the proposition "It is not true that today is Sunday," or more simply, "Today is not Sunday." *Not* is truth-functional, because whether "Today is not Sunday" is true is entirely a function of whether our original proposition, "Today is Sunday," is true. If "Today is Sunday" is true, then "Today is not Sunday" is false, and if "Today is Sunday" is false, then "Today is not Sunday" is true. Another way of putting this is to say that if you know the truth-value of any proposition, that is, if you know whether it is true or false, then you will know simply as a matter of logic, and without checking on the facts, the truth-value of the proposition that is formed by performing the logical operation of negation on the original proposition. If there's no doubt in your mind that "Minnesota is north of Florida" is true, then simply as a matter of logic, there can be no doubt that "Minnesota is not north of Florida" is false. And if you know that "Oregon is not north of California" is false, then you also know that "Oregon is north of California" is true.

In using *not* to negate words and phrases, special care needs to be taken as to where the *not* is placed. The expression "All. . .were not. . ." is confusing; it is sometimes used to mean "Not all. . .were. . . ," but strictly speaking, it means "None . . .were. . . ." Thus, strictly speaking, "All of the people present were not Christians" means that every person among those present was not a Christian. When people say things like this, however, they often mean "Not all of the people present were Christians," or equivalently, "Some of the people present were not Christian." Sometimes you can tell from the context which they mean, but if not, you will need to ask them which they mean. In general, it is best to avoid this construction in your own writing. If you want to say, for example, that it is not the case that any rabbits are white, say "None of the rabbits were white." If, on the other hand, you simply want to claim that it was not the case that all were white, say "Some of the rabbits were not white."

The results of what we have just discovered about the logical operator *not* can be represented schematically in the following truth tables for *not*.

P	-P
T	F
F	T

-P	P
T	F
F	T

These tables, like the succeeding ones, should be read as follows: Look first for the truth-values of a proposition, *P*, in the column directly below that operator. Then the corresponding values for the compound proposition in which that logical operation has been performed will be found in the column under the symbol for that operator. Thus, in the left-hand table for *not*, when the truth-value for *P* is *True*, the truth-value for *Not-P* (*Not* being represented here with a dash) is *False*. In the right-hand table, when *Not-P* is *False*, the truth-value for *P* is *True*.

And.   The *and* operator is almost as easy as *not*. In English, the rules for the use of *and* are such that for any compound proposition using this operator to be true, both of the simple propositions out of which it is constructed (called the *conjuncts*) must be true. Otherwise it is false. Thus the whole proposition "New York is north of Florida and Oregon is north of California" is true, because both of the conjuncts to which the "and" operator was applied are true. But "New York is north of Florida and Oregon is south of California," as well as "New York is south of Florida and Oregon is north of California," are false, because one of the conjuncts in each of the compound propositions is false. Furthermore, "New York is south of Florida and Oregon is south of California" is false, because both of the conjuncts are false. In all of these examples, "and" is used to join two simple propositions, but it can be used to join together any larger number of propositions as well. When it is, the rule for its truth-functionality will remain the same: In order for the whole proposition to be true, every one of the conjuncts comprising it must be true. Otherwise, it is false.

Notice that there are other words in English that function to tie two propositions together the same way *and* does. "Bill is angry, but Ted is pleased," just like "Bill is angry and Ted is pleased," is true only when both conjuncts are true. Therefore we can treat *but* as being logically equivalent to *and*, although of course they do not have exactly the same meaning; *but* usually serves to contrast two situations whereas *and* does not. Based on what we have just said, the truth table for *and* is as follows:

P	Q	P & Q
T	T	T
T	F	F
F	T	F
F	F	F

Either–Or.   The rules for propositions using the *either–or* operator are slightly more complicated. Any proposition using *or*, or the equivalent expression *either–or*, will be true if either one or both of the simple propositions out of which it is composed (called the *alternatives*) is true. Otherwise, it is false. Thus, "Either Lincoln was the 16th president of the United States, or Johnson was" is true, because Lincoln was, and "Either Lincoln was the 17th president or Johnson was" is true, because Johnson was, and "Either Lincoln was the 17th president or Johnson was the 16th" is false, because both alternatives are false. Usually, we count propositions in which both alternatives are true as true. Thus, "Either Lincoln was the 16th president or Johnson was the 17th president" is true. Sometimes, however, we count propositions in which both alternatives are true as being false. We see how to deal with these propositions shortly. For now, though, we need to note that the convention we adopt throughout the remainder of this text, is the following: We understand all propositions using the *either–or* operator as being true when both alternatives are true. With this understanding in mind, see the truth table for the *either–or* operator looks like this:

P	Q	P or Q
T	T	T
T	F	T
F	T	T
F	F	F

Not Both.   Having examined the truth tables for the *not* and *and* operators, we can turn now to an operator that is a combination of the two—the *not both* operator. To see how this logical operator works, consider the case of an uncertain identifier of birds, who thinks the bird in the tree is perhaps a crested flycatcher, but also that it is a western kingbird. In response, another person might say, "But it can't be both!" The latter person is saying that the only thing that is impossible is the situation where the bird is of both varieties. Of course, this leaves it open whether it is either of them, or neither. So the *not both* operator will be false in case both halves (called *disjuncts*) are true, but otherwise true. Notice that the following truth table, which represents this operator, is a combination of the *and* and *not* truth tables, insofar as the truth values for the *and* table have simply been negated. For this reason, in the language of computer design this operator is referred to as a "NAND-gate," which is short for "Not and."

P	Q	Not both P and Q
T	T	F
T	F	T
F	T	T
F	F	T

Either–Or But Not Both.   Introducing the *not both* operator allows us to return to the situation in which someone wants to say that either A or B is true, but not both. Under the convention we have adopted, to say that either A or B is true is to allow that both may be. But now we want to go on to exclude that possibility. So all we need to do is to combine the *either–or* and *not both* operators. In doing so we will have formed an *alternative-disjunct*. It is this operator that we are using when we say to someone, for example, "I am either going to the symphony this weekend or to a movie" (which so far leaves it open as to whether we might do both), "but not both" (which forecloses that possibility). The truth table for *either A or B but not both* is a combination of the truth tables for alternatives (either–or propositions) and disjuncts (not both propositions).

P	Q	Either P or Q but not both
T	T	F
T	F	T
F	T	T
F	F	F

If, Then.   Of all the logical operators we examine, the most useful for purposes of argument, but the most difficult to master, is the *if, then* operator. Propositions of the form "If. . . , then. . . ." are called *hypothetical propositions* or *conditional statements*. That part of the proposition immediately following the *if* is called the *antecedent*, and that part immediately following the *then* is called the *consequent*. An example of a hypothetical proposition is "If you have a key, then you will be able to get in." In this proposition "You have a key" is the antecedent, and "You will be able to get in" is the consequent.

To see how *if, then* is truth functional, consider under what circumstances someone who had uttered the previous proposition would be judged to have said something false. If the antecedent is false, that is, the person being addressed does not have a key, then it certainly wouldn't be fair to say that the *if, then* proposition was false, for all it states is what will be true if the person has a key. Because, then, when the antecedent is false, the entire proposition cannot be indicted, we have to count it as true. Now if the antecedent is true, there are two possibilities: The consequent can be true, or it can be false. If the consequent is true, that is, when the person being addressed does have a key and can get in, then the entire proposition must be true. But if the consequent is false (while the antecedent is true), then that whole proposition will be false, because it said that if the person had a key then the person could get in, but we have a situation where the person has a key but can't get in. So the only situation in which the whole hypothetical proposition is false is the one in which the antecedent is true but the consequent is false. Otherwise, the hypothetical proposition will be true.

These facts about the rules for *if, then* can be represented on a truth table for *if P, then Q,* as follows:

P	Q	If P, then Q
T	T	T
T	F	F
F	T	T
F	F	T

Be careful at this point to remember that *if, then* is simply a logical operator used to join two propositions to form a compound proposition. It is not a way of expressing an argument. "If A, then B" is not equivalent to "A, therefore B." The latter is an argument, and is either sound or unsound, but the former is merely a hypothetical proposition, and is either true or false, depending on what propositions are substituted for A and B. We use hypothetical propositions extensively as premises in arguments, but we must be careful not to confuse them with arguments themselves. Another way of putting this is to say that when a salesperson selling tools says to a buyer, "If you'll give me $25, I'll let you have the plane," that salesperson is not presenting evidence for the truth of any proposition. What the person is doing is making a statement, which is either true or false. If the person reneges when the buyer presents the $25, then the proposition was false, and if the person hands over the plane when the buyer presents the $25, then the proposition was true. But nothing is being argued for, any more than if the seller had said "This plane was made by the Stanley Tool Works."

Another factor that you should take note of when using hypothetical propositions is that the A and B propositions *cannot be reversed.* "If A, then B" is not the same as "If B, then A." For example, "If you take I-10 west, you'll wind up in California" is true, but its reverse, "If you wind up in California, you've taken I-10" is often false. This is not to say, of course, that the entire proposition "If A, then B" cannot be reversed. "B, if A" is the same as "If A, then B." (Note how this differs from the previous example. In this case the *if* stayed with the *A.*) "You'll wind up in California if you take I-10" does say the same thing as "If you take I-10, then you'll wind up in California." Other alternative ways of saying the same thing include: "Given A, then B," "B, on the condition that A," "Whenever A, then B," "A guarantees B," "A is sufficient for B," "A will give you a B," "B is the result of A," and so on. There are many other ways as well, but the general rule is the same for them all: You cannot reverse the A's and B's within an *if, then* proposition, no matter what form it takes.

Although there are many different ways of representing the *if, then* relationship in English, for the purposes of consistency in this chapter, we represent them in standard form as "If A, then B." Thus, we will rewrite "B, provided that A" as "If A, then B," and "C will give you a D" as "If C, then D," and so on.

Only If.   *If* needs to be very clearly distinguished from *only if.* The proposition "If you have a key, then you can enter the room" does not mean the same thing, nor are its truth conditions usually the same as, "Only if you have a key can you enter the room." If you have the right key, and the lock is not broken, the first proposition is usually true. But the second is often false. Perhaps there's another door, or an open window that you can enter through. In dire straits, pipe wrenches, crow bars, and sledge hammers will get you through many doors. We have learned the truth table for *if, then*, and how to convert various other formulations of this relationship into standard form. But how do we represent *only if, then* logically? The answer is that all *only if* propositions can be converted into standard *if, then* form, and then treated simply as those kind of propositions are treated. But this conversion is tricky, and although at first sight there may appear to be a simple formula for it, you will find it more reliable to learn to think through the relationship each time than to try to apply a rote formula.

To see how to convert *only if* propositions into *if, then* propositions, let us reflect upon the logic of the proposition, "Only if you have taken organic chemistry will you be admitted to medical school." You can see at once that this is not the same as "If you have taken organic chemistry, then you will be admitted to medical school," for the first proposition is true of most medical schools, whereas the second is false. Most medical schools do require organic chemistry, but none will admit you just because you have taken it. So "Only if A, then B" cannot simply be converted into "If A, then B." We must look elsewhere for a method of converting one into the other. When we were discussing *if, then* propositions we said that one way of saying "If A, then B" was to say "A guarantees B." Let us ask what it is in the *only if* proposition that is guaranteed. Consider some people who have been admitted to medical school. Is there anything that we're *guaranteed* about them, such that logically it must be so? Well, if the original proposition is true, and if they have been admitted, it must be true that they've taken organic chemistry. So if they've been admitted, they must have taken organic chemistry. But now we've constructed a standard form *if, then* proposition: "If you've been admitted to medical school, then you've taken organic chemistry," which is what we were trying to do. Notice what has happened to the word order in making this translation: "Only if A, B" has become "If B, then A." Using this reasoning, we can convert other forms of *only if* propositions into standard form hypothetical propositions. "I'll sell you the horse only if you promise to give it a good home," becomes "If you've been sold the horse, then you have promised to give it a good home," or, symbolically, "A, only if B" has become "If A, then B." (Notice in this example why it won't work to memorize a simple rule such as "Turn the A's and B's around.": "Only if A, B" becomes "If B, then A," but "A, only if B" becomes "If A, then B.")

Understanding and recognizing the distinction between "if" and "only if" statements enables us to understand another logical distinction—that between what are called *necessary conditions* and *sufficient conditions*. Something is a necessary condition for something else when the first is required for the second to be present or to occur. Something is a sufficient condition for something else when the first guarantees that the second will occur or be present. Thus, it is a requirement (and so a necessary condition) for baking bread that we have a source of heat, and it is a requirement (a necessary condition) for being rectangular that a figure have four sides. But neither of these conditions will guarantee that the second state or event will occur, and so neither is a sufficient condition. Just having heat present does not guarantee that we will wind up with bread—we also need the proper ingredients for bread, as well as the knowledge of how to blend them together and cook them, and so on. And having four sides does not guarantee that we will have a rectangular figure (trapezoids, for example, have four sides but are not rectangular). In contrast, falling into a lake is, in ordinary circumstances, a sufficient condition for getting wet, and being over 7 ft in height is a sufficient condition for being tall. But it is not necessary that one fall into a lake to get wet (there are other ways), and it is not necessary that one be over 7 ft in height to be tall.

Understanding that the *if* operator functions logically to guarantee the occurrence of an event or state, we can now see that *if* statements present us with sufficient conditions. "If you present a valid ticket, you will be admitted" guarantees that admission will occur following the presentation of a valid ticket, and so it states that the one is a sufficient condition for the other. We have also seen that *only if* statements present requirements, and so present necessary conditions. "You can be president only if you're 35 or older" states one requirement for being president, and so states a necessary condition for being president.

Unless.   *Unless*, like *only if*, is a logical operator that can be converted into standard hypothetical form. Consider the example: "You must pay a late fee of $10 unless we receive payment by June 15." The key to translating this into *if, then* form is to imagine what will happen if something else does not happen. In this case, if the payment is not received by June 15, then a late fee will be owed. Symbolically, letting "A unless B" represent the original proposition, it can be converted into "If not B, then A."

We can deal with *not unless* propositions in a similar fashion. Letting "Not A unless B" stand for the proposition "You will not graduate unless you maintain an average GPA above 1.5," we ask ourselves what will not happen if something else does not happen. Here, you will not graduate if you do not receive the 1.5 average, or "If you do not receive a 1.5 average, then you will not graduate," which is "If not B, then not A."

If and Only If.   Sometimes it is necessary to combine the *if* and the *only if* operators. Imagine parents who tell their children "You may watch TV if you clean up your room." The parents have guaranteed what will happen if another thing happens, and upon cleaning up the room the children have every right to expect to watch TV. But the parents have not said that cleaning up the room is the only way they will be able to watch TV. Precociously logical children might try to watch TV without cleaning the room. The children would then be logically correct in saying that the parents had not ruled out the possibility of watching TV without cleaning the room. If the parents had wanted to say that, they should have said "Only if you clean your room may you watch TV." Then watching TV without having cleaned the room would have been forbidden. But then of course if the parents had only said "Only if you clean your room can you watch TV," the children would not have been guaranteed nearly as much as they might think (unless they were logically precocious). For this does not guarantee the children that if they clean up, they may watch TV. The only solution that will guarantee the parents what they want (TV only if a clean room) as well as what the children want (if a clean room, then TV) is for the parents to say in the beginning "If and only if you clean your room may you watch TV." The way to see this is to break the *if and only if* proposition down into its two constituent parts—"If you clean the room, you may watch TV," and "Only if you clean the room may you watch TV." The first part, a standard hypothetical proposition, guarantees the children that cleaning will be followed by TV. The second part, an *only if* proposition, guarantees the parent that if TV is being watched, that must have followed the room cleaning.

Propositions using the words *if and only if* do not occur very frequently in ordinary English discourse, probably because people such as the aforementioned parents do not realize that they often mean *if and only if* when they say simply *if*. But this is no reason for us, who have now learned the distinction between *if, only if*, and *if and only if* not to be logically meticulous. In the remainder of this text we use each operator only when it is the one that is called for logically. The adoption of this policy outside the confines of this text and course is highly recommended.

We saw earlier that *if* statements present sufficient conditions, and that *only if* statements present necessary conditions. It should come as no surprise, then, that *if and only if* statements present necessary and sufficient conditions. "You are a bachelor if and only if you are an adult unmarried male" states the requirements for being a bachelor, and also guarantees that you are a bachelor if you fulfill them. Notice that the example just presented is a definition. Writers of definitions, as well as those who must compose rules and laws, must be especially careful to distinguish between necessary, sufficient, and necessary and sufficient conditions. "If you present a valid ticket, you'll be admitted" states a sufficient condition, but the concert promoter who prints it on the ticket will probably wish it had been written as a necessary condition when the first drunk appears at the turnstile. And the college registrar who makes a high school diploma a necessary condition for attendance will thereby have prevented admission to a prodigy of 14 who has yet to finish high school.

Now that we have seen how various logical operators work, let us put them to use in learning some elementary forms of logical argument. We investigate three groups of the forms of propositional logic: immediate inferences, hypothetical syllogisms, and alternative and disjunctive syllogisms. (All of the forms that we introduce are summarized in Table 3.1 at the end of the chapter. You may want to refer to this table as you go through the chapter.)

Immediate Inferences

Immediate inferences are arguments that have only one premise. The conclusion in these arguments is said to follow directly from that one premise, so that one does not have to combine information from two or more premises. We discuss three forms of immediate inference in this section: double negation, what we call conversion, and the De Morgan laws.

Double Negation.   The logical rule known as *double negation* simply states that the negation of the negation of a proposition is the same as the original proposition. Any time we encounter a proposition, then, we can replace it, if we choose, with its double negation; any time we encounter a double negation, we can replace it with an unnegated proposition. Put into symbols, the rule thus says that the following arguments are valid:

$$\frac{A}{\therefore --A \text{ VALID}} \qquad\qquad \frac{--A}{\therefore A \text{ VALID}}$$

These two inferences may seem to be quite trivial, but you will find them necessary when we have introduced some more complicated rules.

Conversion.   Recall that when we discussed the rule for the *if, then* operator, we saw that "If A, then B" is not the same as "If B, then A." There is, however, a rule of logic that will allow us to derive a statement that reverses the A and the B in a hypothetical proposition. What it says is that when we do so, we must add negation signs to both the A and the B. Thus, the following inference is valid:

$$\frac{\text{If A, then B.}}{\therefore \text{ If -B, then -A.}} \qquad\qquad \text{VALID}$$

Let us see why this inference is valid. We begin with the proposition that A guarantees B, or that if we have an A, we have a B. Let us suppose that we know that B is not true, that is, that -B. Now if we know that if we have an A, we will have a B; but we don't have a B, so we can't have an A (otherwise we'd have a B, which is what we don't have). As an example, consider the relationship between being a bachelor and being unmarried. If you're a bachelor, then you must be unmarried. Now suppose we know that some man is married. If that person is married, then we can be sure he's not a bachelor. Otherwise, he couldn't be married. So, given that if a person is a bachelor, then he's unmarried (If A, then B), we can immediately infer that if he's married, then he's not a bachelor (If -B, then -A), which is what the rule of conversion says is the case.

Notice that this is not the same as the following, which is an invalid reference:

$$\frac{\text{If A, then B.}}{\therefore \text{ If -A, then -B.}} \qquad\qquad \text{INVALID}$$

If your car is drivable, then it must have four wheels on it. But this does not imply that if it is not drivable, that it does not have four wheels. All sorts of other factors could account for your car's being undrivable.

Already we can see a use for the double negation rule we just learned if we ask ourselves whether the valid inference rule of conversion works in reverse, that is, whether "If -B, then -A" implies "If A, then B." Let us begin with "If -B, then -A." The rule of conversion says we can reverse the order of the A and B, so long as we negate both of them. Doing that to "If -B, then -A," we obtain "If --A, then --B." But the rule of double negation says that we can replace the --A with A, and the --B with B. Doing so, we get "If A, then B." Therefore, "If -B, then -A" does imply "If A, then B," and we can write:

> If -B, then -A.
> ∴ If A, then B.   VALID

The De Morgan Laws.   One of the trickiest pieces of logic arises when one combines *not* with either *and* or *or*. Consider the sentence

> It is not the case that both the president and the vice president will be on the flight to Cincinnati.

What this entails is that at least one of the two, the president or the vice president, will not be on the flight to Cincinnati. Thus, the following inference is valid:

> It is not the case that both the president and the vice president will be on this flight to Cincinnati.
> ∴ Either the president will not be on this flight or the vice president will not be on this flight.

More generally, the following form is valid:

> Not both A and B.
> ∴ Not A or not B.

When the *not* that was originally applied to the whole disjunctive statement is distributed over the two parts of the statement, the *and* must be replaced by an *or*.

Using this example, we can see how a mistake is made if we do not replace the *and* with *or*. In that case we would make the following inference:

> It is not the case that both the president and the vice president will be on this flight to Cincinnati.
> ∴ The president will not be on this flight and the vice president will not be on this flight.(= Neither the president nor the vice president will be on this flight.)
> INVALID

But this is clearly not valid, because the premise could be true and the conclusion false. For example, the premise is true if the president but not the vice president is on the flight. But then the conclusion is false.

The same principle applies in reverse if we start with a *not* applied to a whole alternative statement: If we distribute the *not* to the two parts, then the *or* should be replaced by an *and*:

> Not either A or B.
> ∴ Not A and not B.

Thus, the following inference is valid:

> I cannot work either Monday or Tuesday.
> ∴ I cannot work Monday and I cannot work Tuesday.

(In this case, if we had not substituted *and* for *or* we would not actually have generated an invalid argument. In the following argument,

> I cannot work either Monday or Tuesday.
> ∴ I cannot work Monday or I cannot work Tuesday.

if the premise is true, the conclusion will also be true. That is because the *or* statement "I cannot work Monday or I cannot work Tuesday" is weaker than the *and* statement "I cannot work Monday and I cannot work Tuesday." If the second statement is true, than both component sentences must be true, and as we already saw, an *or* statement is true if one or both alternatives is true. But whereas this argument is not invalid, it is quite misleading, because it leaves open the possibility that one could work both days, something ruled out by the premise.)

These argument forms are known as the *De Morgan laws* after the 19th-century logician/mathematician Augustus De Morgan, who codified them into a system of logic. They also apply if we start with a premise in which a *not* is distributed. Then they enjoin us to change the *and* to *or* or vice versa in the conclusion. Thus, the following two forms represent the correct inference in the situation in which *not* is distributed in the premise:

> Both not A and not B.   Either not A or not B.
> ∴ Not either A or B   ∴ Not both A and B

Failure to make the substitution in the second case results in the invalid inference:

> Either not A or not B.
> ∴ Not (A or B)   INVALID

In the following example, we see that this form could have true premises and a false conclusion, and so is not valid:

Either Atlanta will not host the 1996 Olympics or it will not host the 2000 Olympics.

∴ It is not the case that Atlanta will host the 1996 Olympics or host the 2000 Olympics.

(For the same reasons noted earlier, failure to make the substitution in the first case does not result in an invalid argument, but it can be misleading.)

Hypothetical Syllogisms

We now come to a set of three valid argument forms that you will find extremely useful in developing your own arguments. In fact, you can construct an argument for almost any conclusion you will need to argue for using either one of these forms, or some combination of these, alternative, and disjunctive syllogisms. What is distinctive about this class of argument forms is that all of them use an initial premise that has the form of a hypothetical proposition (hence the name *hypothetical syllogisms*). Two of them, *modus ponens* and *modus tollens*, allow one to derive a conclusion about either the antecedent or consequent of the hypothetical premise. The other, which we call a *conditional syllogism,* allows us to conclude from two hypothetical premises a hypothetical conclusion.

Modus Ponens.   The first form of valid hypothetical syllogism goes by the Latin name *modus ponens* or the English expression *affirming the antecedent.* The English name gives us a clue as to how the syllogism is constructed. We begin with a hypothetical proposition in the first premise, such as "If A, then B." Then in the second premise we affirm the antecedent of that first premise. To do this, we simply assert that A, the antecedent, is true. The rule allows us to conclude that B, the consequent of the first premise, must be true. It should come as no news to you that B must be true, because we have already said that "If A, then B" means that A guarantees B. Because we have an "If A, then B" proposition in the first premise, and an "A" in the second, we can validly conclude "B." Knowing that if you're a music major, you must take a theory course, and that you're a music major, you can conclude that you must take a theory course. Symbolically, we can express this valid argument form as:

If A, then B.   modus ponens
A_____   VALID
∴ B

The A's and the B's in the previous formula are of course only *dummy* letters. They can stand for any proposition whatever, ranging from "The car is red" to "This property costs $12,500 per acre." But they can also stand for compound propositions, such as "This car is not red," or "This property consists of 25 acres, is located in the mountains, has 3 springs on it, with a National Forest Service boundary on

2 sides, and it costs $12,500 per acre." Thus, the following syllogisms are both examples of modus ponens arguments:

> If this car is not red, then I don't want to buy it.
> This car is not red.
> ∴ I don't want to buy it.

> If this property consists of 25 acres, is located in the mountains, has 3 springs on it, with a National Forest Service boundary on 2 sides, and it costs $12,500 per acre, then, although it would be nice to own, I can't afford to buy it.
> This property consists of 25 acres, is located in the mountains, has 3 springs on it, with a National Forest Service boundary on 2 sides, and it costs $12,500 per acre.
> ∴ Although it would be nice to own, I can't afford to buy it.

If you were to put the first of these syllogisms into standard form, you might represent it as:

> If -A, then -B.
> -A
> ∴ -B

The important point here is to see that this is just as much an example of modus ponens as:

> If A, then B.
> A
> ∴ B

Both of these are examples of modus ponens because in both cases the second premise affirms the antecedent of the first premise. In one case the antecedent happens to have a negation sign in front of it, but so long as we affirm that assertion (i.e., state -A), and then conclude the consequent (i.e., -B), we will have used the form modus ponens. Indeed, all of the forms of argument listed here are equally good examples of modus ponens, for the same reasons we have just considered:

If A, then -B.	If -A, then B.	If --A, then -B.	If A, then --B.
A	-A	--A	A
∴-B	∴B	∴-B	∴--B

Likewise, the example of the property purchase might be symbolized as:

> If A and B and C and D and E, then, although E, -F.
> A and B and C and D and E.
> ∴ Although E, -F.

But it could also be symbolized as

> If A, then B.
> A_____
> ∴ B

Again, so long as we are careful in the second premise to affirm the antecedent of the first exactly as it appeared, then we can conclude the consequent of the first, exactly as it appeared. To check your understanding of this principle, write in the following blank space exactly what the second premise and the conclusion of a modus ponens argument would be that had as its first premise:

> If Sally gives the promotion to Robert, and Rachel does not quit or file a grievance, and neither Ted nor Ned are fired, then there's a good chance that if I receive a promotion, it will be to assistant vice-president of sales.

Your second premise should read: "Sally gives the promotion to Robert, and Rachel does not quit or file a grievance, and neither Ted nor Ned are fired," and your conclusion should be, "There's a good chance that if I receive a promotion, it will be to assistant vice-president of sales."

Notice that we have said that to use modus ponens, the second premise must affirm the antecedent exactly as it appeared in the first premise, and the conclusion must assert the consequent exactly as it appeared in the first premise. Modus ponens, as well as the other valid forms of hypothetical syllogisms, are valid only when these conditions are strictly met. Otherwise, the syllogism commits what can be called the *fallacy of three terms*. Modus ponens works on the principle that the first premise contains a hypothetical proposition, the second premise the exact antecedent of that proposition, and the conclusion the exact consequent of that proposition. Thus, only two *terms*, the antecedent and the consequent, are used. Just as the following are not examples of modus ponens, because they contain three terms instead of two, so any change or slippage in the antecedent or consequent when they appear in the second premise or conclusion will commit this fallacy:

> If A, then B.   If A, then B.
> E_____   A_____
> ∴ B   ∴ D

In a subsequent chapter we learn how to use probabilistic qualifiers, such as *probably*, *extremely likely*, *highly improbable*, and so on, in hypothetical propositions. Special care must be taken to preserve these in both the second premises and conclusions of hypothetical syllogisms. Thus the following argument is valid:

> If there's good evidence that the testator was delirious when she signed the will, then the court will probably not validate it.
> There's good evidence that the testator was delirious when she signed the will.
> ∴ The court will probably not validate it.

But the following one commits the fallacy of three terms in two places:

> If there's good evidence that the testator was delirious when the will was signed, then the court will probably not validate it.
> There's some evidence that the testator was delirious when the will was signed.
> ∴ The court will not validate it.

Modus ponens provides an effective but simple argument form to use to convince someone of a simple claim. What you do to construct such an argument is to find a condition under which the claim in question is true. State this as your first premise. Then show that this condition is met, in the second premise. In the conclusion you can then assert the claim. (The second step may of course require another argument of its own, unless its truth is obvious to the person you are trying to convince.)

We saw in the last chapter that enthymemes are arguments in which one or more of the premises or the conclusion is missing. An effective way to learn the valid forms of argument discussed here is for you to complete enthymematic arguments by supplying the missing premises necessary to produce a valid argument. As we discuss each argument form in this section, you are presented with an opportunity to get some practice with that form by completing enthymemes. To get some practice with modus ponens, you should fill in the missing premise in the following incomplete argument:

> If I complete this enthymeme correctly, then I will have a valid argument.
> _____
> ∴ I have a valid argument.

The only second premise that will make this argument valid is "I completed this enthymeme correctly." Notice that sometimes you will need to change the tense of verbs between the various premises and conclusion in order to produce meaningful English sentences. Such changes are allowable, and do not commit the fallacy of three terms.

In the previous example the second premise was the missing part of the enthymeme. But often it is the first premise that has been left unstated. Provide the hypothetical proposition that is needed to complete the following enthymeme:

> It is raining today.
> ∴ The rally will be moved into the gym.

Here you should have supplied, "If it is raining today, then the rally will be moved into the gym," as the first premise.

Having completed enthymemes with missing first and second premises, let us now supply both of the premises necessary to complete a valid modus ponens argument. Suppose you want to argue that Plan 12b-1 of the U.S. securities law should be repealed. Your principal objection to it is that it deceives investors by making them think they are not being charged a fee, when in fact they are. You should begin by writing your conclusion, leaving the premise lines blank for the time being:

∴ Plan 12b-1 of the securities law should be repealed.

At this point, having decided to use a modus ponens form, you know that the conclusion will be the consequent of the major premise, so you can write that in:

If   , then Plan 12b-1 of the securities law should
     be repealed.

∴ Plan 12b-1 of the securities law should be repealed.

All that is then left to do is to state the reason you have for repealing the plan, in both the antecedent of the first premise and as the second premise. There are several ways to state your principal objection. You could say, "If Plan 12b-1 deceives investors, then it should be repealed," as your first premise. This would imply that you objected in general to plans that deceive investors. It might be the case that you felt that way, but in the principal objection as it was originally stated, the reason given was more limited. There the reason was that it deceived investors by making them think they were not being charged a fee when in fact they were. This is a narrower reason than the one just listed, in that it details exactly what kind of deceit is objectionable. As a *general* rule of thumb, you should never give a broader reason than is necessary for the conclusion at hand. The reason for this is that if you are called on to defend your major premise, the narrower it is, the easier it will be to defend. So in this case, it will be preferable to state the first premise as, "If Plan 12b-1 deceives investors by concealing a fee, then it should be repealed." Placing this back into the format we have already created, and using pronouns to replace some otherwise clumsy noun phrases, we then obtain the following complete syllogism:

If Plan 12b-1 deceives investors by concealing a fee, then it should be
     repealed.
Plan 12b-1 deceives investors by concealing a fee.
∴ Plan 12b-1 should be repealed.

This, as we have seen, is an example of modus ponens, a valid form of hypothetical syllogism. We must be very careful to distinguish it from an invalid form of argument with which it is often confused. This form is called *affirming the consequent*, which looks like this:

> If A, then B.   affirming the consequent
> B _____
> ∴ A   INVALID

When we say that an argument form is invalid, we are saying that even if the premises of it are true, we cannot, on that basis alone, assert that the conclusion must be true. That is, the argument does not compel us to assert or believe the conclusion in the way that true premises in a valid argument do. This is not to say that a conclusion of an invalid argument might not, for all that has been said, be true. Accidentally, so to speak, someone might wind up with a true conclusion in an invalid argument. Consider the following argument:

> If you are a psychology major, then you are required to take statistics.
> You are required to take statistics._____
> ∴ You are a psychology major.

This example of affirming the consequent (like affirming the antecedent, so named because of what the second premise does in relation to the first premise) shows that although the conclusion might be true, it is not guaranteed by true premises. Take the case of Beth, who is a psychology major. Suppose that, at her university, the first premise is true. Then the second premise is true of her, and the conclusion is true. But in the case of Roger, a sociology major whose university requires statistics of both psychology and sociology majors, the first premise is true, the second premise is true, and the conclusion is false. Clearly no truth is guaranteed by the two premises when one commits this fallacy, although the conclusion might be true.

Modus Tollens.   The second form of hypothetical syllogism discussed here is also known most often by its Latin name, *modus tollens*. Its English name, *denying the consequent*, however, is helpful in giving us a clue as to how it works. Thus, the second premise denies (or negates) the consequent of the first premise, and then goes on to conclude the denial (the negation) of the antecedent of the first premise. Symbolically, it looks like:

> If A, then B.   Modus tollens
> -B _____
> ∴ -A   VALID

Using the same first premise as in the argument we just considered, an example of modus tollens would be:

> If you are a psychology major, then you are required to take statistics.
> You are not required to take statistics._____
> ∴ You are not a psychology major.

Suppose that you are not required to take statistics, and the first premise is true at your university. Then does the truth of those two premises guarantee the truth of the conclusion? That is, is there any way the conclusion could be false of you? Well, let us try to suppose that it is false. In that case, you *are* a psychology major. But then notice what that, combined with the major premise, means. Modus ponens will tell you that you are required to take statistics. But that contradicts the second premise! So in order for the conclusion to be false, one of the premises must be false, which means that two true premises could not ever be followed by a false conclusion, in this form of argument. And that is exactly what we mean when we say that the form is valid.

Once again, some practice in completing enthymemes that require this form may help you to learn it. Supply the necessary premise to complete the following enthymeme:

If today is Tuesday, Ellen will be in the library tonight.

_____

∴ Today is not Tuesday.

You should have denied the consequent of the first premise in the second, and supplied "Ellen is not in the library tonight." Try one now in which the first premise is missing:

I am not a citizen of the United States._____

∴ I am not eligible to receive a Pell grant for college expenses.

Because the second premise will have denied the consequent of the first premise, that consequent must have been "I am a citizen of the United States." Because the conclusion must be the negation of the antecedent of the first premise, that antecedent must be "I am eligible to receive a Pell grant for college expenses." Putting these together, the missing premise must have been, "If I am eligible to receive a Pell grant for college expenses, then I am (or must be) a citizen of the United States."

As with modus ponens, modus tollens is valid even if the antecedent or consequent has a negation within it. There is only one requirement: Whatever form the consequent takes, it must be denied in the second premise, and the conclusion must be the negation of the antecedent. Thus, the following forms are all valid instances of modus tollens:

If -A, then B.	If A, then -B.	If -A, then -B.	If -A, then --B.
-B_____	--B (or B)___	--B (or B)___	---B (or -B)__
∴--A (or A)	∴-A	∴--A (or A)	∴--A (or A)

Also, as with modus ponens, modus tollens can be used on hypothetical statements with complex antecedents or consequents. Thus this is an example of modus tollens:

> If the weather report indicates that Boston will have either sleet or snow or freezing rain tomorrow, then, provided that I can get a ticket, I will fly to either Phoenix or Miami tomorrow.
> It is not true that, provided that I can get a ticket, I will fly to either Phoenix or Miami tomorrow.
> ∴ The weather report does not indicate that Boston will have either sleet or snow or freezing rain tomorrow.

Again, as with modus ponens, modus tollens requires that when the consequent is denied in the second premise, it appear in exactly the same form as it did in the first premise, and that the antecedent negated in the conclusion appear in exactly the same form as it did in the first premise. If either of these does not occur, then the fallacy of three terms is committed. For example, if the second premise in the previous example read "It is not true that I will fly to either Phoenix or Miami tomorrow," then the omission of the availability of the ticket proviso would render the argument fallacious.

Let us now try to construct an argument toward a given conclusion, using this form. Suppose we want to argue that, contrary to someone else's expressed belief, George is not a poor student. Filling in the conclusion line with that proposition, we have:

> _____
> ∴ George is not a poor student.

Because we are using modus tollens, we know that the conclusion must be the negation of the antecedent in the first premise. So we can fill that in as well:

> If George is a poor student, then
> _____
> ∴ George is not a poor student.

Now all we have to do is to find a reason that would, if true, make George a poor student, but that in his case is false. We will fill in this reason as the consequent of the first premise, and then deny that the reason is true in the second. One sign of a poor student is a low grade point average (GPA), so we can check George's record first to see what it is. Because it is 3.8, a high average on a 4.0 scale, we can use this as the reason. We can then complete the syllogism as follows:

> If George is a poor student, then he would have a low GPA.
> George does not have a low GPA.
> ∴ George is not a poor student.

Another way of achieving this same end would have been to put the reason negatively in the first premise, and then state it positively in the second:

If George is a poor student, he would not have a high GPA.
George has a high GPA.
∴ George is not a poor student.

To be sure you know how to use modus tollens, try to supply two true premises to argue that you are not rich. To do this, write a first premise claiming that something would be true if you were rich. Then in the second premise state that this thing is not true:

If I were rich, then
It is not true that
∴ I am not rich.

As with modus ponens, there is an invalid form of argument with which it is easily confused. It is called *denying the antecedent*, named again after what the second premise does to the first. Its structure is:

If A, then B.   Denying the antecedent
-A
∴ -B   INVALID

You can convince yourself that this is an invalid form of reasoning by producing an argument using this form that has true premises and a false conclusion. Here is an example:

If I am a Nobel Prize winner, then I am a human.
I am not a Nobel Prize winner.
∴ I am not a human.

Because Nobel Prizes are not given to plants, animals, or inanimate objects, the first premise is true. Unless you have been hiding something from the registrar of this university, the second premise is true, and unless you have been hiding something from your parents and everyone else, the conclusion is false. So it is possible to produce an argument in this form with true premises and a false conclusion, thereby proving that it is invalid.

Conditional Syllogisms.   We call the third kind of hypothetical syllogism *conditional syllogism*. These take their name not from the second premise, as do modus tollens and modus ponens, but from the conclusion. Because the conclusion of a conditional syllogism is a conditional, or hypothetical, proposition, this form of argument is particularly useful when you need to establish that something is true if something else is true: "Thus, if you do so-and-so, so-and-so will result," or "So, on the condition that A occurs, B will occur," and so on. The general form of this argument is:

If A, then B.
If B, then C.
∴ If A, then C.

An example is:

If I fly to San Francisco tonight, then I must change planes in Dallas.
If I change planes in Dallas, there's a greater chance of losing my luggage
than if I fly nonstop tomorrow.
∴ If I fly to San Francisco tonight, then there's a greater chance of losing
my luggage than if I fly nonstop tomorrow.

Although this syllogism contains three terms, one of them *cancels out* in the
conclusion. Because B, which follows upon A, itself guarantees C, we can, so to
speak, disregard it. That is in essence what this form of syllogism allows you to
conclude. And there is no reason that this "cancellation" process cannot go on
indefinitely. "If A, then B; if B, then C; if C, then D; if D, then E; if E, then F," will
allow you to conclude, "If A, then F." Notice: It will allow you to conclude, "If A,
then F," not simply "F." The conclusion of a conditional syllogism is always a
hypothetical proposition, never a simple assertion. It is easy to forget this, especially when the antecedent of the first premise seems obviously true. The temptation
is tacitly to supply it, and then use a modus ponens to infer the consequent of the
last premise as the conclusion.

As before, some practice with enthymemes will help you to learn this form.
What premise is required to complete the following enthymeme?

If I am to start my car, then I must find the ignition key.
∴ If I am to drive my car, then I must find the ignition key.

The antecedent of the conclusion should contain the antecedent of the first
premise, and the antecedent of the second premise should contain the consequent
of the first premise, so the entire first premise should read, "If I am to drive my car,
then I must start my car."

Now complete the following enthymeme:

If I learn this material, I will do well on the assignments.

∴ If I learn this material, I will get a good grade.

Here the second premise should be constructed of the consequent of the first
premise, and the consequent of the conclusion. Therefore it should be, "If I do well
on the assignments, then I will get a good grade."

The next enthymeme requires you to invent a proposition that will act as a logical
"go-between" for the antecedent and consequent of the conclusion:

If I don't keep a record of my checks, then
If _____ , then I am likely to overdraw my account.
∴ If I don't keep a record of my checks, then I am likely to overdraw my
account.

Here the missing proposition needs to link the antecedent of the first premise with the consequent of the second. So what is needed is a proposition that follows from the first, but guarantees the second. Perhaps you thought of something like, "I won't (don't) know how much money is in my account."

As a last exercise, try completing your own conditional argument for the following conclusion:

_____

∴ If I'm to finish the job on time, then I must skip lunch.

To complete this, begin by filling in the antecedent of the first premise with the antecedent of the conclusion, and the consequent of the second premise with the consequent of the conclusion, as was done for you in the last example. Then find a single proposition that will link the first and second premises. One example would be, "I need 6 more hours working time."

As with the other forms of hypothetical syllogism, there is an argument form that is quite similar to conditional syllogism, but it is invalid. Its form is:

If A, then B.
If A, then C.
∴ If B, then C.   INVALID

To see that this is invalid, consider an example with true premises and a possibly false conclusion:

If Sam plays for the Atlanta Braves, Sam is a baseball player.
If Sam plays for the Atlanta Braves, Sam works for Ted Turner.
∴ If Sam is a baseball player, Sam works for Ted Turner.

Assume Sam plays for the Pittsburgh Pirates. Then the premises would both be true and, although Ted Turner might wish the conclusion were true, it would not be. So the argument must be invalid.

Alternative and Disjunctive Syllogisms

This last set of valid propositional logic forms uses the *either–or, and,* and *not* operators to construct arguments. The three kinds examined here are called *alternative syllogisms, disjunctive syllogisms,* and *alternative-disjunctive syllogisms.*

Alternative Syllogisms.   Alternative syllogisms, like modus ponens, modus tollens, and the basic form of conditional syllogisms, have two premises and a conclusion. But whereas those three forms of hypothetical syllogism all have *If,* *then* propositions as their first premises (hence the name hypothetical syllogisms), this form of syllogism has, as its name might suggest, an alternative proposition as its first premise. Recall from our discussion of the *either–or* operator earlier in this chapter that another name for an *either–or* proposition is an alternative proposition, and that its two halves are each called alternatives. So an alternative syllogism will state either that one thing is the case or that something else is. As its second premise, it will state that one of those alternatives is not true. Because the first premise says that (at least) one of them has to be true, we can conclude that the other must be true. Symbolically, we have:

Either A or B.	Either A or B.	Alternative syllogism
-A	-B	
∴ B	∴ A	VALID

So there will be no misunderstanding, we have included both forms of the argument, negating both the first and then the second alternative in the second premise. There is nothing special about the order of the two alternatives in the first premise, so it makes no difference which we negate in the second premise, so long as we go on to conclude the other alternative in the conclusion.

Neither is there anything special about the number of alternatives that has been presented in these examples. Suppose we knew that at least one of *four* different things were true. Then we should be able to validly conclude that if one of them were not true, then at least one of the other three would have to be, and that if two of them were not true, then at least one of the remaining two would have to be true, and so forth. That is, the following are all valid forms of alternative syllogism:

Either A or B or C or D.	Either A or B or C or D.	Either A or B or C or D.
-D	-C and -D	-B and -C and -D.
∴ Either A or B or C.	∴ Either A or B.	∴ A

Alternative syllogisms are particularly useful forms of argument when you are certain of the number of alternatives, and are able to eliminate some. Much puzzle solving is based on this form of syllogism. You know that a piece of the puzzle fits somewhere, but you don't know where, so you try several places, find that it doesn't fit there, and conclude that it must fit in the remaining place. Think of picture puzzles, or of the kind of reasoning you do when you have a set of keys, one of which you know fits a lock. If you're not sure which one it is, then you will probably proceed to find out by eliminating alternatives, trying first one key, then the next, until you've found the right one. If you reason this way, you've used an alternative syllogism. Or if the police are certain that one of five persons under arrest committed a crime, but they don't know which, they might deduce which person did it if they find that four of them have unshakable alibis.

In order to make your practice with enthymemes a little more challenging this time, first look at the invalid, or fallacious form of this argument. It is extremely easy to commit, and probably is responsible for more invalid conclusions than any other fallacy we study. It takes the form:

Either A or B.

A _____

∴ -B   INVALID

We can see that this form is invalid if we recall the truth table for *either–or*. It is the very first line of this truth table that causes the problem: People often forget that to assert that either one thing is true, or another is, is to leave open the possibility that both may be. If I tell you that I may paddle the Chattooga River this weekend, or the Chauga, I will not have lied if it turns out that I paddle both. One alternative's being true does not rule out the possibility of the other's being true. If one wishes to do so, one can always add, "but not both." As becomes obvious when we turn to that form of argument (i.e, alternative-disjunctive syllogisms), the invalid form listed previously is in that case *not* a fallacy. But that is another story that we get to soon enough.

As practice, supply the missing premise to make the following enthymeme valid:

Either we will negotiate with the terrorists or they will kill our hostages.

_____

∴ They will kill our hostages.

Because the second alternative was deduced to be true, a valid form requires that the first alternative have been stated to be false. Thus, "We will not negotiate with the terrorists" is required. Now try to supply the missing premise for a similar argument:

Either we will negotiate with the terrorists or they will kill our hostages.

_____

∴ They will not kill our hostages.

Did you supply "We will negotiate with the terrorists"? If so, then you have joined the ranks of thousands who have committed the fallacy just mentioned. You were probably assuming that negotiations would prevent the hostages from being killed, that is, that both alternatives couldn't co-exist. But that assumption cannot be made with an *either–or* proposition. No second premise can be supplied that will make this argument valid. You should have tried, and found it impossible to do.

Try to supply the missing premise for this alternative argument:

It won't sleet.

∴ It will snow.

This is a very common form of enthymeme. Whenever people deduce that something will occur simply from something else's not occurring, the chances are that they are assuming an alternative proposition as a first premise. Here that alternative proposition must be: "It it will either sleet or snow."

One of the important reasons for learning enthymemes is so that you can be sure what assumptions other people have behind their arguments. Often, by way of criticism, those assumptions can be challenged. And when you are dealing with enthymematic arguments in which the first premise of an alternative proposition has been omitted, the chances are very high that there is room for criticism. This is because of a tendency many people have to understate the real number of alternatives in any situation. We encounter the fallacy of false alternative again in a subsequent chapter, but for the present let us note that in the previous example the real number of possible alternatives is very likely to be larger than the number stated. Ordinarily there is some likelihood, for example, that it also might rain, or that there might be no precipitation at all. If there is such a likelihood, then the original missing premise—"Either A or B"—is false, and some other premise—"Either A or B or C or D," for example—is true.

The obverse of the advice given—to look for false alternatives when people use enthymematic alternative arguments in which the first premise is missing—is that you need to be very careful yourself when you construct such arguments. If other alternatives than the ones you list do exist, then you will have constructed an argument with a false premise.

As one last example, you should employ this advice in supplying the missing premise to make the following enthymematic argument valid:

John is either   or over 6 ft tall.

_____

∴. He is over 6 ft tall.

Did you supply "John is either under 6 ft tall or over 6 ft tall" as your first premise? If so, then you committed the fallacy of false alternative, for you left out the possibility that he might be exactly 6 ft tall. Notice that when that is included in the first premise, the second premise must be expanded too in order to produce a valid syllogism:

John is either over 6 ft tall, under 6 ft tall, or 6 ft tall.
He is not under 6 ft tall, and he is not 6 ft tall.
∴. He is over 6 ft tall.

Disjunctive Syllogisms.   Disjunctive propositions are used when we want to rule out the possibility that two propositions might both be true. To do this, we use the operator, "Not both A and B" (or some equivalent thereof). This gives rise to a useful kind of argument, for if we know that one of the propositions is true, we can validly conclude that the other is not. Symbolically, we have:

Not both A and B.   Disjunctive syllogism
A_____
∴ -B   VALID

As with the previous form, it doesn't matter which order the A and the B appear in, so long as one is affirmed in the second premise, and the other is negated in the conclusion. The following argument illustrates this form:

> Elaine cannot both be a convicted felon and have a gun permit.
> Elaine is a convicted felon._____
> ∴ Elaine cannot have a gun permit.

Try this one yourself:

> Carol cannot be both a citizen of the United States and a citizen of Germany.
> _____
> ∴ Carol is not a citizen of the United States.

Here, Carol must have been a citizen of Germany in order for it to be concluded that she was not a citizen of the United States.
  Supply the missing first premise here:

> John is married._____
> ∴ John is not a Catholic priest.

Here the first premise must be: "John couldn't be both married and a Catholic priest."
  As a final exercise, supply two premises that imply the conclusion:

> _____
> ∴ Joan will not buy a new computer.

  To solve this you need to think of some situation that is incompatible with Joan buying a new computer. State that incompatibility in the first, disjunctive, premise. Then state that that situation occurred, in the second premise. That will allow you to conclude that the other situation, Joan's buying a new computer, could not have occurred. An example of the first situation might have been Joan's buying a new car.
  As usual, there is a fallacious argument that closely resembles a valid disjunctive syllogism. Remembering the truth table for *not both* will help you to see how the fallacy arises. This time it is the last line of the truth table that causes the problem, for we often tend to forget that although it may not be possible for two things to occur together, that leaves open the possibility that neither may occur. The general form of the fallacy is:

Not both A and B.
<u>-A   </u>
∴ B   INVALID

An example of this is a variation of an earlier syllogism:

Elaine cannot both be a convicted felon and have a gun permit.
<u>Elaine does not have a gun permit.   </u>
∴ Elaine is a convicted felon.

Clearly, she could fail to be a convicted felon *and* not have a gun permit.

Alternative-Disjunctive Syllogisms.   As the name suggests, alternative-disjunctive syllogisms are a combination of alternative syllogisms and disjunctive syllogisms. Their first premise is always in the form of an alternative-disjunctive proposition: "Either A or B, but not both." If the second premise then asserts that A (or B) is the case, then because of the "not both" phrase, we can conclude that B (or A) must not be the case. If the second premise asserts that A (or B) is not the case, then because of the either–or phrase, we can be guaranteed that B (or A) must be the case. Symbolically, we have:

Either A or B, but not both.   Either A or B, but not both.
<u>A   </u>   <u>-A </u>
∴ -B   ∴B

As an example, suppose we see an international driving symbol on the rear of someone's car, in the form of the letter *S*. We've forgotten whether that means Sweden or Switzerland, but we know it stands for one of the countries, and we're sure it can't stand for both countries. If we now learn that it stands for Sweden, we can conclude that it doesn't stand for Switzerland, as the aforementioned form on the left shows. But as the form on the right shows, if we learn that it does not stand for Sweden, we can infer that it does stand for Switzerland.

Because, given either an A or a -A, or a B or a -B, *something* follows from an alternative-disjunctive's first premise, there is little opportunity to commit a fallacy with this form of argument (unless of course one inferred from A that B was true, or from B that A was true). But in addition to this virtue, this argument form is also extremely useful, and widely used. Very often when it is used, the linguistic operators *either–or, but not both* are not explicitly stated, but implied by the context. Thus, if you are awarded an airline ticket for a free roundtrip passage to either Paris or London, the implicit meaning is that you cannot use the ticket to fly to both places. A lawsuit that tried to establish that you should be allowed to, based on the logical grounds that *either–or* allows both possibilities to occur, and *not both* was not included in the statement of the award, would not stand a chance in a court. And this is rightly so. The contexts of propositions should be taken into account when determining what their utterers meant. Very often speakers do mean to include *not both* when they utter *either–or* statements, but fail to do so. If we wish to give them the benefit of the doubt when we try to understand them, we will often have to assume that they meant an alternative-disjunctive syllogism when quite literally all they stated was an alternative syllogism. Giving others the benefit of the doubt, logically speaking, is a practice that has much to recommend it. Doing so does not indicate a *failure* to be logical, but a logical awareness of the importance of contexts. Only an insensitive and poorly trained logician would ever say, as one sometimes hears, "But you didn't *say* so-and-so, so you couldn't have meant it."

⚟ CATEGORICAL LOGIC ⚟

So far in this chapter we have been learning the rules for the use of certain logical operators, and then learning how to combine propositions that use those operators into logically valid arguments. Having come this far, you should congratulate yourself on being able to understand how propositions can be logically combined. Now it is time to turn to another area of logic—what is known variously as *class logic*, or *Aristotelian logic*, or *classical logic*, or by the name we use, *categorical logic*.

Let us look at an example of categorical logic to see how it differs from sentential or propositional logic. Here is an example of a valid syllogism of categorical logic:

> None of Beethoven's piano sonatas are trite.
> <u>The *Waldstein* is a piano sonata by Beethoven.</u>
> ∴ The *Waldstein* is not trite.

Some aspects of this example should seem familiar to you, whereas others should not. It certainly looks like what we have come to know as a syllogism, for it has two premises and a conclusion, such that the premises seem to imply the conclusion. But exactly how these premises imply the conclusion is not something we are at this point prepared to deal with. *Not* is the only logical operator in it with which we are familiar. And its form clearly is not an immediate inference, nor any of the hypothetical syllogisms, nor any of the alternative or disjunctive syllogisms.

What these considerations mean is that we need another way of assessing the validity of arguments such as the previous one. Unless we are content with just guessing whether each new case of a categorical syllogism was valid—and in the previous example we might guess correctly that it is valid—we need a means of *taking apart* the premises, so that we can see how they do or do not fit together. There are two ways of doing this. One is long, involved, detailed, requires a completely new set of rules from the ones we have already learned, and will enable us to deal meticulously with any categorical syllogism. The other is short, relatively simple, does not require another set of rules for validity, and will enable us to deal with only the most frequently used categorical syllogisms. It is the second method of analyzing categorical syllogisms that we learn here. This method allows us to *translate* most categorical syllogisms into hypothetical form. Then we are in a position to use the rules for hypothetical syllogisms to evaluate the validity of the arguments.

In categorical logic, most propositions are of four forms:

All A's are B's.
No A's are B's.
Some A's are B's.
Some A's are not B's.
(For example,)
All politicians are honest.
No politicians are honest.
Some politicians are honest.
Some politicians are not honest.

It is the first two kinds of propositions that you will most often be using in your arguments, and so it is those you learn how to translate and how to treat syllogistically. Symbolically, translations of them look like this:

CATEGORICAL	HYPOTHETICAL
All A's are B's.	If something is an A, then it is a B.
No A's are B's.	If something is an A, then it is not a B.

Whenever you see a syllogism in which a premise reads, for example, "All elephants are large," you can write in its place the more familiar, "If something is an elephant, it is a large thing," or for short, "If something is an elephant, it is large." And when you see "No mice are large," you can write, "If something is a mouse, it is not large." These two translations alone will enable you to deal with several different kinds of syllogism. It is easy to show that those that are valid categorically are valid hypothetically, and those that are invalid categorically are invalid hypothetically. Here are a few examples:

CATEGORICAL		HYPOTHETICAL
All A's are B's.		If something is an A, then it is a B.
All B's are C's.	VALID	If something is a B, then it is a C .
∴All A's are C's.		∴If something is an A, then it is a C.
All A's are B's.		If something is an A, then it is a B.
No B's are C's.	VALID	If something is a B, then it is not a C.
∴No A's are C's.		∴ If something is an A, it is not a C.
All A's are B's.		If something is an A, then it is a B.
No A's are C's.	INVALID	If something is an A, it is not a C.
∴No B's are C's.		∴If something is a B, it is not a C.

All A's are B's.		If something is an A, then it is a B.
All C's are B's.	INVALID	If something is a C, then it is a B.
∴ All A's are C's.		∴ If something is an A, then it is a C.

You can see that the hypothetical equivalents of these categorical syllogisms are all in the form of conditional syllogisms. You can also see that all those categorical syllogisms that are labeled valid categorically are valid hypothetically (because they follow the valid form of hypothetical syllogism), and all that are invalid categorically have no valid hypothetical counterpart.

There is another kind of proposition that occurs in categorical logic for which you need a hypothetical equivalent. Consider the following categorical argument:

All Floridians are Americans.
Jerry is a Floridian.
∴ Jerry is an American.

This has the form:

All A's are B's.
x is an A.
∴ x is a B.

Whereas up to now all categorical propositions have referred to classes of things, such as Floridians, elephants, and large objects, the second premise is a proposition referring to a particular person, or to what is called a *particular*. The question that arises is how to deal with this hypothetically. What you obviously need is a rule that will allow you to substitute the name of an individual in any position where the word *something* has occurred. Thus, you need to be able to regard "Jerry is a Floridian" as affirming the antecedent of "If something (or better, *someone*) is a Floridian, then it (that person) is an American." It will be legitimate to do this only by fudging slightly on the fallacy of three terms, for strictly speaking, the only way to affirm the antecedent of "If someone is a Floridian, then that person is an American" is by saying, "Someone is a Floridian." But we want to replace the second "someone" in this proposition with "Jerry." What licenses us to do so is the fact that "someone" means "Any one person you pick, such as Susan, Ellen, John, or Jerry." Because you choose here to pick Jerry as the someone, you can regard "Jerry is a Floridian" as affirming "Someone is a Floridian." When you do this, you can then go on to conclude that the same someone, namely Jerry, is an American. Thus you find that the previous categorical syllogism is valid in hypothetical form, for it is equivalent to:

If someone is a Floridian, then that person is an American.
Someone (namely, Jerry) is a Floridian.
∴ Someone (namely, Jerry) is an American.

Notice that it *would* constitute the fallacy of three terms were you to conclude, in this argument, that Elisa is an American. In that case our conclusion would not affirm the exact consequent of the first premise, because the "that person" in that premise is supposed to refer to the same someone who is a Floridian.

So long as you are clear what does and what does not commit the fallacy of three terms in examples such as these, you can write them in a shorter form than that given earlier. You can eliminate the "Someone, namely" phrase from the second premise and the conclusion, and write the example as:

> If someone is a Floridian, then that person is an American.
> Jerry is a Floridian.
> ∴ Jerry is an American.

Let's try to evaluate another categorical argument by translating it into hypothetical form. Consider the argument:

> All A's are B's.
> x is not a B.
> ∴ x is not an A.

Translating this into hypothetical form, we have

> If something is an A, then it is a B.
> x is not a B.
> ∴ x is not an A.

This uses the form modus tollens, and so it is valid.

So far we have worked through the translations for six forms of categorical argument, and seen that four are valid and two are invalid. The following is a list of 14 of the most common forms of categorical syllogism (including the ones already discussed). On the left are listed valid forms, and on the right invalid forms. Although this list will serve as a reference tool, there is no substitute for knowing on your own how to determine whether a given categorical syllogism is valid. Therefore, as practice you should translate each of these categorical forms into hypothetical syllogisms, making sure you can tell why those labeled *valid* are valid, and those labeled *invalid* are invalid.

VALID FORMS	INVALID FORMS
No A's are B's.	All A's are B's.
∴ No B's are A's.	∴ All B's are A's.
All A's are B's.	All A's are B's.
x is an A.	x is a B.
∴ x is a B.	∴ x is an A.

All A's are B's. x is not a B. ∴ x is not an A.	All A's are B's. x is not an A. ∴ x is not a B.
No A's are B's. x is an A. ∴ x is not a B.	No A's are B's. x is not an A. ∴ x is (or isn't) a B.
All A's are B's. All B's are C's. ∴ All A's are C's.	All A's are B's. All A's are C's. ∴ All B's are C's.
All A's are B's. No C's are B's. ∴ No A's are C's.	All A's are B's. All C's are B's. ∴ All A's are C's.
All A's are B's. No B's are C's. ∴ No A's are C's.	All A's are B's. No A's are C's. ∴ No B's are C's.

If you were able to translate each of these syllogisms into its corresponding hypothetical form, then at this point you should feel comfortable in your ability to migrate from one form to the other. It is important that you have this ability, for it will allow you to express your arguments in a variety of ways. Sometimes the context of what you are saying or writing seems to *demand* that you speak the language of categorical logic, whereas at other times hypothetical forms will seem to fit the context better. Logically, of course, so long as you are careful to use equivalent and valid forms, it makes no difference whether you use a categorical or a hypothetical form.

In addition to the previous list of common valid and invalid categorical forms, it may be helpful to have a list (see Table 3.1) of the valid and invalid forms of immediate inference, hypothetical syllogism, and alternative and disjunctive syllogism that we have studied.

COMBINATIONS OF SIMPLE FORMS OF ARGUMENT

Having had an opportunity to learn the truth tables for the various operators that go into these arguments, having discussed the general form, as well as examples, of the arguments themselves, and having had some practice discovering the missing premises of enthymemes that use these arguments, you should now be quite conversant with them. (If not, you will get more practice in the exercises for this

TABLE 3.1
Forms of Inference

Valid Argument Forms			Invalid Argument Forms
Immediate inference			
Conversion	If A, then B. ∴If −B, then −A.		If A, then B. ∴If −A, then −B.
Double Negation	A ∴ −−A	−−A ∴A	
De Morgan Laws	−(A or B) ∴ −A and −B −A and −B ∴ −(A or B)	−(A and B) ∴ −A or −B −A or −B ∴ −(A and B)	−(A and B) ∴ −A and −B −A or −B ∴ −(A or B)
Hypothetical syllogism			
Modus Ponens	If A, then B. A ∴B	Affirming the Consequent	If A, then B. B ∴A
Modus Tollens	If A, then B. −B ∴ −A	Denying the Antecedent	If A, then B. −A ∴ −B
Conditional Syllogism	If A, then B. If B, then C. ∴If A, then C.		If A, then B. If A, then C. ∴If B, then C.
Alternative and disjunctive syllogism			
Alternative	Either A or B. −A (−B) ∴B (A)		Either A or B. A (B) ∴ −B (−A)
Disjunctive	Not both A and B. A (B) ∴ −B (−A)		Not both A and B. −A (−B) ∴B (A)
Alternative-Disjunctive	Either A or B, but not both. A (B) (−A) (−B) ∴ −B (−A) (B) (A)		

chapter.) You will often find it useful to use the simple forms listed in Table 3.1 as models for arguments you want to construct. But often you will also find it helpful to combine various forms, and to use various logical operators together with these forms. The number of possible combinations is obviously very large, and we cannot cover here the complete range of possibilities. But we finish this chapter by taking a brief look at some examples.

Modus ponens can be used together with both the *and* and the *either–or* operators. One can claim, for example, "If A and B and C and D are true, then E will be." To affirm this antecedent one needs of course to know that A and B and C and D are all true. Or one can claim, "If either A or B or C or D were true, then E would be." Because of the way the *either–or* operator works, to affirm that antecedent one would only have to know that one of those elements was true. Symbolically, then, we have:

If A and B and C and D, then E.	If either A or B or C or D, then E.
A and B and C and D.	Either A or B or C or D.
∴ E	∴ E

Sometimes hypothetical propositions are combined with other hypothetical propositions. Thus, "If you are filing a joint return, then if your joint income is less than $25,000, you should use schedule A." Let us call such a proposition an *iterated hypothetical proposition*. A modus ponens that would use this as the first premise could be symbolized this way:

If A, then if B, then C.
A
∴ If B, then C.

If B, then C.
B
∴ C

Notice that it takes A's being true and B's being true to infer C from the first premise. This might suggest to you another way of putting the original proposition: "If you are filing a joint return and your income is less than $25,000, then you should use schedule A." Let us call such a proposition a *conjunctive hypothetical proposition*. Symbolically, the syllogism would be:

If A and B, then C.
A and B
∴ C

Notice that here as well it took A's being true and B's being true for C to be inferred, so a syllogism that uses an iterated hypothetical proposition can always be converted into one that uses a conjunctive hypothetical proposition. For most purposes, you and your audience will find conjunctive hypothetical propositions easier to deal with.

Another combination of forms, which occurs frequently enough to have been given a name, is the use of an alternative proposition together with a pair of hypotheticals, in the following way:

Either A or B.
If A, then C.
If B, then D.   Constructive dilemma
∴ Either C or D

This form, called (for no particularly helpful reason) *constructive dilemma*, can occur in two specialized versions. Sometimes the same consequent follows from either of the disjuncts. Then its form is this:

> Either A or B.
> If A, then C.
> If B, then C.
> ∴ C

Sales presentations and advertisements often employ this form of reasoning: "Whether it's A or B that you want, our product offers them both, so our product is the one you ought to buy."

A second form of constructive dilemma that is particularly effective occurs when the second disjunct is a negation of the first. The form of such an argument is:

> Either A or -A.
> If A, then C.   Arguing in the alternative
> If -A, then C.
> ∴ C

Lawyers are extremely fond of this form of argument, and have given it the name *arguing in the alternative*. It combines an alternative proposition in the first premise with two hypothetical propositions, both of which have the same conclusion. Because the first premise includes two mutually exclusive alternatives, it makes the conclusion appear absolutely inevitable. It's somewhat like saying, "Here's my evidence that B is true: A. But if you think that A is false, that's fine too, because -A implies B as well. So either way, B must be true." The trick to using this form lies of course in finding a proposition such that it *and its negation* imply the conclusion you want. Such a proposition is usually by itself very difficult to find. Here's an example: "Either the defendant killed the deceased or he didn't. I've given evidence to show that he didn't. And if he didn't, then of course you shouldn't convict him. But if you don't accept that evidence, then you should accept the evidence I've presented that he was insane the night of the murder. So even if he did kill the deceased, then you should not convict him. Either way, he should not be convicted."

The effectiveness of this particular argument of course depends on the strength of the evidence showing both that the defendant didn't commit the crime as well as that the defendant was insane the night of the crime. But the logical strategy used here, in which one "covers all the bases," is very powerful.

4

The Basic Argumentative Essay: Identifying Your Audience and Developing Your Conclusion

On some occasions you will be able to achieve your objectives in arguing for a conclusion directly through the use of the valid argument forms presented in the last chapter. For example, if someone asks you why they should support a particular candidate, you might answer, "Because she has been supportive of environmental measures and is fiscally conservative." As we have learned, this is an enthymeme with a suppressed premise such as, "If a candidate has been supportive of environmental measures and is fiscally conservative, then you should support her." If your interlocutor agrees with both your stated premise and the suppressed premise, you will have established your conclusion. But many of the conclusions you will want to argue for cannot be established this easily. One reason is that your audience might not assent to one of the premises you use in such an argument. (This might be true in the previous example: Someone might not already agree that the candidate has been supportive of environmental measures, or that this is a reason for supporting that candidate.) In this case, you will have to present an argument to convince someone of the premise of your argument before you can employ it.

When simple arguments are not sufficient, then you must combine the simple forms to make more complex structures. This, in a nutshell, is what is involved in constructing an argumentative essay. In this chapter and the next we are concerned with the basic skills involved in writing an effective argumentative essay. An argumentative essay is different from several other types of essays (e.g., descriptive essays or narrative essays) you might write. The difference lies in the fact that in an argumentative essay you are trying to convince someone to agree with a claim you are making and for which you are offering logical arguments. The difference is manifested in the fact that an argumentative essay has a *conclusion* or *thesis*. In setting out to write an argument, it is important to be extremely clear about your conclusion. In an argumentative essay, everything you say should be directed to demonstrating the truth of this conclusion. Moreover, what you say must be adequate to the conclusion. Hence, a major task in constructing an argumentative essay is to formulate your conclusion. This task is our central focus in this chapter. But before turning to it, there is a preliminary point we must deal with. The goal of an argumentative essay is to convince an *audience* of a claim. Thus, throughout the task of constructing an argument we must be cognizant of who our audience is. We begin with a brief discussion of what you need to know about your audience in constructing an argumentative essay.

KNOWING YOUR AUDIENCE

If you carefully consider what happens when we use valid argument forms, you realize that all they guarantee is that if you start with true premises, you reach a true conclusion. If a valid argument is to convince someone, that person must already accept that your premises are true. Even as we learn to combine argument forms into more complex structures, we still face the same limitation: We can only show people that a conclusion is true if they already accept the truth of the premises with which we start. This has an important consequence: You can only convince someone through logic to accept a conclusion not already accepted if that person already agrees with you on *some premises*. Arguing with someone who agreed with absolutely nothing that you believed would be a futile task, for every premise you advanced would have to be defended by advancing some other argument. Arguing with children is sometimes like this. They are notoriously good at continuing to challenge whatever reasons or premises you advance. "Why is that so?" they ask, and you respond "Because of this." "But why is *that* so?" they ask. "Because of this," you say, thinking that this will satisfy them. But it doesn't, and often the only way out of their incessant questions seems to be to stop talking altogether. There is so much to explain to them, but not enough time to do it. Taken to the limit, the lesson we learn from explaining or arguing with children is that arguments *can* go on forever.

Fortunately, however, most people with whom we argue do share *some* beliefs and assumptions with us. Clearly they do not share all of our beliefs, for if they did, there would be nothing to argue about. "Let me prove to you that X" is said only against a background assumption that the person to whom you are speaking does not already believe X, or at least that they do not believe it for the same reasons you do. (Sometimes people do respond, "I already think X is true too, but go ahead and tell me *your* reasons for it.") Usually, though, if other people already believe what you are about to prove to them, they will tell you so, and you will then save your breath.

We proceed to give other people an argument for our view. Then, we assume that they share some beliefs with us, but not the belief in the conclusion we are about to prove. Insofar as we know or can determine what those shared beliefs are, we will have found appropriate stopping places for our argumentative chains. Often we make assumptions about what others believe. We say to a friend, "You're going to buy that product from company X? Don't you know that this company advertises on pornographic television shows?" In so doing, we assume that the friend shares our view about television shows that we deem to be pornographic, and our belief that a company that advertises on such shows ought to have its products boycotted. We assume, that is, that what we have pointed out will furnish an "ultimate" premise for our argument, such that if the friend accepts the fact that the company does advertise on the television shows in question, that will be all it will take to convince that friend not to buy its products. Our friend may of course surprise us and say, "Well, so what?" Obviously we are then going to have to do some more arguing to convince the friend not to buy the product. Friends, even close friends, can surprise us in this way, making our argumentative day longer than we thought it was going to be.

In oral argumentation, the only penalty we have to pay for being wrong about the assumptions and beliefs we share with the people to whom we are talking is the job of having to do some more arguing. But in written argumentation, the case is different. We write a letter to the editor of our local newspaper, hoping to persuade its readers of the foolishness of a proposed piece of legislation, but often we have no idea how effective or ineffective our letter may have been. To ensure that it is as effective as possible, what is necessary is to know what are the *assumed premises* on which we should rest our argument. Assumed premises are the stopping points beyond which we need not go because we can safely assume our audience shares our belief in them. But in order to know what those points are, we need to know some things about our audience.

There are two points at which knowing your audience can be extremely important in developing your argument. We have been emphasizing one of them: You must know your audience in order to determine what premises it will accept as assumed premises. In the process, though, we have alluded to a second reason: It would be futile to argue for a conclusion that your audience already accepted. Thus, you must also know your audience in order to determine that your conclusion is something for which an argument is needed.

In reviewing your audience there are many things that you might focus on. The following points are most likely to be relevant in determining whether they accept your premises or conclusion:

Initial attitude toward the subject
Age
Occupation
Socioeconomic status
Educational level
Intellectual and cultural interests
Moral views
Political views
Social views
Religious views
Possible self-interested motives

In any particular case, some of these will be relevant, others irrelevant.

Let us look at a few of these factors, and see how they might influence the course of an argument. Suppose you have been elected president of your neighborhood homeowner's group, and the job of presenting your group's case against a proposed zoning change has fallen to you. Suppose the zoning change would allow a new topless night club, bar, and package store to be built on the edge of your neighborhood. There may be several audiences you would wish to address: your fellow citizens of the county, a group of clergy whose support you hope to enlist, a local club of teenagers, the realtor who is handling the sale of the property, the person who is president of your local chamber of commerce, and the zoning commission itself, which will have to rule on the matter in a few weeks. The conclusion you are going to argue for will be the same for each group: The zoning should not be changed to allow the club.

The first thing you need to know about your various potential audiences is what attitude they already have toward the change. Perhaps some of them have no view at all, and perhaps others have very strong views on either side of the issue. Clearly, your time is poorly spent arguing with those who already agree with you. *Preaching to the converted* is the name commonly given to such useless activity, although here we might rename it *arguing to the convinced*. Suppose that you find, for example, that the group of clergy agrees with you, and is opposed to the change for many of the same reasons that you are, but that the chamber of commerce president is in favor of the zoning change. Your time is going to be better spent arguing with that person rather than the clergy. However, it will only make sense arguing with the chamber of commerce president if you can find a basis for argument on which the president might be convinced. On some issues, unfortunately, you will find that some audiences are so inalterably set in their ways that they cannot be moved by argument.

If you decide to argue against the chamber of commerce president, it is important that you find out not only why the president is in favor of the rezoning but also some of the other factors listed previously. Finding out the president's reasons for favoring it will be necessary for structuring a critique of the president's arguments (which we discuss in chapter 7), but finding out "what makes the president tick" will help you in structuring your demonstrations. The president will probably be very interested in the economic aspects of the rezoning, so if you can show the president that there are economic advantages to not changing the zoning for the club, you may have the basis for convincing the president to support your side. However, the same argument may not be successful with other audiences who do not find the economic consequences to be of major importance in deciding on the zoning. For example, it is unlikely that the local club of teenagers will be moved by them. On the other hand, the age of the teenagers is quite relevant to the reasons you may give them against the rezoning. Pointing out to them that the club will be restricted to admitting only those over 21 years of age, and the package store will only serve those who have already been admitted to the club, may serve to dampen their enthusiasm for the club (if that is indeed what you found their initial attitude to be). However, such facts would probably not serve as reasons for the members of the zoning commission to deny the request for a change. That the club will admit only those over 21 and serve only those already admitted may, in their eyes, be a reason *in favor of* the rezoning.

Again, if you wish to argue against the rezoning to your fellow citizens of the county, you may find that an inexpensive but effective way of doing this is to write letters to the editors of the various newspapers in the county. But then some research into who reads those newspapers is going to be a prerequisite for structuring your argument. The readers of a large metropolitan daily will have different characteristics than the readers of a small suburban neighborhood weekly. And the interests, views, politics, educational level, and so forth of these two readerships may in turn be different from those of the readers of a small weekly that serves a rural part of the county whose inhabitants are mostly lower-middle-income people with little education. Even the language you use, including your vocabulary, is going to have to be different for these various newspapers. Certainly the shared assumptions, beliefs, and values that you may have with the various readers are going to be different, and you are going to need to determine what they are in order to know what assumed premises you can rely on as a basis for your argument.

Let's be clear what taking your audience into account does and does not entail. Some people have interpreted remarks such as the ones we have made in this section as meaning that good arguers cater to the particular audience being addressed, and in essence tell it what it wants to hear. But this would mean that the arguers have no standards of their own, and merely adopt the whims, biases, and prejudices of others. To cater to the audience instead of advancing one's own views seems, in short, to make arguers into modern sophists, the counterpart of those ancient Greek rhetoricians who would argue any side of an issue, adopting views they did not believe just to win an argument. And surely (so the objection goes) logic ought to enable us to rise above this level.

If what we have said did amount to this, logic would be in trouble. But it is not. We are not recommending that the good arguer should tell the audience what it wants to hear, nor are we recommending that you ever argue for something based on a belief you do not have. To begin with, you are trying to convince your audience to believe something it does not already believe, so you are not simply telling people what they want to hear. Moreover, in considering your audience while you are deciding our your premises, the goal is to find those *shared* beliefs that you can base your arguments on. You share many of your beliefs with many different people, but you won't share all of your beliefs with all people, nor is it likely that even any one person will have exactly the same set of beliefs that you do. What we have tried to stress is that there is no one argument that in each case is going to prove its conclusion to all people. Arguments require premises to support them, and it is very unlikely that any one premise that is at all interesting is going to be agreed on by everyone. Assumed premises are not *ultimate* in any metaphysical sense. They are simply the ones that the argument in question will rest on, at least temporarily. If someone wants to challenge them, then more argument may be required. Or, alternatively, perhaps there is such a profound difference in beliefs that no premise can be assumed to be accepted by all parties to the argument. In this case, no argumentation is possible. And if that is so, then it should be acknowledged, and the argument broken off. What should not happen is for you to change your beliefs just to win the argument. Realizing that some people need the conclusion demonstrated to them in different ways from other people does not require us to be sophists.

FORMULATING A CONCLUSION

The goal of an argumentative essay is to convince your audience of a conclusion. Thus, you must be making a claim of some kind. In the sample argumentative essay in chapter 1, for example, the claim was that Mytown should institute a program of curbside recycling of glass, plastics, and newspaper. Insofar as it makes a claim, a conclusion is not the same as a *topic* or subject matter for an essay. You might choose as a topic *cats* or *psychology* or *taxation*. But specifying such a topic does not yet specify a claim that you are trying to demonstrate to your audience. A conclusion must state something about the topic. For example, "cats should be kept indoors" is a possible conclusion. "Social psychology is a stimulating course" is another. These are claims that one person might try to demonstrate to another person.

You will need to come up with conclusions for each argumentative essay that you are asked to write in this course. For some students this can be an obstacle. But it is actually very simple. Begin with a topic or subject matter about which you are interested and know something. This may be an academic subject in which you have taken a course, or an activity in which you enjoy participating. Or it may be a problem you recognize in your college or society. The task now is to find a claim that you believe to be true, but that is not already believed to be true by your audience. Notice there are two clauses here, both of which must be satisfied. The claim for which you argue ought to be one you take to be true. Otherwise, it will not be possible for you to produce a sound argument for the claim. Second, it must be one that your audience does not already believe. If they already believe it, there is no point to the argument.

There is a further factor that you need to bear in mind in developing a thesis for an argument. This is the amount of room you have in which to present your argument. If you are writing an argumentative essay of five pages or less, you will not want to argue for an overly broad or complex conclusion, because you will not be able to marshal sufficient arguments to convince someone of that conclusion. Thus, you will not want to argue for the repeal of all your country's welfare programs, or that your country should institute a program of national health insurance. Either one of these might be the conclusion of an interesting argument, but such an argument will require a substantially longer essay. In writing a short essay you need to *focus* or *limit* your thesis to something that can be reasonably established within five pages. You might try to show that a particular welfare program is having adverse consequences that outweigh its benefits, or that one type of health care benefit (e.g., a vaccine for a contagious disease such as AIDS) should be provided by the national government.

Students sometimes worry that if they restrict their topic, they will not have enough to say to make a paper. But in fact, the opposite is usually true: The more focused your conclusion, the more material you will be able to identify from which to construct arguments. This is a consequence of the fact that a more specific claim provides a better memory cue, and thus makes it easier to come up with reasons.

Let us work through a couple examples of constructing the conclusion of an argument. First we must identify a topic or subject matter. Perhaps you are concerned with the cost of attending school. You might try immediately to formulate a position on this topic: *The cost of attending my college is too high.* This certainly is an arguable claim. But it is a very general claim. There are a variety of different costs associated with attending a college, and there are numerous different standards against which you might evaluate whether the costs are too high. Consider how you might focus this conclusion. You might focus on one of the costs of attending college—for example, the fee charged for extracurricular activities. The following will then be your conclusion: *The fees charged for support of extracurricular activities at my college are too high.* This provides one tentative conclusion for an argumentative essay. In the next section we consider some ways to test it for adequacy before we set out to construct arguments.

Let us develop one more example. This time we might choose as our topic the surge of commercial development in our neighborhood. We might be upset about it and consider how we might argue against it. This topic, however, is extremely broad, and we need to restrict it before we can develop an effective argument. If we realize that one place to direct our opposition is to the county zoning board, that might help us narrow it. Our topic becomes county zoning policy. Now we must consider what exactly we want to claim about county zoning policy. Here are three possibilities:

1. The county zoning board ought to put an end to any more commercial development in the county.
2. The county zoning board ought never to rezone residential areas in the county to make them commercial.
3. The county zoning board ought not to rezone a particular piece of property.

These are all possible conclusions, but they are clearly not equivalent. In the next section we consider some means for deciding between them.

TESTING POSSIBLE CONCLUSIONS

Once you have formulated a possible conclusion, you are getting close to the point at which you can begin to formulate your argument. But before you do so it is useful to test your conclusion to insure that it is appropriate for the kind of essay that you intend to write. In this section we present *seven rules for evaluating the conclusion* you have proposed. As you consider these rules, you may be led to revise your conclusion.

1. Never Argue for a Broader Position than Is Necessary

First, we can differentiate claims in terms of how broad or general they are. Some claims apply to many more objects or events than others. Consider the three conclusions about zoning policy we introduced at the end of the previous section. The first conclusion is far more sweeping than the second, for it prohibits commercial development in areas that are now zoned for commercial development. There might be justification for such a policy, but it raises substantial questions beyond those raised by the second conclusion. For instance, the value of land purchased with commercial zoning might go down precipitously, raising the question of whether commercial land owners are being treated fairly. The second conclusion does not raise this issue (except with respect to those who have bought land on the speculation that the zoning might subsequently be changed). Not only is the first thesis far broader, but it might be much more than is required for your purposes. You might be able to halt the growth of commercial development sufficiently by restricting the rezoning of land now zoned as residential. If so, then you are far better off arguing for the second conclusion than the first one, for with the first one you take on a much greater burden of proof. Thus, the first rule to employ in evaluating possible conclusions is: Never argue for a broader position than is necessary.

2. Never Argue for a Narrower Position than Is Necessary

Now consider the difference between the second and third conclusions. Conclusion 2 is again far more sweeping than Conclusion 3. It might be far easier to establish Conclusion 3 than Conclusion 2. But in this case Conclusion 3 might not be adequate for your objectives. It might stop one commercial development, but that is not likely to affect the rate of commercial development in your area significantly. Thus, it would also be a mistake to argue for a conclusion that was narrower than that you needed to establish. So the second rule for evaluating possible conclusions is: Never argue for a narrower position than is necessary.

These first two rules focus on the *scope* of your conclusion. In the context of writing papers for a course, you are largely in control of the scope of your conclusion. You will want to choose a scope broad enough to make the conclusion interesting, but narrow enough that you can deploy a convincing argument for it. When you are developing arguments in the real world, however, you do not have this luxury. When your boss instructs you to prepare a memo recommending the best computer for your company, the conclusion is going to have to be that such-and-such is the best computer. Your choice as to what the conclusion will be is very limited. In this context, the length of argument you will need to develop is determined by the nature of the conclusion for which you are arguing, rather than the other way around. But even in the practical world, you will want to give some thought to the scope of your conclusion. Within the bounds of what is assigned to you there may still be some latitude in determining your particular conclusion. Subtle differences in wording can often broaden or restrict your conclusion. For example, you might restrict the scope of your conclusion that such-and-such is the best computer for your company by building in some qualifications. You might argue that it is the best computer *given* available resources for capital expenditures and what computers are available through local vendors. You hereby limit yourself to a specific set of brands and to computers in a certain price range.

3. Make it Clear Whether Your Conclusion is a Demonstration, Critique, or Defense

In addition to evaluating whether your conclusion is too broad or too narrow, you need to test whether the conclusion captures the sort of argument you intend to make. Is your intent to prove or demonstrate that something is or isn't the case, or is it merely to show that someone's argument for a different conclusion is inadequate? Or do you intend to show that someone's critique of an argument on behalf of a conclusion is inadequate? Using the terminology introduced in chapter 1, the first case, in which we are trying to show that something is or isn't the case, presents an instance of a *demonstration*. If, however, the goal is to show that someone else's argument for a different position is inadequate, then we are concerned with developing a *critique*. Finally, if we are rebutting someone else's critique, we are engaged in *defense*. As we have worded our possible conclusions in this chapter, they will all constitute demonstrations. If what we seek to do, however, is critique someone else's argument in favor of permitting continued rezoning of residential land, then we need to word our conclusion differently. We will no longer be showing that the county zoning board ought never to rezone residential areas to commercial, but only that the argument in question does not show that this practice should be continued. Thus, we might word our conclusion: *Commissioner Doolittle's argument in favor of continued rezoning is inadequate*. If instead we want to rebut a critique of a previously made argument, our conclusion might be *Commissioner Doolittle's objections to our case for no further rezoning are inadequate*.

The third rule for evaluating possible conclusions, therefore, is: Make it clear whether your conclusion is a demonstration, critique, or defense. In some cases our mission will be more comprehensive: We might be putting forward an argument for a position (a demonstration), raising an objection to an argument for a contrary position (a critique), and defending against a critique of our position all at once. Notice for example that the sample essay in chapter 1 included a demonstration, but also considered possible critiques of that demonstration, and provided a defense against them. In that case, the author's conclusion was worded as in the case of a demonstration. But in additional sentences in the introduction, the author alerted the reader to the multiple tasks that were undertaken in the essay.

4. Make Clear the Kind of Statement for Which You Are Arguing

The fourth consideration focuses on the type of claim you are making in your conclusion. Are you arguing that a particular condition holds or that a state of affairs is true? If so, then the conclusion states a fact, and we will call it a *description*. It is sometimes claimed that you cannot argue about facts, but this is false. If they are well known, of course we won't bother arguing for them. But any time the facts are in dispute, we can try to demonstrate them. In fact, we often argue to show that something is the case: You might argue that a higher percentage of land has been rezoned from residential to commercial than vice versa. On the other hand, our conclusion might propose an *evaluation*. If we contended *too much land is being rezoned from commercial to residential*, we would be arguing for an evaluative conclusion. The words *too much* are the key terms that indicate the conclusion is evaluative.

Your conclusion might also take a variety of other forms. You might argue for a *prediction*, that is, for the claim that something will come to be true. An example would be arguing for the conclusion that *Property values for residential homes in this neighborhood will drop over the next 5 years.* Or you might argue for a *causal claim* in which you contend that one thing caused another. Thus, you might contend that *Current zoning practices have already caused property values to decline.* Another option is to argue for a *hypothetical* statement. You should already be familiar with hypothetical claims from the previous chapter. They state that *if* certain conditions are true, certain other conditions will also be true. In arguing for a hypothetical claim, you are not arguing that either the antecedent or the consequent is true, but that, should the antecedent be true, then the consequent will also be true. An example of a hypothetical conclusion would be: *If the county zoning board does not stop rezoning residential land to commercial, this community will become an undesirable community in which to live.* (You may note that predictions and hypothetical statements are often closely connected: We generally specify conditions under which a prediction will hold, and these might constitute the antecedent of a conditional.)

Your conclusion may also take the form of a *recommendation*. You might argue that some action should be taken. Your conclusion then takes the form of an *advice statement*. In other contexts you might be arguing on behalf of a certain policy, in which case your conclusion has the form of a *policy statement*. The difference between these is that an advice statement is generally focused on a particular situation. If you were arguing against rezoning a particular tract of land from residential to commercial, that might take the form of advice. A policy statement, on the other hand, once it is adopted, makes certain other conditions true. If the zoning board adopts a policy of never rezoning residential land to commercial, for example, then that would mean that no further rezoning of this sort will take place. Thus, the possible conclusion that the county zoning board ought never to rezone residential areas in the county to make them commercial represents a recommendation as to a policy.

It is important to make clear the sort of statement for which you are arguing, because these statements are very different, and will require different kinds of arguments. For example, note that some commissioners might be convinced that the predictions or hypothetical claims that you advance concerning what will happen if rezoning is allowed to continue are correct, but they might not agree with your policy recommendation. They might claim that although there are undesirable consequences of permitting rezoning, there are even worse consequences of prohibiting rezoning. They might foresee that the county could become involved in prolonged legal controversies that will require enormous tax increases if they adopt the policy. This shows that more needs to be done to prove the policy recommendation than the prediction.

5. Make Sure the Conclusion Is an Arguable Statement

Your goal is to argue for your conclusion, so you need to make sure it is something that can be argued for. As we have seen, there are a wide variety of kinds of statements for which you can argue. What kind of statements, then, are not arguable? There are three kinds of statements that are particularly worth noting: (a) subjective statements, (b) statements that are obviously true, and (c) narrative statements. *Subjective statements* often begin with words such as *I believe, I think,* or *It seems to me that.* It may be of interest that the speakers do or do not believe something, and it will be true or false that they do or do not believe it, but such statements do not constitute appropriate conclusions for arguments. They do not call for proof or evidence of a logical sort. Thus, it is not usually the business of argument to treat them as conclusions in need of demonstration. Notice, however, that it is usually possible to reword a subjective statement into an assertion that can be argued for. If someone asserted as a conclusion, *I believe that the county zoning board ought never to rezone residential areas in the county to make them commercial,* one could reword it by deleting the words *I believe that.* Now the truth of the statement does not turn on the subjective state of the speaker, but on whether the proposed policy is correct.

The second kind of unarguable assertion is one we have already discussed. You should not argue for an assertion that is *obviously true* or *known to be true* by your intended audience. The goal of an argument is to convince people to accept as true something they do not now believe. For example, if it is widely known that the county zoning board has recently rezoned several pieces of property from residential to commercial, and if it is generally accepted that this rezoning has had adverse consequences, then the statement, *The county zoning board has recently rezoned properties from residential to commercial, often with negative consequences* would not be arguable.

The third kind of unarguable assertion is a *narrative statement.* A narrative statement reports on a series of events. Generally, it is not controversial that these events occurred, and hence one need not argue that they did occur. Thus, a narrative such as, *The county zoning board met, and after reading and approving of the minutes from the previous meeting, considered whether to accept the application to rezone the Harrison property for purposes of building a shopping center,* is generally not controversial. As with all rules, there might be exceptional cases. If the event in question is one in the distant past, or there is some doubt about the order of events, one might proceed to develop an argument. Typically, however, a narration of an event does not require argumentation.

6. Make Sure the Conclusion is Definite

We noted earlier that your conclusion is not just a subject matter; it is a claim. You need to state your claim as precisely and as definitely as possible. If you are recommending the policy of never rezoning land from residential to commercial, then say so. Do not say, "I am going to discuss whether the county zoning board should rezone residential land for commercial use." Because you are going to argue that it should, commit yourself to defending this position at the outset. If you do not do this, the chances are very great that your argument will wander. Deciding exactly what it is you are going to argue for at the beginning will help to avoid this. If you do not have a claim to advance, then you have no business arguing.

The whole goal of argumentation is to convince your audience. If you are not explicit as to what conclusion you are arguing for, however, you probably won't convince them of the statement you want them to believe. For example, if your goal is to get a salary increase, but you only say you are going to discuss how you are rewarded for your work, your boss may conclude you merely want more acknowledgment, not an increase in salary. To have a chance of succeeding, your readers must know what it is you are trying to demonstrate. In fact, because getting them to accept your conclusion is the major goal, being explicit about the conclusion is actually as important as the arguments you give. Although you want your readers to accept your conclusion because of the arguments you put forward for it, what matters most is that they accept the conclusion. To have a chance of doing this, your reader must know what your conclusion is, and thus you must make sure the conclusion is definite.

7. Determine Whether the Conclusion Requires Qualification

After formulating your conclusion as clearly as possible, determine whether it requires qualification. It may be that you cannot prove the conclusion you would like to, but that you *are* able to prove a qualified version of it. The evidence you have at hand may just not support the conclusion that an expenditure of $2 million in advertising *will* produce increased sales revenues of $4 million, but the evidence may suggest that it is very likely that it will. If your evidence supports only this strong likelihood, then make your argument support the conclusion that an expenditure of $2 million in advertising will have a strong likelihood of producing increased revenues of $4 million. Perhaps this projection is based on past data relating expenditures and revenues. Because examples from the past never *guarantee* what the future will be like, you should qualify your projection. If you are using modus ponens as your basic argument form, for example, you might want your first premise to read, "If advertising expenditures last year of $1.5 million produced increased revenues of $3 million, then advertising expenditures next year of $2 million are very likely to produce increased revenue of $4 million." Notice the qualifier in this sentence: You did not say that increased advertising expenditures *would* produce increased revenues, but that they *are very likely* to do so. Your second premise will affirm the antecedent, and your conclusion will retain the qualification: "Advertising revenues next year of $2 million are very likely to produce increased revenues of $4 million." Your evidence here did not guarantee that $4 million would result, so you have compensated for the weakness in your evidence by weakening your conclusion.

Many people are afraid or hesitant to write qualified conclusions, perhaps out of the feeling that such conclusions "don't say enough." But usually what qualifying your conclusion (and the appropriate premises to support it) amounts to is following a policy of honesty. If you can't prove the stronger conclusion you want because the evidence just doesn't support it, then you are being dishonest if you say that you can. Honesty requires that you qualify the conclusion until it *is* supported by the evidence you have. Beyond honesty, however, there are practical reasons to make sure you have qualified your conclusion appropriately. If you claim more than you can prove, you open yourself up to a critique on just this point.

There are many ways of qualifying conclusions. The example we have just seen uses a *probabilistic qualifier*, which states that there is a chance of something being true. If you have done a statistical study and are able to do so, you should use mathematical terminology to express the chances of something's being true. For example, you might be able to conclude, as a result of a study, that the probability that the variable *V* has the value *S* is .35. But more often our inferences in everyday life are not based on statistical surveys, and we have to be content with using as qualifiers such ordinary English expressions as *somewhat likely, rather (or fairly) likely, likely,* and *very (or quite) likely* to indicate increasing degrees of probability over 50%, and their counterparts, *somewhat unlikely, rather (or fairly) unlikely, unlikely,* and *very (or quite) unlikely* to indicate decreasing degrees of probability under 50%. This list is a fairly intuitive one, but you may find it helpful to memorize the order of the terms in it if you are not familiar with them. On a scale of probabilities ranging from 0% (0.00) to 100% (1.0), these words occupy roughly the following positions in the list of ordinary English probabilistic qualifiers:

100%	Certain
	Very (Quite) Likely
	Likely
	Rather (Fairly) Likely
	Somewhat Likely
50%	Tossup, Even Chance
	Somewhat Unlikely
	Rather (Fairly) Unlikely
	Unlikely
	Very (Quite) Unlikely
0%	Impossible

In addition to probabilistic qualifiers, you will sometimes find it helpful to use other words such as *at least, at most, minimally, maximally,* and so on. One qualifying phrase that lawyers and academics are fond of using and that we can adapt is *ceteris paribus*. Most audiences will not know what it means, so unless you are trying to impress them with your knowledge of Latin, it is best not to use the phrase, but to use its English equivalent, *other things being equal*. In the previous example of projecting the effects of increased advertising examples, our uncertainty as to $2 million in expenditures producing $4 million in income was based on not being sure that next year would be just like the last. There are a variety of factors that could make the outcome different. For example, if there is an unexpected recession or a major war, the revenues might be a good deal less. We can allow for these other factors in stating our conclusion, however, by saying, "Other things being equal, $2 million in advertising expenditures will produce $4 million in revenue." Again, using this phrase only acknowledges the truth—that there are factors that could undercut our prediction. Such honesty in argument has much to recommend it. If nothing else, it prepares for a critic who will want to highlight possible ways in which the prediction could be falsified.

FURTHER EXAMPLE OF TESTING A CONCLUSION

Because setting up an appropriate conclusion is an extremely important aspect of developing a successful argumentative essay, we will go through one more example of evaluating a conclusion. In an earlier section we developed the possible conclusion: *The fees charged for support of extracurricular activities at my college are too high.* Let us evaluate this conclusion using the seven rules developed in the previous section. Consider first whether it is too broad. We in fact arrived at this conclusion by narrowing another possible conclusion, *The cost of attending my college is too high* for a short paper. But it might still be too broad. If your real concern is with the access to college of students from low-income households, then perhaps the thesis needs to be narrowed further. The following is one possible restriction: *The fees charged for support of extracurricular activities should be reduced for students on financial aid.*

The second rule requires us to examine whether the conclusion is too narrow. Depending on your objectives, even the final conclusion we ended up with might be too narrow. Your concern, for example, might be with the overall impact of college fees on students and families, not with one particular fee. If that is your concern, then even the narrowing we considered will be inappropriate, and you will have to return to the broader thesis, *The cost of attending my college is too high.* The consequence is that you may need to write a longer argument.

The first two rules clearly point in opposite directions. There are no absolute guidelines as to when a proposed thesis is too broad or too narrow. Ultimately, you must decide what it is important for you to establish, and weigh this against the amount of space you have in which to present your argument.

Turning now to our third rule, the thesis we are considering rather clearly takes the form of a demonstration. We do not try to critique another argument, or defend against someone else's critique. If that were our purpose, we would need to modify the conclusion. For example, if someone else had argued for raising fees, and we intended to critique that person's argument, we might word our conclusion as follows: *Carleton's arguments on behalf of increasing fees for extracurricular activities are flawed.* In this case the claim that fees are already too high would not be our conclusion, but might be one of the premises we use in developing our critique of Carleton's argument.

The fourth rule requires us to consider what kind of statement our conclusion is. The words *too high* make it clear that the conclusion is an evaluative one. You might, however, intend a different kind of conclusion. For example, you might be concerned to show what sorts of effects these fees are having on students and their parents. Then your conclusion will have a descriptive form, such as, *Current fees for extracurricular activities are forcing families of students to forego essential health care.* Similarly, you might intend a hypothetical conclusion, such as, *If fees for extracurricular activities were reduced, it would have little adverse effect on campus life.* Make sure you intend to argue for the evaluative conclusion, not one of these other options.

Fifth, your conclusion must be arguable. The greatest danger is that your conclusion should be presented in a subjective statement, such as, *I think that fees for extracurricular activities are too high.* The conclusion that *the fees charged for support of extracurricular activities at my college are too high* is not worded in a subjective manner, so it does not violate this constraint. Another concern is whether your conclusion is already well known. In this case, that will depend on your audience. If the argument is addressed to students committed to protesting the fees for extracurricular activities, then that audience presumably already believes the conclusion and it will not be arguable. But for other audiences the conclusion might well be arguable.

Sixth, one must make sure the conclusion is definite. That involves taking a position. In this case, you have clearly taken a position by arguing that the fees for extracurricular activities are too high. The conclusion might be spelled out in yet more detail by specifying how high they are, but as it stands the conclusion for the argument takes a position and so is sufficiently definite.

Finally, we need to consider whether the conclusion requires qualification. In this case qualification is probably not needed. You intend to make the strong claim that the fees are definitely too high, so you don't want to qualify it by saying that they are only *probably* too high. But if you were arguing for some of the alternatives we have just considered, then qualification is needed. Note, for example, that the word *little* in the hypothetical conclusion, *If fees for extracurricular activities were reduced, it would have little adverse effect on campus life,* is such a qualifier. A cut in fees almost certainly will have some adverse effects, but you may be able to argue that these are, after all, fairly minimal. The conclusion, *Current fees for extracurricular activities are forcing families of students to forego essential health care*, is one that does require qualification. In all likelihood, you will only be able to show that *some* families have had to forego health care, not a large number.

5

The Basic Argumentative Essay:

Generating a Logical Diagram and Written Prose

In the previous chapter we dealt with two essential preliminaries to writing an argumentative essay: identifying your audience and developing your conclusion. With these behind us, we are now in a position to develop our arguments and to craft these arguments into written prose. These are the topics of this chapter. The focus of our endeavors is the *logical diagram* of our argument. A logical diagram is an expansion of standard form, which we developed in chapter 2, that not only shows the relation between premise and conclusion, but the relation between the different arguments that are marshaled to establish the conclusion. This logical diagram shows the full structure of your argument and provides the basis for structuring your argumentative essay.

In this chapter we develop two sample essays for two different conclusions. One is a conclusion very similar to one you might develop for your class assignment: *The cost of books required for college courses should be included in tuition.* We take as our audience for this argument the administration of your college or university, especially the vice president for financial affairs. (As an exercise, you should evaluate this conclusion using the criteria of the previous chapter.) The second conclusion is one you might confront in your work. Imagine that your boss has asked you to review the application of an individual named Alpers for a job. You have come to the conclusion that your boss should not hire this person, and you need now to present your arguments to your boss.

There are several steps involved in developing a good argumentative essay for such conclusions. We begin by considering the process of developing arguments, then turn to the generation of a logical diagram for the essay, and finally to the writing of the essay itself.

DEVELOPING ARGUMENTS

Brainstorming for Reasons

The first task in developing arguments for your conclusion is to construct a set of *reasons*. Reasons are not yet arguments, but eventually they will become the premises of arguments. Reasons are statements that indicate to you that the conclusion is true. Your first task should be to *brainstorm* to come up with a wide variety of reasons. At this point be inclusive as possible. Ask yourself, "How many reasons can I think of to support this conclusion?" List every reason you can think of, even if you are not absolutely sure of the truth of each one. Brainstorming for reasons is the most creative part of developing an argument, and you should not stifle your creativity by becoming overly fussy about how good the reasons you list actually are. There is a virtue to listing reasons you already recognize to be bad or mediocre: They may help bring to mind much better reasons. The job of sorting out which reasons to include and which to omit can be left until later.

It is important to do your brainstorming on paper. First of all, you don't want to forget the reasons you have already constructed. Second, the very act of putting reasons on paper and rereading them serves as a useful stimulus for coming up with better reasons.

It is important to allow yourself adequate time to brainstorm your argument. Start this activity considerably before you must produce the final argument. What you want to do is let your mind wander a bit in order to come up with a variety of ideas. If you wait until the last minute, you won't be able to do this. As a result you may fail to come up with what might be some of the most fruitful ideas for developing arguments.

You can make use of a variety of sources in brainstorming. See what has been said about your conclusion in newspaper or magazine articles or editorials. If you choose a topic related to a course you are taking, you might find reasons, or information that prompts you to think of reasons, in your textbook. A further source of reasons is discussion with friends. Using published material or conversations with other people in the process of brainstorming for reasons does not constitute cheating or plagiarism as long as you do the work of developing the reasons and building effective arguments around them. Of course, if the reason someone else advances is original and creative, and you decide to use it, you should give credit to the originator for the idea. If you utilize reasons or factual information developed by others, you should note their source in your list of reasons so that you can credit them when you write your essay.

Let us brainstorm for reasons to support our conclusion: *The cost of books required for college courses should be included in tuition.* If we do so, we might arrive at the following:

A. The books required for college courses now cost too much.
B. If colleges and universities negotiated with publishers regarding costs, they would be able to provide books at less expense.

C. Professors do not give enough attention to the price of books they assign.
D. If the costs of required books were included in tuition, professors would be required to choose reasonably priced books.
E. If the costs of required books were included in tuition, professors would only order books that will actually be used.
F. Students would be more inclined to keep the books from their college courses and consult them again later if there weren't a ready resale market at college bookstores.
G. Student performance will increase because students will no longer try to get by in courses without the books.
H. College tuition will more honestly reflect the cost of taking courses.

Take some time now to come up with a few additional reasons of your own. You can then follow through the various steps in developing arguments with your own reasons as well as the ones offered here.

Evaluating Your Reasons

After developing your list, you need to evaluate statements on the list, modifying and pruning as necessary. The first step is to ask yourself whether each statement is true. If it is, you can leave it on the list for now. If it isn't, ask yourself whether it can be modified to be made true. If the answer is *yes*, then modify your list.

Consider the first item, *The books required for college courses now cost too much.* Although that may seem to be true of some or even many books required in college courses, you probably can think of some *counterexamples*—books you used in college courses that were inexpensive or reasonably priced (perhaps some paperback novels used in a literature course). This item clearly requires modification and qualification. You might modify the item as follows:

A'. *Many of* the books required for college courses now cost too much.

This qualified statement is much more likely to be true. (The same considerations we discussed in the previous chapter with respect to qualifying conclusions apply here to the reasons we put forward.) If you believe it, and think that your audience will also accept it, then you can leave this statement on your list.

You should go through the whole list in a similar fashion. If a statement requires modification for you to accept it as true, supply the necessary modifications. Sometimes on further reflection you may decide that a reason is simply false. For example, as you reflect on Reason F, *Students would be more inclined to keep the books from their college courses and consult them again later if there weren't a ready resale market at college bookstores,* you may begin to have some doubts. What is the likelihood of students actually consulting their course books again later even if they did keep them? Moreover, even if they could not sell their books back to the college bookstore, you might suspect that some other avenue might open up for resale of course books. For example, some enterprising students might set up a company to buy back books and sell them to colleges to provide to their students at lower prices than the book publishers. If these doubts convince you that the premise is no longer true, you should remove it from the list.

So far you have focused only on whether *you* find the reasons to be true. You need also to consider whether your audience will accept them. This requires reviewing the list a second time, arriving at one of the following verdicts about each item:

Acceptable to my audience as is.

Not acceptable to my audience initially, but I can convince them of it.

Not acceptable to my audience, and not something of which I can convince them.

Determining which judgment applies requires you to examine each reason from your audience's perspective and carefully consider whether they will take the claim to be true. Items that fall into the third category should now be removed from your list. You may also decide as you proceed that you need to make further revisions to the way in which items were worded.

Let us review some of the items on your list. A′ states, *Many of the books required for college courses now cost too much.* Unless you have heard your administration already discuss this issue, you probably have little reason to believe that they will already accept this claim. In fact, you can almost hear your administrator respond "And what is *too* much?" Reflecting on what you had in mind, you might answer that the price charged for books is heavily marked up beyond what it costs to produce them. This might lead you to reword the reason as

A″. Books required for college courses currently cost much more than they cost to produce.

This is still a potentially controversial claim, but perhaps it is one you feel your audience will accept or that you can defend.

You need to go through the complete list in the same manner. Whenever you find an item on the list that you believe is true but that you will have to argue for in order to convince your audience, you should note that fact. One way to indicate it is to put an asterisk in front of the item. When you have finished this second review of your list, you will have a set of reasons for your conclusion. But you still don't have complete arguments. At best you have enthymemes. You now need to add premises to the individual reasons to create valid arguments.

To construct valid arguments out of your reasons, make use of the forms developed in chapter 3. Let us do this with the reasons on our list. In most cases, it will be very natural to use modus ponens. Thus, take Reason A″: *Books required for college courses currently cost much more than they cost to produce.* To create a valid modus ponens argument we need to add the following premise: *If books required for college courses currently cost much more than they cost to produce, the cost of books required for college courses should be included in tuition.* These two premises, taken together, now generate the following argument:

If books required for college courses currently cost much more than they cost to produce, the cost of books required for college courses should be included in tuition.

Books required for college courses currently cost much more than they cost to produce.
_____

∴ The cost of books required for college courses should be included in tuition.

This task needs to be carried out with each reason on your list. To add variety to your argument, you might consider whether some of the arguments might be better stated using a form other than modus ponens. Sometimes modus tollens or alternative syllogism might seem more natural. Sometimes, when you are arguing for a negative conclusion, modus tollens is the more natural form to use. For example, if you want to show that the president will not veto a certain piece of legislation, you might base your argument on the premise that *If the president were going to veto it, he or she would already have spoken out against it*, and then use the fact that the president has not spoken out against it to complete the modus tollens argument. If you restrict yourself to the valid forms discussed in chapter 3, though, you will not have to worry about the validity of any of your arguments.

Establishing the soundness of our arguments requires a bit more work. You have already evaluated the second premise of each argument and determined that you think it is true, and either your audience agrees with it or can be convinced to accept it. So we need not question that premise further right now. However, for your arguments to be sound, both of the premises must be true. Thus, you must review all of the additional premises you have now added to make your reasons into valid arguments, asking whether you think they are true, and whether your audience will accept them, or can be convinced to accept them as true. Consider the premise we just added to make a valid argument out of Reason A": *If books required for college courses currently cost much more than they cost to produce, then the cost of books required for college courses should be included in tuition.* If you give some thought to this conditional, you may recognize that it is not obviously true. Granting that the price of books required for college courses is much greater than the cost of producing them (and that this is a problem) does not suffice to demonstrate that the correct way to solve the problem is to include the price of books in tuition. You, and especially your audience, are likely to wonder what the antecedent has to do with the consequent. What good would it do to have the cost of books included in tuition? Won't students still have to pay the same amount in the end? Thus, as it stands, the premise we have added to make this argument valid does not seem to be true. As a result, this argument will not be sound.

At this point we must choose one of three options. The first is to completely eliminate the argument. One reason to have brainstormed broadly was to generate a large collection of reasons so that we might abandon those that do not result in sound arguments. The second option is to see if we might modify the wording of the premises so that we can preserve the validity of the argument and yet make both premises true. The third is to ask ourselves whether in fact the markup for required course books was an *autonomous* reason for our conclusion, or whether it might be coupled with some other reasons.

The first option is a safe one, but might rob us of an effective part of an argument. So, before we give up on an argument too quickly, we should explore the second and third options. The third option, in fact, is sometimes our most powerful one. Your audience might not be convinced that the markup in the price of course books is a good enough reason, *taken by itself*, for having the cost of books included in tuition. Nor might your audience find some of your other reasons to be sufficient, *in themselves*, to justify your conclusion. But your audience might agree that when some of these reasons are *taken together*, they are enough. For example, it might be the fact cited in the second reason, that if colleges and universities negotiated with publishers regarding costs, they would be able to provide books at less expense, which helps explain why building the cost into tuition would help solve the problem identified in the first reason. Therefore, in this case we might get a stronger argument by grouping the first two reasons together and having a conjunct antecedent to the conditional premise of the modus ponens argument:

> If books required for college courses currently cost much more than they cost to produce and if colleges and universities negotiated with publishers regarding costs, they would be able to provide books at less expense, then the cost of books required for college courses should be included in tuition.
>
> Books required for college courses currently cost much more than they cost to produce.
>
> If colleges and universities negotiated with publishers regarding costs, they would be able to provide books at less expense.
>
> ∴ The cost of books required for college courses should be included in tuition.

This argument is much more likely to be sound than either of the arguments that might have been constructed separately.

Reasons C, D, and E might similarly need to be grouped in order to present a compelling argument. For example, Reason C alone could give rise to the following argument:

> If many professors do not give enough attention to the price of books they assign, then the cost of books required for college courses should be included in tuition.
>
> Many professors do not give enough attention to the price of books they assign.
>
> ∴ The cost of books required for college courses should be included in tuition.

(Note that the word *many* has been added to this reason. At what stage would it have been added and why?) This argument has the same problem as the one constructed on the basis of Reason A alone: What reason is there to believe the conditional? Even if you believe that many professors do not give enough attention to the price of books they assign (and that this is a problem), why should that lead one to subsume the cost of books under tuition? There might be other ways of getting professors to attend to the price of books they assign. For example, because most professors are not even informed of the price of books before ordering them, it might suffice to require them to put the price on the order form and total the prices for all their books when they order books for their classes. But in this case Reasons D and E, when combined with C, give a far more compelling argument:

> If many professors do not give enough attention to the price of books they assign, and if including the cost of required books in tuition would cause professors to choose reasonably priced books and to order only books that will actually be used, then the cost of books required for college courses should be included in tuition.
> Many professors do not give enough attention to the price of books they assign.
> Including the cost of required books in tuition would cause professors to choose reasonably priced books.
> Including the cost of required books in tuition would cause professors to order only books that will actually be used.
> ∴ The cost of books required for college courses should be included in tuition.

This argument is far more likely to be sound than an argument constructed from just one reason alone. But there is a disadvantage to conjunct conditionals: They are often difficult for audiences to follow. Therefore, when you have developed an argument with a conjunct conditional, you might want to consider whether you can simplify its structure. One way to do this is to paraphrase the various components of the antecedent in one expression. Thus, in the case of the first argument, the claims that there is currently too much profit built into the price of books required for college courses and that if colleges and universities negotiated with publishers regarding costs, they would be able to provide books at less expense might be captured in the statement, *having colleges handle the purchasing of books required in college courses would lead to an overall savings for students*. This permits us to present the first argument as follows:

> If having colleges handle the purchasing of books would help solve the problem of excessive prices now charged for books required in college courses, then the cost of books required for college courses should be included in tuition.
> Having colleges handle the purchasing of books would help solve the problems of excessive prices now charged for books required in college courses.
> ∴ The cost of books required for college courses should be included in tuition.

The two claims that originally went into the second premise will now be held in reserve for the point when we need to provide support for the second premise. In a similar fashion, the second argument can be simplified as follows:

> If it is an effective way to alleviate current problems resulting from professors not being price conscious in ordering books for their courses, then the cost of books required for college courses should be included in tuition.
> Having the price of books required for college courses is an effective way to alleviate current problems resulting from professors not being price conscious in ordering books for their courses.
> ∴ The cost of books required for college courses should be included in tuition.

One advantage of boiling these arguments down in this manner is that we realize that they both have to do with lowering the cost of required course books for college students. Because the contents of the two arguments are so closely linked, this might lead us to combine these two arguments into one argument as follows:

> If having colleges handle the purchasing of books required for college courses would lead to an overall savings for students, then the cost of books required for college courses should be included in tuition.
> Having colleges handle the purchasing of books required for college courses would lead to an overall savings for students.
> ∴ The cost of books required for college courses should be included in tuition.

Once again, the two arguments from which we started will provide support for the second premise of our argument. Moreover, the first premise of this argument seems quite plausible. Thus, from our initial list of reasons we have developed one reasonably compelling argument for our conclusion. You should consider whether other arguments can be crafted from the initial list of reasons, or from those you added to the list. We leave this example for now, but return to it later.

CONSTRUCTING A LOGICAL DIAGRAM

After you have developed one or more arguments for your conclusion, you need to begin to develop the overall logical structure for your essay. What you will be doing is connecting arguments. There are two ways of doing this. The first is employed if you have more than one separate argument that you want to use to support your conclusion. We call this *multiple arguments to the same conclusion*. When you use multiple arguments, the arguments are totally independent. Each alone is sufficient to establish the conclusion. These arguments may all be of the same simple form, say, modus ponens, or they may have different forms, one using modus ponens, another modus tollens, another disjunctive syllogism.

To illustrate how we might employ multiple arguments to the same conclusion, we turn to our second example conclusion. You have been requested by your employer to recommend whether an individual named Alpers should be hired by your company, and you have reached the conclusion that your employer *should not hire* Alpers. Through the process of brainstorming and formulating arguments, you may have developed four arguments for not hiring Alpers:

1. If a person has a felony record, we should not hire the person.
    Alpers has a felony record.
    ∴ We should not hire Alpers.

2. If a person's last employer is unwilling to recommend the person, we should not hire the person.
    Alpers's last employer is unwilling to recommend him.
    ∴ We should not hire Alpers.

3. If people refuse to state that they will abide by departmental regulations, we shouldn't hire them.
    Alpers refuses to state he will abide by departmental regulations.
    ∴ We should not hire Alpers.

4. If a person doesn't have a high school diploma, we shouldn't hire the person.
    Alpers doesn't have a high school diploma.
    ∴ We should not hire Alpers.

Just as we used *standard* form to make clear the structure of individual arguments, we use an extension of standard form to make clear the *relation* between simple arguments in more complex arguments. This involves the construction of what we call a *logical diagram*. To show that all four arguments have the same conclusion, we write them in four columns next to each other. We then draw *one* line beneath all four sets of premises and write the conclusion once, centered below all of the arguments. The logical diagram for the aforementioned four arguments will look like this:

| If a person has a felony record, we should not hire the person. | If a person's last employer is unwilling to recommend the person, we should not hire the person. | If people refuse to state that they will abide by departmental regulations, we shouldn't hire them. | If a person doesn't have a high school diploma, we shouldn't hire the person. |
| Alpers has a felony record. | Alpers' last employer is unwilling to recommend him. | Alpers refuses to state he will abide by departmental regulations. | Alpers doesn't have a high school diploma. |

∴ We shouldn't hire Alpers.

In developing a logical diagram for yourself, *always start at the bottom of the page*. Put your main conclusion at the very bottom, and the arguments supporting it directly above. As we shall see soon, it is often necessary to develop additional arguments as you proceed. Thus, leave plenty of space further up on the page to work with as you go.

Note that each column contains a complete, valid argument. The point of using separate columns is to indicate that each argument is intended to stand on its own. When using multiple arguments, each of which stands on its own, you must be sure that each is *sufficient* to establish the conclusion *by itself*. In the previous example Alpers' felony record is presented as a sufficient reason for not hiring him. Thus, even if it turned out that his previous employer was willing to giving him a glowing recommendation, that Alpers was more than willing to state that he will abide by departmental regulations, and that he not only had a high school diploma, but a college degree, the first argument is still offered as sound, and hence sufficient to establish the truth of the conclusion. If, under this hypothetical situation, you would change your mind and think Alpers should be hired, you need to reexamine the argument. Because you agree that Alpers has a felony record, and that the argument is valid, the only way you could dissent from the conclusion is if you did not accept the premise, *If a person has a felony record, we should not hire the person*, as true. That premise said that a felony record was a sufficient reason not to hire the person, but in this scenario you apparently do not believe that a felony record is sufficient. Hence, you must withdraw the first premise.

The previous paragraph presents a strategy that you should consider any time you present multiple arguments to the same conclusion. You should examine each argument separately for soundness. One way to do this is to *imagine* that the claims put forward in the other arguments are false. Then ask yourself whether the argument under consideration is sufficient to establish the conclusion. If not, then the argument does not really stand on its own. One remedy at this point is to consider combining the arguments into fewer arguments. Consider again the previous case. Perhaps on further consideration you will determine that what makes Alpers undesirable is not any one of the factors in isolation, but all four taken together. If so, then you will end up with only one argument in which the conditional premise will have a complex antecedent:

> If a person has a felony record, the person's last employer is unwilling to recommend the person, the person refuses to abide by departmental regulations, and the person does not have a high school diploma, we should not hire the person.
> Alpers has a felony record.
> Alpers' last employer is unwilling to recommend him.
> Alpers refuses to state he will abide by departmental regulations.
> Alpers doesn't have a high school diploma.
> ∴ We should not hire Alpers.

In this case, the second, third, fourth, and fifth premises are the same as they were before. But the first premise is considerably different. It now asserts that if all four conditions are met, then we should not hire the person. It tells us nothing about what should happen if only one or two of the conditions is met.

The previous example is not meant to show that you should never use multiple arguments. Sometimes each argument will stand on its own. If so, then there is actually an advantage to multiple arguments. Because each of the arguments is independent, and each is sufficient to establish the conclusion, then if it should turn out that you are wrong about one of the premises in one of the arguments, that does not undercut your whole argument. Imagine that you did view each of the previous four factors as sufficient for not hiring Alpers. Then if it turned out that he did have a high school diploma, you would still have three sound arguments for hiring Alpers. (Of course, you should withdraw the argument that you now know to have a false premise!) Thus, having multiple arguments is like having extra protection. In marshaling multiple arguments to provide backup protection, you should exercise some caution. Even though each argument must suffice on its own, in your audience's mind, the presence of bad arguments may taint the better ones you have. Thus, if you have doubts about the soundness of an argument, don't use it in as an additional multiple argument.

Except for giving you such backup protection, multiple arguments are no stronger than single arguments that use our simple valid forms. For a simple valid argument to be effective in establishing a conclusion, all premises must be accepted as true by both you *and* your audience. Here is where we most often confront problems. Imagine you have presented the previous set of four multiple arguments for not hiring Alpers to your supervisor, who might well respond to you:

> I know that having a felony record is grounds for not hiring a person, but are you sure that Alpers has such a record? I am also not convinced that we should take the lack of a recommendation from his previous employer too seriously. Perhaps he left the position having exposed the improprieties of his employer, and so the employer holds a grudge against him. Further, what is the evidence that he states he will not abide by departmental regulations? And lastly, why should a high school diploma be necessary for this job?

What your supervisor is doing is questioning the premises of your argument. Before finding your argument convincing, the supervisor needs to be convinced of the premises. This is the point at which we encounter our second means of connecting arguments together, a method we will call *chain arguments*.

In chain arguments (also known by their Greek name as *sorites*, pronounced sore-eye-tees), the premises of one argument are themselves supported by other arguments. To answer, you will need to provide such arguments for the premises that the supervisor was not already prepared to accept. Note that some of the supervisor's challenges were directed against the first premises of arguments, others were directed against the second premises (in some cases, challenges could be directed against both premises). We have reprinted the logical diagram of this argument in the following with the questioned premises marked by asterisks.

If a person has a felony record, we should not hire the person.	*If a person's last employer is unwilling to recommend the person, we should not hire the person.	If people refuse to state that they will abide by departmental regulations, we shouldn't hire them.	*If a person doesn't have a high school diploma, we shouldn't hire the person.
*Alpers has a felony record.		*Alpers refuses to state he will abide by departmental regulations.	Alpers doesn't have a high school diploma.
	Alpers' last employer is unwilling to recommend him.		

∴ We shouldn't hire Alpers.

Let us consider how we might answer these challenges from your supervisor. Presumably Alpers did not indicate the felony record on his application. If he had done so, you would only need to draw this to your supervisor's attention. But if things are not that simple, you will have to provide your evidence that he had a felony record. Perhaps you had done a background check, and one of Alpers' references indicated that he had done time for a felony crime. One source of this sort, however, is not sufficient to establish his record. So you also confirmed the fact via a search of police files. What you will do now is construct an argument such as the following:

> If one of his references as well as police files indicate that Alpers has a felony record, then he has one.
> One of his references indicated that he had a felony record.
> Police files indicate that he does have a felony record.
> ∴ Alpers has a felony record.

Because this argument does not directly demonstrate the overall conclusion, but rather a premise in an argument that in turn establishes the conclusion, we refer to this as a *subordinate argument*. To incorporate a subordinate argument into your diagram and show that it supports a premise in an already given argument, put it above the argument whose premise it supports. Then, to make it clear how the line of support goes, draw an arrow from the conclusion of the subordinate argument to the premise in a later argument that it supports. When we incorporate the previous argument into our diagram, it will look like the following:

If one of his references as well as police files indicate that Alpers has a felony record, then he has one.
One of his references indicated that he had a felony record.
Police files indicate that he does have a felony record.
∴ Alpers has a felony record.

If a person has a felony record, we should not hire the person.
Alpers has a felony record.

If a person's last employer is unwilling to recommend the person, we should not hire the person.
Alpers' last employer is unwilling to recommend him.

If people refuse to state that they will abide by departmental regulations, we shouldn't hire them.
Alpers refuses to state he will abide by departmental regulations.

If a person doesn't have a high school diploma, we shouldn't hire the person.
Alpers doesn't have a high school diploma.

∴ We shouldn't hire Alpers.

Note carefully how the arrow is used in this diagram. It goes from one occurrence of a statement as a conclusion to a second occurrence *of the same statement* as a premise. Arrows do not go between premises and conclusions, but only between conclusions of subordinate arguments and premises in subsequent arguments. Moreover, the two statements it connects are worded exactly the same.

Because your supervisor also questioned premises in the other arguments, you now need to develop subordinate arguments demonstrating each of these premises. Note in particular that in some cases it is the conditional premise that must be supported. For example, your supervisor challenged the following premise: *If a person doesn't have a high school diploma, we shouldn't hire the person.* In developing a subordinate argument that has this statement as its conclusion, you might use a basic form such as modus ponens. But as the statement itself is a conditional, it sometimes is more natural to employ a conditional syllogism. To do this you might set up the following argument structure:

If a person doesn't have a high school diploma, then
If   , then we shouldn't hire the person.
∴ If a person doesn't have a high school diploma, we shouldn't hire the person.

Now what you need to do is fill in the blank with a phrase that shows why not having a high school diploma is reason for not hiring a person. Perhaps the job requires communication and computation abilities that can only be assured if the person has a high school diploma. Then you would complete your subordinate argument as follows:

> If a person doesn't have a high school diploma, then we cannot be sure of the person's communication and computation skills.
> If we cannot be sure of a person's communication and computation skills, then we shouldn't hire the person.
> ∴ If a person doesn't have a high school diploma, we shouldn't hire the person.

You need to construct subordinate arguments for each of the premises your supervisor challenged. When you have done this, you might end up with something like what appears in the next logical diagram.

When you are constructing an argument, you may realize that one of your premises in fact requires support, but that you cannot construct a good argument for it. In that case, you should consider dropping that line of argument. For example, when you consider some of the reasons that a previous employer might not be willing to recommend a person, you may decide that this is not a line of argument to pursue. In that case, you should drop the argument. This is a further reason to have done a thorough job of brainstorming when you began. If you have more reasons on your initial list than you can possibly use, then you can afford to eliminate some when the arguments do not pan out.

If one of his references as well as police files indicate that Alpers has a felony record, then he has one.
One of his references indicated that he had a felony record.
Police files indicate that he does have a felony record.
∴ Alpers has a felony record.

If a person has a felony record, we should not hire the person.
Alpers has a felony record.

If a person's last employer is unwilling to recommend the person, that indicates that the person probably did not do a good job.
If evidence indicates that a person probably did not do a good job, then we should not hire the person.
∴ If a person's last employer is unwilling to recommend the person, we should not hire the person.

If a person's last employer is unwilling to recommend the person, we should not hire the person.
Alpers' last employer is unwilling to recommend him.

If, when presented with the *Departmental Regulation Manual*, people indicate they cannot accept the regulations having to do with client confidentiality, then they have refused to state they will abide by departmental regulations.
When presented with the *Departmental Regulation Manual*, Alpers indicated he could not accept the regulations having to do with client confidentiality.
∴ Alpers refuses to state he will abide by departmental regulations.

If people refuse to state that they will abide by departmental regulations, we shouldn't hire them.
Alpers refuses to state he will abide by departmental regulations.

If a person doesn't have a high school diploma, then we cannot be sure of the person's communication and computation skills.
If we cannot be sure of a person's communication and computation skills, then we shouldn't hire the person.
∴ If a person doesn't have a high school diploma, we shouldn't hire the person.

If a person doesn't have a high school diploma, we shouldn't hire the person.
Alpers doesn't have a high school diploma.

∴ We shouldn't hire Alpers.

Chain arguments can be as long and as complicated as you need them to be, and can even incoporate multiple arguments to the same conclusion. You might want, for example, to give further evidence that a high school diploma is required for your job and so you construct the following independent argument:

> If a person doesn't have a high school diploma, then the person does not show a drive for self-advancement.
> If a person does not show a drive for self-advancement, then we should not hire the person.
> ∴ If a person doesn't have a high school diploma, then we should not hire the person.

We would then incorporate this into our diagram by putting the two arguments for the conclusion—*If a person doesn't have a high school diploma, then we should not hire the person*—in separate columns, with one line beneath both of them, and then center the conclusion below that line. These are both subordinate arguments, so we would then draw an arrow from their joint conclusion to the place where the same statement appears in a premise in a later argument.

In the argument we have been developing, as in any chain argument, some of the premises have been argued for, and others have not. We call premises in a complex argument that have been argued for elsewhere in the argument *demonstrated premises,* and premises that have not been argued for elsewhere in the argument *assumed premises.* In your logical diagram, any demonstrated premise will have an arrow pointing to it. As the argument for not hiring Alpers has expanded in the last few paragraphs we have turned some assumed premises into demonstrated premises. And this of course has generated new assumed premises, which might be argued for as well. Thus, there could be multiple links in a chain.

At this point you may wonder, "But couldn't this go on forever?" Because the remaining assumed premises have not been argued for, and because the premises that might be assumed in order to argue for them might themselves be argued for, the correct answer to the question is, "Theoretically, yes." But, practically, we must terminate this process at some point. We do this at the point at which we have premises that we accept as true and believe our audience will accept as well. A particular premise may be so obvious to your audience that it will not require an argument to prove it. But if you are in doubt as to whether it is acceptable to your audience without argument, then by all means use a chain argument to support it. Obviously this will require you to have a good idea of which premises the particular audience you are addressing will find acceptable, and this means that you will need to know your audience (see chapter 4).

It is important to notice that all of this really amounts to saying that the very practice of arguing is ultimately based on nonarguments. Arguments require, in order to begin, that certain premises be assumed to be true without argument. If, in a given argument, certain premises cannot be assumed to be true, then certain other premises will have to be. Without agreement on *some* premises, arguments will have no place to begin. But you need to be careful in deciding whether a premise can stand as an assumed premise. Ask yourself seriously: *Is the person I am trying to convince, who does not already agree with my conclusion, likely to agree to this premise?* Perhaps your audience does not accept your conclusion because it does not accept your premise. If you assume a premise that is in fact the source of contention about the conclusion, then you will have committed the fallacy of *begging the question*, which we discuss in a subsequent chapter. To avoid this, you must consider your audience seriously and ask, will this premise be agreed to by my audience?

DEVELOPING THE COLLEGE COURSE BOOK LOGICAL OUTLINE

Let us return to our other sample essay conclusion, *The cost of books required for college courses should be included in tuition*, and consider how we will develop our logical outline for that conclusion. In our earlier examination of our initial reasons we boiled several of them down to one argument. We might decide to build our essay around this argument alone. In that case we would do as we do here, examining each of the premises and offering support for those that need it. But there were some other reasons on our list that we did not use. We might make use of these as additional arguments, ending up with three arguments.

If having colleges purchase and include the cost of books required for college courses in tuition would lead to an overall savings for students, then the cost of books required for college courses should be included in tuition.

Having colleges handle the purchasing of books required for college courses would lead to an overall savings for students.

If having colleges purchase and include the cost of books required for college courses in tuition would lead to improved student academic performance, then the cost of books required for college courses should be included in tuition.

Having colleges purchase and include the cost of books required for college courses in tuition would lead to improved student academic performance.

If having colleges purchase and include the cost of books required for college courses in tuition would result in college tuition more honestly reflecting the cost of taking college courses, then the cost of books required for college courses should be included in tuition.

Having colleges purchase and include the cost of books required for college courses in tuition would result in college tuition more honestly reflecting the cost of taking college courses.

∴ The cost of books required for college courses should be included in tuition.

In this argument we have three multiple arguments for the same conclusion. There is no proper number you should have. In some cases you might have only one main argument. In others you might have two or four main arguments. (Unless you are developing a fairly long essay, you probably should not have more than three or four multiple arguments.) You might think of some additional arguments that might be advanced for this conclusion. If so, you would diagram them in additional columns.

We proceed with just these three main arguments. Our next task is to consider which of the premises in the diagram would not receive immediate assent from our audience. These are ones for which we will need to develop subordinate arguments. Earlier we boiled several of our initial reasons down to one reason, *Having colleges handle the purchasing of books required for college courses would lead to an overall savings for students*. This might be a statement that is not obvious to our intended audience, but the way in which we arrived at this statement will suggest how we might support it. We developed this claim from two other claims: *Having colleges purchase and include the cost of books required for college courses in tuition would help solve the problem of excessive prices now charged for books required for college courses,* and *Having colleges purchase and include the cost of books required for college courses in tuition would be an effective way to alleviate current problems resulting from professors not being price conscious in ordering books for their courses*. We can now use these as supporting reasons for the second premise in our first main argument. In setting up this argument, though, we must remember that the conclusion now is not the final conclusion, but the premise in our main argument that *Having colleges handle the purchasing of books required for college courses would lead to an overall savings for students*. Thus, the argument is structured as follows:

> If having colleges purchase and include the cost of books required for college courses in tuition would help solve the problem of excessive prices now charged for books required for college courses and be an effective way to alleviate current problems resulting from professors not being price conscious in ordering books for their courses, then having colleges handle the purchasing of books required for college courses would lead to an overall savings for students.
>
> Having colleges purchase and include the cost of books required for college courses in tuition would help solve the problem of excessive prices now charged for books required for college courses.
>
> Having colleges purchase and include the cost of books required for college courses in tuition would be an effective way to alleviate current problems resulting from professors not being price conscious in ordering books for their courses.
> _____
> ∴ Having colleges handle the purchasing of books required for college courses would lead to an overall savings for students.

Note that in this argument we have kept the two reasons separate. This permits us to provide an argument for each one separately. Such arguments, based on our initial reasons, are shown in Fig. 5.1. They are positioned higher in the diagram, and arrows connect their conclusions to those in this subordinate argument.

The second premise of the first main argument has now been supported, but we must also consider the first premise of that argument, *If having colleges purchase and include the cost of books required for college courses in tuition would lead to an overall savings for students, then the cost of books required for college courses should be included in tuition.* Our overall goal is to convince your college administration, and so we must ask whether they would be likely to agree to this premise. Your case may be particularly helped by the fact that there is currently great concern over the cost of education. You may, in fact, have heard your administration present holding down the cost of education as a major goal. If so, you can support the conditional premise with the following conditional syllogism:

> If having colleges purchase and include the cost of books required for college courses in tuition would lead to an overall savings for students, then this policy would contribute toward the administration's stated goal of holding down the cost of education.
> If this policy would contribute toward the administration's stated goal of holding down the cost of education, then the cost of books required for college courses should be included in tuition.
> ∴ If having colleges purchase and include the cost of books required for college courses in tuition would lead to an overall savings for students, then the cost of books required for college courses should be included in tuition.

This argument has also been included in Fig. 5.1. This process of constructing subordinate arguments for each premise in arguments that need support must be continued until you produce a logical diagram in which each assumed premise (a premise with no arrows leading into it) is one you can trust your reader to accept. Figure 5.1 provides an example of how this might look.

PRESENTING YOUR ARGUMENT IN WRITTEN FORM

Once you have your logical diagram in place, you are in position to put your argument into written prose. You should not attempt this, however, until you are totally satisfied that your logical diagram presents an argument that your audience will find to be logically sound. In terms of logic, your written essay cannot be any better than your logical diagram. If there are shortcomings in your logical diagram, they will weaken your written argument as well. If you discover these after beginning to write your essay, you will have to return to your logical diagram to make corrections. This may require you, in turn, to rewrite parts of your essay. So make sure your logical diagram presents an argument your audience will find to be sound before attempting to put your argument into prose form.

If college books currently sell for much more than they cost to produce and if having colleges negotiate directly with the publisher for large orders of books would reduce the cost of required books to students, then having colleges purchase and include the cost of books required for college courses in tuition would help solve the problem of excessive prices now charged for books required for college courses.

College books currently sell for much more than they cost to produce.

Having colleges negotiate directly with the publisher for large orders of books would reduce the cost of required books to students.

∴ Having colleges purchase and include the cost of books required for college courses in tuition would help solve the problem of excessive prices now charged for books required for college courses.

If having colleges purchase and include the cost of books required for college courses in tuition would help solve the problem of excessive prices now charged for books required for college courses and be an effective way to alleviate current problems resulting from professors not being price conscious in ordering books for their courses, then having colleges handle the purchasing of books required for college courses would lead to an overall savings for students.

Having colleges purchase and include the cost of books required for college courses in tuition would help solve the problem of excessive prices now charged for books required for college courses.

Having colleges purchase and include the cost of books required for college courses in tuition would be an effective way to alleviate current problems resulting from professors not being price conscious in ordering books for their courses.

∴ Having colleges handle the purchasing of books required for college courses would lead to an overall savings for students.

If professors now generally do not take price into account when ordering books for their courses, and sometimes order books that are never actually used, and if the proposed policy would cause professors to take more care in ordering books for course, then having colleges purchase and include the cost of books required for college courses in tuition would be an effective way to alleviate current problems resulting from professors not being price conscious in ordering books for their courses.

Professors now generally do not take price into account when ordering books for their courses.

Professors sometimes order books that are never actually used.

The proposed policy would cause professors to take more care in ordering books for courses.

∴ Having colleges purchase and include the cost of books required for college courses in tuition would be an effective way to alleviate current problems resulting from professors not being price conscious in ordering books for their courses.

If under the proposed policy colleges would have an incentive to keep the overall costs of textbooks down and would put pressure on professors, then the proposed policy would cause professors to take more care in ordering books for courses.

Under the proposed policy colleges would have an incentive to keep the overall costs of textbooks down and would put pressure on professors.

∴ The proposed policy would cause professors to take more care in ordering books for courses.

If having colleges purchase and include the cost of books required for college courses in tuition would lead to an overall savings for students, then this policy would contribute toward the administration's stated goal of holding down the cost of education.

If this policy would contribute toward the administration's stated goal of holding down the cost of education, then the cost of books required for college courses should be included in tuition.

∴ If having colleges purchase and include the cost of books required for college courses in tuition would lead to an overall savings for students, then the cost of books required for college courses should be included in tuition.

If having colleges purchase and include the cost of books required for college courses in tuition would lead to an overall savings for students, then the cost of books required for college courses should be included in tuition.

Having colleges handle the purchasing of books required for college courses would lead to an overall savings for students.

If students and parents primarily base their decisions about college finances on tuition and fail to consider the cost of required books and if this misleads them as to the true cost of attending college, and if this produces a feeling of dishonesty on the part of the college, then having colleges purchase and include the cost of books required for college courses in tuition would result in college tuition more honestly reflecting the cost of taking college courses.

Students and parents primarily base their decisions about college finances on tuition and fail to consider the cost of required books.

Failing to appreciate the cost of books misleads students and parents about the true cost of attending college.

Being misled about the true cost of attending college does produce a feeling of dishonesty on the part of the college.

∴ Having colleges purchase and include the cost of books required for college courses in tuition would result in college tuition more honestly reflecting the cost of taking college courses.

If colleges want to gain respect for their honesty and integrity, then if having colleges purchase and include the cost of books required for college courses would result in college tuition more honestly reflecting the cost of taking college courses, then the cost of books required for college courses should be included in tuition.

Colleges want to gain respect for their honesty and integrity.

∴ If having colleges purchase and include the cost of books required for college courses would result in college tuition more honestly reflecting the cost of taking college courses, then the cost of books required for college courses should be included in tuition.

If students who are not able to buy the required books often fail to read their assignments because they cannot easily get access to the books, then these students would do better in their classes if they had the required books.

Students who are not able to buy the required books often fail to read their assignments because they cannot easily get access to the books.

∴ These students would do better in their classes if they had the required books.

If some students now do not buy the required books because they cannot afford them and these students would do better in their classes if they had the required books, then having colleges purchase and include the cost of books required for college courses in tuition would lead to improved academic performance.

Some students now do not buy the required books because they cannot afford them.

These students would do better in their classes if they had the required books.

∴ Having colleges purchase and include the cost of books required for college courses in tuition would lead to improved academic performance.

If having colleges purchase and include the cost of books required for college courses in tuition would lead to improved student academic performance, then this policy would contribute to fulfilling one of the major missions of any college.

If this policy would contribute toward fulfilling one of the major missions of any college, then the cost of books required for college courses should be included in tuition.

∴ If having colleges purchase and include the cost of books required for college courses in tuition would lead to improved student academic performance, then the cost of books required for college courses should be included in tuition.

If having colleges purchase and include the cost of books required for college courses in tuition would lead to improved student academic performance, then the cost of books required for college courses should be included in tuition.

Having colleges purchase and include the cost of books required for college courses in tuition would lead to improved student academic performance.

If having colleges purchase and include the cost of books required for college courses in tuition would result in college tuition more honestly reflecting the cost of taking college courses, then the cost of books required for college courses should be included in tuition.

Having colleges purchase and include the cost of books required for college courses in tuition would result in college tuition more honestly reflecting the cost of taking college courses.

∴ The cost of books required for college courses should be included in tuition.

FIG. 5.1. Logical diagram—Books.

Your logical diagram provides the basis for your written essay. You will incorporate into your essay all of the arguments included in your diagram. Moreover, you will not include any additional argumentative content in your essay that is not in your logical diagram. There are, however, some things that you must do in putting your argument into prose that you did not need to do in your logical diagram. One of the most important of these is to provide verbal indicators as to how the various arguments relate to each other. The relation between arguments was indicated in your logical diagram by the way in which you laid arguments out on a page: You indicated that two or more arguments were multiple arguments to the same conclusion by placing them in parallel columns, and you showed that subordinate arguments provided support for premises in subsequent arguments by writing the subordinate arguments above the main arguments, and connecting their conclusions to the premises in the subsequent arguments. In your written argument you will need to use verbal cues to indicate that two arguments are intended to offer multiple arguments to the same conclusion or that the conclusion of one argument is serving as a premise in a subsequent argument. The examples that follow illustrate some ways to show these relations between arguments.

As with other styles of writing, there are no absolute rules as to how to structure an argumentative essay. However, the following section outlines a rather typical structure for a demonstration, whether it takes the form of a letter to an editor, a memorandum, a letter, a recommendation, a one-page pamphlet, advertising copy, a legal brief, a college essay, or even a lengthy thesis.

COMPOSITIONAL STRUCTURE FOR DEMONSTRATIONS

1. Introduction
   Background to the topic
   Presentation of the conclusion
   Foreshadowing of the argument

2. Body
   Presentation of the main argument(s)
   Presentation of subordinate arguments

3. Summary
   Restatement of the conclusion

This structure has three basic parts. As a very rough guide, two thirds of the composition should be devoted to the *body*, and the remaining one third divided more or less equally between the *introduction* and the *summary*. Let us discuss the contents of these three parts in more detail. We then go through our two examples and show how we might turn their logical diagrams into argumentative essays.

Introduction

As the previous list indicates, there are three tasks to be performed in the introduction to an argumentative essay. The first is to set the stage for the argument by providing a brief discussion of the context in which the argument arises. The main point in writing this part is to make sure your audience knows why you are bothering to argue the point at all. Often this is a good place to point out the importance of the issue you are addressing. In this part you should introduce your audience members to the subject, and try to get them interested in it. Although this part of your composition should not be very long, it is absolutely essential to it. Without it, your audience is thrust into the middle of things, with no idea of where you've come from, where you're going, or why you're trying to get there. Think of what you experience when you turn on a movie on television in the middle of the program. The disorientation you experience ("Who *is* that man? Why did he say that to that other man? Is he his brother or a friend? Is what he said to be understood comically or seriously?") often results in your turning the show off. An argumentative composition without an introduction, or with a poorly written one, will usually have the same effect on your audience. And if the stage you set in the introduction causes your audience to *turn off* or *tune out*, then all your efforts at developing sound arguments are going to have been wasted.

Many times in real-life contexts, such as business, you will be developing an argument as part of an ongoing activity. For example, you may receive a memo from your boss asking you to come up with a recommendation as to what brand of car your company should purchase. You can then provide an adequate introduction to your argument by referring to the earlier memo that your boss had sent. Your first sentence might be something like, "In response to your memo of September 12, asking for a recommendation for three new cars to purchase for use by our company's sales representatives. . . . " Notice that this first sentence does more than merely mention the memo. It also states briefly what it said, namely, that it had requested a recommendation for three new cars. This helps to nail down exactly what is at issue: which cars to buy. *That* will be what this memo is about. A *back-reference* such as this to an earlier discussion, memo, or letter, and so on, is often a good way to locate the context of the argument.

There are various other ways to introduce the topic of your argumentative essay. Sometimes a purely *historical reference* is helpful: "In 1964 the Congress of the United States passed the Civil Rights Act, making racial discrimination illegal. In this essay I shall argue that. . . ." At other times an *analogy* will help to gain your readers' attention: "Prior to the stock market crash of 1929, the average price of stocks had an uninterrupted series of increases. Today the Dow-Jones has continued to increase over the last 5 years. In this essay I shall argue that. . . ." Sometimes an *example* that illustrates the topic will set the stage: "John, 16, lies comatose in a hospital bed, the victim of. . . ." Sometimes a *statistic* will provide a context for your argument: "At any time, 10% to 20% of all American children fall into the 'clinically depressed' category. . . ." There are many other strategies you can use to get your readers' attention and to introduce them to the topic you wish to argue about. The important thing is that you do so, as the first order of business in your written argument.

The second major task of a good introduction is to state precisely the conclusion for which you are going to argue. This is perhaps the most important part of the introduction. The reason you are arguing is to convince your audience of something. If you do not inform your audience what claim you are trying to convince it to accept, it may well draw a different conclusion from your arguments. You will then have failed in your argumentative endeavors. Moreover, if you do not inform your readers of your conclusion, they are going to have to do too much work as they read through your composition. They are going to have to (a) follow the argument through its presentation in the body, and (b) try to imagine where that argument is going to lead them. An argumentative composition is not a mystery novel, and there's nothing to be gained by hiding the identity of your conclusion throughout the work, only to "spring" it on your readers at the end. Stating your conclusion at the beginning of your composition will take all the wonder out, and will allow them to keep track of the steps of your argument. They now know *where* it's going to go, and all they have to do is see *how* it will get there.

The third component of your introduction is to give your reader a guide as to the arguments that will follow. This is not the place for you to state your arguments, but only to *foreshadow* what form they will take. The point of doing this is to prepare your reader to assimilate as easily as possible the substantive arguments you will make in the body of your essay. You want to reduce as much as possible the chances that your reader will be led astray in the course of your argument. In a short essay you might only indicate in the introduction that you will be advancing a specific number of multiple arguments for the conclusion. In a somewhat longer essay you might indicate *very briefly* the content of each of these arguments. If there is to be only one argument, and most of the body of the essay will be devoted to supporting the premises of this argument, you might tell your reader that you are going to first establish two particular claims, and then use these to justify the conclusion.

Body

In the *body* of your composition, you need to spell out the logical arguments already worked out in your diagram. Insofar as your diagram reflects valid logical form, writing the body of your argument ought to be easy. Much of what you need to do is simply to work through each of the main arguments and subordinate arguments of your diagram, constructing complete, grammatically correct English sentences out of the individual premise and conclusion lines in the diagram. But there is something additional that is extremely important: You must make it absolutely clear to your reader how the various parts of your overall argument fit together.

One part of making clear how the pieces fit together is to use the premise and conclusion *indicator words* listed in chapter 2 to make it clear what statements are to be taken as premises, and what conclusions follow from them. It is *extremely* important that you use these words in your written argument, for they indicate that there is an argument going on. Without them, your audience will be as lost as someone giving directions would be without the words *left* and *right*. *Hence, for this reason*, and *this shows that* are the directional indicators you need to use to guide your audience through your argument. Without them, your reader is likely to take all statements as having equal status. In particular, they are likely to take issue with your conclusion (remember, the conclusion is not something they will initially agree with) without realizing that they have been given reasons to accept it. In order to avoid boredom, you will occasionally want to vary the order of the premises and conclusion. Sometimes, for example, you will want to say "Premises A and B imply that C is true," whereas other times you will want to state this as, "C is true; this is because A and B are true." The list of premise and conclusion indicator words in chapter 2 will furnish you with several different ways of saying the same thing, but you should not be afraid to use other words not on the list to tie together your premises and conclusion. The important point is to make sure your reader appreciates the relation between premises and conclusions that you intend and that you have indicated in your logical diagram. Your reader won't be able to look into your mind or at your logical diagram for this, and so you must make it clear with the use of indicator words.

The second part of the task of making clear how the pieces of the argument fit together is to show the relation between arguments. What was shown by the use of parallel columns and arrows in the logical diagram must now be conveyed in prose in your essay. Think of the logical diagram as a road map on which you have traced out a route. The geometry of the map makes it clear whether you are to turn left or right at a certain spot, and what the relation is between different points at which you must turn. Your argumentative essay is comparable to a verbal representation of the directions. In giving verbal directions you must translate the information provided in the geometry of the map into words. Similarly, in the argumentative essay you must use words to make the relation between different multiple arguments, or between different arguments in a chain, clear. When you are constructing multiple arguments to the same conclusion, words such as *first, second, moreover, furthermore*, and *finally* are particularly helpful in keeping the various arguments separate from each other. They tell your reader that one line of argumentation is complete and it is time to move on to the next. They also serve as a stimulus for those who have not followed the current argument to go back and make sure they understand it before proceeding to a new line of argument.

When you are using chain arguments, words that indicate that some statement is a conclusion, but is now going to be used as a reason for another conclusion are necessary. These are words such as, *Having seen that A, we can see that this means that B*, and *So C is true. But this, together with D, means that E is true.* Sometimes it will be quite awkward to repeat the same statement in the position in which it appears as conclusion and in the later position in which it serves as a premise of another argument. Sometimes you can use pronouns to refer to the statement: *Having established this point, we can combine it with Consideration F to arrive at Conclusion G.* However, we must make sure it is absolutely clear to the reader what the points are to which we are referring.

We know that for an argument to be valid, all the necessary premises must be in place. In developing your written argument, though, it may get awkward and tedious to state all the premises explicitly. Thus, occasionally you might want also to use an enthymeme, particularly if the premise or conclusion you leave out will be clearly understood by your audience. But you need to judge this by what you have determined about your audience. If they do not supply the missing part, your logical point has been lost, and your enthymeme has worked to your disadvantage. Thus, be very careful in using enthymemes in written prose. And never use enthymemes in your logical diagrams. Only when you are in the process of putting the logical diagram into prose should you consider omitting a premise or conclusion of an argument. When you do decide to omit a premise, indicate the fact in your logical diagram by putting that premise in parentheses.

The diagram you have drawn for your argument will furnish you with a strong clue as to how to divide the body into paragraphs. Except in the case of the very shortest argument, each main argument you have written down generally should be developed in its own paragraph. Sometimes you will be able to include the subordinate arguments that support the premises of that argument in the same paragraph. In other cases, you may need to use separate paragraphs for the subordinate arguments. If your argument is at all complex, you may need at various points to summarize the argument to that point so that your reader will be absolutely clear about what you have demonstrated so far. For example, if the overall structure of your argument involves three arguments to the same conclusion, each with subordinate arguments, it may be practical to develop each main argument together with its subordinate arguments in a paragraph. At the end of each paragraph you should make it clear that you have developed one line of argument for your conclusion. For example, you might conclude a paragraph in the argument for not hiring Alpers: *Thus, I have shown that, because Alpers does not have a high school diploma, we should not hire him.*

Summary

The last section of your argumentative essay is the *summary*. The summary should always include a statement of your conclusion. This is the last chance you have to impress on your audience members the conclusion you are trying to convince them to accept. When you are in the process of writing your argument, you may find that what you intended to argue for has changed, and that the conclusion you have arrived at is slightly different from what you thought it was going to be. When this happens, be sure to return to your introduction and rewrite it so that the conclusion you say you are going to arrive at is the same as the one you actually do arrive at. In addition to reiterating your conclusion, you can use the summary to remind your reader of the structure of your argument. If you have advanced three different arguments for your conclusion, you can remind them of that fact and perhaps even indicate in a couple words what was the focus of each argument. Finally, the summary is also often a good place to clarify your conclusion, and to distinguish it from other conclusions with which it might be confused. Forestalling confusion, preventing any misreading of what you have said, and showing the limits of the claim(s) that you have made are all perfectly appropriate activities to engage in when writing an argumentative essay. Better that you do these things than that your audience or critic have the opportunity to become confused, misread you, or point out the limits of your argument.

EXAMPLE ARGUMENTATIVE ESSAYS

Let us return now to the logical diagrams we constructed for our sample conclusions and see how we might develop essays from these examples. Our first example was for the conclusion *We should not hire Alpers*. As you recall, we initially developed a very simple diagram for this conclusion, using four arguments to the same conclusion. If we do not worry for now about the subordinate arguments subsequently advanced to support the premises in this argument, you might write your whole argument in one paragraph. First, you must be sure to introduce your argument. This can be done in a sentence or two in which you introduce the subject of your argument and announce the conclusion. For example, *You requested that I review Alpers' application for employment. My recommendation is that he not be hired by our department.* You can now turn to presenting the arguments included in your logical diagram. There are two things you will need to do. The first is to prepare your reader for the fact that you will be presenting multiple arguments. You can do this by introducing the arguments with a comment such as *I will give four reasons for this* or *There are several reasons for this*. The second is to give your reader sufficient guideposts as to when you are progressing from one argument to the next. Here you will want to use words like *first, second*, and so forth. Using these principles, we can construct a paragraph to present the previous argument:

> You requested that I review Alpers' application for employment. My recommendation is that he not be hired by our department. There are several reasons hiring him would be a bad idea. First, we should not hire people with felony records, and Alpers has such a record. Second, Alpers' last employer refuses to give him a recommendation, and we should not hire people whose last employer is unwilling to give them a recommendation. Third, no people should be hired who refuse to sign a statement saying that they will abide by departmental regulations, and Alpers refuses to sign such a statement. Finally, Alpers lacks a high school diploma, and no one without a high school diploma should be hired.

Because the argument is so short, we do not need a summary, although we could add one like the following if we choose: *Thus, for these four reasons we should not hire Alpers*.

Note that in this short paragraph we have incorporated both premises in all four arguments in our outline. In some cases we might choose to use an enthymeme. For example, we could state the first argument: *First, Alpers has a felony record* and leave it to your boss to supply the other premise, *We should not hire people with felony records*. Most of the time, however, we are better off including the premise rather than relying on our audience to supply it.

We expanded our simple diagram to provide support from some of the premises in the main arguments. We also dropped the second line of argument on the grounds that one of the premises in it was not likely to be true. Thus, we ended up with the final logical diagram:

If one of his references as well as police files indicate that Alpers has a felony record, then he has one.
One of his references indicated that he had a felony record.
Police files indicate that he does have a felony record.
∴ Alpers has a felony record.

If, when presented with the *Departmental Regulation Manual*, people indicate that they cannot accept the regulations having to do with client confidentiality, then they have refused to state that they will abide by departmental regulations.
When presented with the *Departmental Regulation Manual*, Alpers indicated that he could not accept the regulations having to do with client confidentiality.
∴ Alpers refuses to state he will abide by departmental regulations.

If a person doesn't have a high school diploma, then we cannot be sure of the person's communication and computation skills.
If we cannot be sure of a person's communication and computation skills, then we shouldn't hire the person.

If a person doesn't have a high school diploma, then the person does not show a drive for self-advancement.
If a person does not show a drive for self-advancement, then we should not hire the person.

∴ If a person doesn't have a high school diploma, we shouldn't hire the person.

If a person has a felony record, we should not hire the person.
Alpers has a felony record.

If people refuse to state that they will abide by departmental regulations, we shouldn't hire them.
Alpers refuses to state he will abide by departmental regulations.

If a person doesn't have a high school diploma, we shouldn't hire the person.
Alpers doesn't have a high school diploma.

∴ We shouldn't hire Alpers.

Given the more complex structure in this diagram, it is no longer reasonable to present the whole argument in one paragraph. However, we can still present a quite short business memo that incorporates the whole argument.

Memorandum

To: Your Supervisor

From: Your Name

Re: Alpers's Application

In your memo of June 10 you requested that I review Alpers' application for employment. Below I offer three reasons why Alpers should not be hired by our department.

The first reason is that we should not hire people with felony records. One of Alpers' references indicated that he had served time for a felony. Further, I have checked police records and they corroborate the fact that he was convicted of a felony. This already gives us adequate reason for not hiring Alpers.

A further reason for not hiring Alpers concerns willingness to abide by departmental regulations. If people refuse to state that they will abide by department regulations, then we should not hire them. When I reviewed with Alpers the *Department Regulation Manual*, Alpers objected to the regulations having to do with client confidentiality and indicated a lack of willingness to conform to this regulation. Thus, because Alpers will not agree to abide by departmental regulations, we have a second reason not to hire him.

Finally, Alpers does not have a high school diploma. We should not hire someone who does not have a high school diploma. There are two reasons for insisting on this policy. First, if a person lacks a high school diploma, then we cannot be sure of the person's communication and computation skills, and we should not hire someone unless we can be sure of these abilities. Second, anyone who lacks a high school diploma does not exhibit a drive for self-advancement, and we should hire someone only if the person exhibits a drive for self-advancement. Hence, our policy of insisting on a high school diploma is a good one. Because Alpers fails to satisfy this condition, we should not hire him.

As you requested, I have reviewed Alpers' file and have found three solid reasons for not hiring this person, one having to do with a felony record, a second with unwillingness to abide by departmental regulations, and third with the lack of a high school diploma. Thus, I strongly recommend that we do not hire Alpers.

There are several points we should note. First, in the header for this memorandum we included the line, *Re: Alpers' Application*. This serves as a title for the essay. Whether you are writing a business memo or a class paper, it is always worth giving your writing a title. In the case of argumentative writing, it serves to focus your reader on the subject matter of the argument, thereby making it easier for the reader to follow your argument. Second, the first paragraph introduced the topic of the argument, stated the conclusion, and provided some orientation for the argument that follows. Third, each paragraph included one main line of argument for the conclusion, and the supporting material. Fourth, these paragraphs all began with indicators that made it clear that they each advanced a new argument. Fifth, all of the crucial premises have been stated in the paragraphs. A couple of premises have been left out, generating enthymemes, but these have been obvious ones (e.g., we left out the premise, *If one of his references as well as police files indicate that Alpers has a felony record, then he has one*). Sixth, each paragraph ends with a statement pointing out how the conclusion that we should not hire Alpers has been established. Seventh, the final paragraph reiterates the main conclusion (in fact, it does so twice) and quickly reviews how this conclusion has been established.

Although this memo is not fancy, it will clearly communicate your argument to your boss. It is very unlikely your boss will not understand clearly what you are recommending, and the basis for your recommendation. If your boss does not agree with your recommendation upon the basis of this memo, then where you have failed is in understanding your audience. The premises you thought could be assumed should have been demonstrated. For if your boss accepted your assumed premises, you have developed a logically compelling case for the conclusion.

Let us now turn to our other sample topic. The following is a sample essay that might be written for your college newspaper's opinion page in hopes of influencing your administration to assume responsibility for supplying required books for courses. Note how it utilizes the arguments from our diagram for this topic.

Required Books Should Be Covered by Tuition

After the first class every term students head to the college bookstore to purchase the books required for their courses. Generally they discover that the books cost far more than they expected. Some students are simply bitter at the surprise extra expense. Others must elect to go without one or more of their required books. Is there anything that can be done about this problem? I will argue that there is. Our college could buy the required books for all students and include the cost in tuition. I will show that such a policy is to be preferred to the current one for three reasons: It will reduce the overall costs of attending college, it will lead to improved student performance, and it will make tuition more honestly reflect the true cost of attending college.

First, and probably the most important reason for adopting this policy is that, even though colleges will pass on the cost of required books in the form of tuition, it will lead to an overall savings for students. It will result in overall savings for two reasons. One is that it will help solve the problem of the excessive prices now charged for books required for college courses. Books required for college courses now sell for much more than what it costs to produce them. If there were effective procedures for negotiating on prices, these prices could be reduced. Although students are in no position to negotiate on prices, colleges would be, because they would be making large orders. Another way in which having colleges handle the purchase of books would help generate overall savings is that it would help overcome problems that now result from professors not considering cost when ordering books for their courses. Notice how many times, when you ask professors how much books will cost, they respond that they do not know? It is pretty clear that they are not aware of the cost of books. Hence, it is not surprising that they sometimes order books that are never actually used. Think how this would be changed under the new policy. Because colleges would want to keep tuition down to be competitive, they would put pressure on professors to limit the cost of books ordered for their classes. One could imagine that each professor would have a budget, and would have to stay within that budget. Thus, professors would know the cost of books, no longer order books that are not needed, and take cost into account when ordering books. The involvement of professors would therefore provide a second means of reducing the overall costs of required books.

What I have established so far is that having our college handle the purchasing of books required for courses would lead to an overall savings for students. But why should an overall savings to students lead our administration to make this change? The reason is very simple. Effecting an overall savings for students would help the administration achieve its often stated goal of holding down the cost of education. Moreover, it is pretty obvious that if it would help the administration achieve such a major goal, then our college could adopt this policy. So we have established that, if it would produce a savings for students, our administration should adopt the policy, and we previously established that this policy would yield such a savings. We therefore have made the case for having the costs of books required for college courses be included in tuition.

There are, however, additional reasons for this new policy. I noted at the outset that some students must forego buying some of the required books because they cannot afford them. It is pretty obvious that these students would do better in their courses if they had the required books. Without owning the books, there are inevitably times when students are not able to borrow the books and consequently do not read their assignments. If this is the case, then having the college purchase the books makes it easier for these students to read their assignments and improve their academic performance. Moreover, if this policy would lead to improved academic performance, it would contribute to one of the major missions of any college. And a college should adopt a policy that helps it fulfill its major missions. So we have a second reason for including the cost of books required for college courses in tuition.

Finally, we can presume that our college wanted to gain respect for its honesty and integrity. So if the policy would result in college tuition more honestly reflecting the cost of taking college courses, then the college ought to adopt it. It is the case that the policy would result in college tuition more honestly reflecting the cost of taking college courses. This is because, as it stands now, students and parents alike focus primarily on the cost of tuition in making their decisions about college finances and do not consider the costs of required books. As a result, students and parents alike are misled about the cost of attending college, and when they discover that they have been misled, they feel they have not been dealt with honestly. Therefore, having colleges purchase and include the cost of books required for courses in tuition is a policy that would result in tuition more honestly reflecting the cost of taking courses, and so is a policy that should be adopted.

I have offered three reasons why our college should incorporate the costs of books required for courses in tuition. The most important reason is that it would reduce the overall costs for students. It would also improve academic performance and make tuition more honestly represent the cost of taking college courses. This is a policy that would impose no additional costs on the college but could both help meet the goals of the college and enhance its reputation for dealing with students and parents honestly. Hence, our college should include the costs of required books in tuition.

6

Evaluation Arguments[1]

The type of argumentative essay that you will most frequently be asked to write is probably an essay of evaluation. In any work activity, for example, it is common for a person to be asked to evaluate an employee, or to evaluate a course of action for an employer. An essay is evaluative because its conclusion measures an object or event against a norm (or standard of excellence). Very often you might state the norm using terms like *good* and *bad*. There are a variety of other words that also present a norm, such as *just, competent, proper, perfect, poor, unsatisfactory*. What is distinctive in each of these cases is that some norm is being set forth and the object or event is being judged by how well it satisfies this norm. The following represent evaluative claims that might be the conclusion of an argumentative essay:

> Connie is a very *competent* plumber.
> The Honda Civic is the *perfect* car for me.
> Taking a week off will be *good* for you.
> Playing golf is an *ineffective* way to get cardiovascular exercise.
> Watching violent TV is *bad* for children.

Arguing for evaluative claims is not difficult. What it requires is simply that you set forth the standards for the kind of evaluation you are performing and then show that the item you are evaluating does satisfy these standards. The challenge in creating a good evaluation is to come up with an appropriate set of standards and to *justify them adequately*. In this chapter we focus on the kinds of standards needed for different kinds of evaluation and the process of justifying them.

There are several different sorts of evaluation one might make. We focus on three common kinds. The first is to evaluate an object as an instrument or item that serves a particular purpose. This is the kind of evaluation you must perform whenever you must decide between different products for purchase. Imagine you

---

[1]The analysis of evaluation arguments presented here is inspired by and modeled after one developed by Milton Snoeyenbos.

are seeking to buy a good lawn mower. Then the following evaluation will give you the information you need:

>*Honda makes a very good lawn mower.*

We refer to this sort of evaluation as an *instrumental evaluation*.

A second sort of evaluation evaluates activities. Activities are frequently evaluated in terms of whether they are projected to have good or bad consequences. Accordingly, we refer to these sorts of evaluations as *consequence evaluations*. You might be asked to evaluate the consequences for your friend Alison of serving as a reporter for your campus newspaper. The following could be the consequence evaluation you arrive at:

>*Serving as a reporter for our campus newspaper would not be a worthwhile activity for Alison.*

A third form of evaluative claim evaluates the ability of people at performing a given activity, so we refer to these as *ability evaluations*. Instead of evaluating the consequences of the activity for Alison, you might be asked to evaluate her ability as a reporter. Here you could come up with the following evaluative claim:

>*Alison would be an excellent news reporter for our campus newspaper.*

In this chapter we explore what is required in arguing for each of these kinds of evaluation.

In addition to having different kinds of evaluation, evaluations can differ according to whether they evaluate something on its own, or in comparison with other things. The most basic form of evaluation is an *absolute* or *noncomparative* evaluation. In this form of evaluation you simply judge whether some object, activity, or person is good or bad, competent or incompetent, worthwhile or nonworthwhile irrespective of other competing objects, activities, or persons. Thus, you would consider whether Alison would make an excellent news reporter for your campus newspaper irrespective of whether Thomas would be as good a reporter or possibly an even better one. For the most part, we focus on such noncomparative evaluations. However, there will often be contexts in which you must determine whether some object, activity, or person is better or worse than another. Thus, you might be asked to judge whether Alison would be better off by serving as a reporter for the newspaper or working on the fund-raising committee for her sorority. Here you must compare two activities and determine which has the better consequences. We refer to such evaluations as *comparative* evaluations. Finally, you might be asked not just to compare an object, activity, or person, against one or a few competitors, but against all available competitors. This would yield a *superlative* evaluation such as:

>*The Chevy Blazer is the best vehicle for our company to purchase for its sales representatives.*

Toward the end of this chapter we discuss some of the special challenges that arise in doing comparative and superlative evaluations.

INSTRUMENTAL EVALUATIONS

Part of the challenge in developing any evaluation is putting the evaluative claim in proper form. This is particularly true of instrumental evaluations. Before you can evaluate an object as an instrument, you must make clear what sort of instrument you are considering it to be. The very same object can be construed as a member of many different categories. Think about your shoe. In addition to serving as footwear, it could be used as a prop to hold a door open, as a weight to hold down papers, or as an object to bang on the table to get attention. Before you can evaluate it, you must know to which of these uses it is to be put. Something may be very good for one purpose and quite bad for another. Notice how your response to the following statements differs:

> *The Ford Escort is a very good practical car.*
> *The Ford Escort is a very good luxury car.*
> *The Ford Escort is a very good sports car.*

In presenting your evaluative claim, you will specify the purpose by stating the kind of object you take the item to be. We refer to the term specifying the category in which you are evaluating the object as a *sortal*. In the previous examples, *practical car*, *luxury car*, and *sports car* were the sortal terms.

In addition to specifying the category in which you are evaluating an object as an instrument, it is important to specify the user for whom you are evaluating the object. Different users make different demands on an object. A car that might be a very practical car for one person might be very impractical for another. For example, the VW Bug was a practical car for many modest-sized people who did not need to carry many passengers. But it was far less practical for someone 6'6" tall, or who regularly had to transport four children. Thus, our statement about the Ford Escort needs to be completed in something like the following manner:

> *The Ford Escort is a very good practical car for a college student.*

Although it is relatively easy to construct instrumental evaluations using terms like *good* and *bad*, these are often not the best evaluative terms to use. The following are some examples of instrumental evaluations that employ other evaluative language:

> *The Allison Acoustics AL-115 is a superb speaker for the sophisticated audio buff.*
>
> *The Panasonic CTM2782S is a poor 27-inch TV for a viewer concerned with sound quality.*
>
> *The AT&T Universal Card is an adequate but not cheap credit card for a person who regularly takes cash advances on a credit card.*
>
> *J.C. Penney's Roberto de Roma blazer is a practical blazer for a price-conscious woman.*
>
> *Glidden Spread Ultra Flat paint is a excellent choice for an interior flat paint for the average do-it-yourself painter.*

Stating your evaluative claim as clearly as possible is important for making an instrumental evaluation, because the claim will provide the conclusion of your argument. Nevertheless, sometimes it is best not to begin the construction of your evaluative essay here. What is important is to determine the sortal that you will be using to categorize the object being evaluated, and the user for whom you are evaluating the object. Then, before determining whether the object in question is a superb, good, adequate, or poor instance of that category for the user in question, you need to proceed to the next, and most crucial step. This involves determining the *criteria* by which objects in the category are to be evaluated.

Determining the criteria by which you will evaluate an object requires careful brainstorming. In carrying out this brainstorming, you should forget about the particular item you are evaluating, and focus on the category of object and the user of the object. Identify the various criteria on which you can evaluate objects in that category. You will generally need to draw up at least two lists. One will identify features that are *necessary* for an object to be *adequate* as a member of that category for that user. Possessing these features alone will not make something an adequate member of the category, but lacking them will disqualify the item. A second list will identify *desirable* features. These are the features that will differentiate between the merely adequate members of the category and the really *good* members. Sometimes the categories of necessary and desirable are not sharply differentiable, the distinction being one only of degree. There may, for example, be a degree something *must* obtain in order to be adequate, but then it may be possible to go beyond this degree. How much it does so may influence our judgment as to how good the item is. For example, if you are buying a used car, four *functional* tires might be a necessary requirement for the car's being adequate, but four *good* tires would be desirable, and might be one of the characteristics that go into making it a good car. Thus, you may want to list the same generic feature in both the necessary and desirable lists, listing one degree of the feature (functional tires) as necessary and a higher level of the feature (good tires) as desirable.

Take as an example a category that is probably familiar to all of us: cold breakfast cereals. We consider a typical college student as our user. What are the important features in evaluating breakfast cereals for college students? Some of these we can come up with by simply reflecting on the category. *Cost* is probably a major consideration for most college students. *Good taste* is probably another. Both of these probably qualify as necessary features.

Whereas some of the criteria for evaluating objects are obvious, there are many that you won't be able to identify just by sitting and thinking about the object. You will likely require some resource material. When dealing with products, it helps to consult the writings of an independent agency (i.e., not one affiliated with the producer of the product) that evaluates products. There are such evaluators for most major consumer items: autos, stereos, computers, and so on. Consumers Union is a nonprofit organization that conducts evaluations of a broad range of products and services and publishes its findings in *Consumer Reports*. In addition to making their own recommendations, magazines like *Consumer Reports* present detailed discussions of the relevant features by which products in different categories should be evaluated and information about how different products do with respect to these features. Thus, in addition to determining what product such a publication ranks best in a particular category, you can use the publication to arrive at your own recommendation. (This may often differ from the publication's recommendation because you may define the category somewhat differently in your sortal and you may have a particular user with particular requirements in mind.) The October 1989 issue of *Consumer Reports* had a report on breakfast cereals. In addition to providing information about cost, it focused on nutritional components of cereals. It explains the importance of high fiber contents and low sugar and fat contents and also provides information about calories and salt contents of various cereals. Based on this information, you may develop a list of necessary and desirable features for a cold cereal for a college student.

Necessary	Desirable
Costs less than 20 cents/oz	Costs less than 17 cents/oz
High fiber content	Less than 100 cal/oz
Low sugar content	High vitamin and mineral content
Less than 20 mg sodium/oz	Attractive taste

Note that you should give very careful thought to what items you place in your list of necessary and desirable features, and where you place them. These will provide the basis for your evaluation. In defending your evaluation, moreover, you will have to defend this list by showing that these are the features that are important for the user you have identified.

With the list of necessary and desirable features in place, you can now begin to develop your evaluation. You need to examine whether the item you have chosen to evaluate possesses each of the necessary and desirable features. In general, to be judged *acceptable* an item should exhibit all of the necessary features. (An exception would be a situation in which you have been so demanding in your list of necessary features that no candidates possess them all. In this case you must either rethink your list of necessary features or accept a lower threshold for being acceptable.) A better than acceptable evaluation, that is, a good or excellent evaluation, generally requires that an item possess a significant number of desirable features as well.

Let us imagine that we had chosen two different cold cereals to evaluate: Nabisco Shredded Wheat'n Bran and Special K. In terms of the data reported in *Consumer Reports* (it is important to indicate where you got your data), Nabisco Shredded Wheat'n Bran possesses all of the necessary features: it costs 18 cents/oz, has high fiber and low sugar content, and has only 5 mg sodium per oz. It also has only 97 cal/oz. From personal experience and talking with others, you might also know that it has an attractive taste. Although it does not meet the criterion of costing less than 17 cents/oz and is ranked only as moderate in terms of vitamin and mineral content, it seems worthy of at least a *good* ranking. Our instrumental evaluation conclusion can thus be worded:

Nabisco Shredded Wheat'n Bran is a good cold cereal for a typical college student.

Special K, on the other hand, costs 22 cents/oz, received a poor ranking in terms of fiber content, and has 230 mg sodium/oz. By virtue of failing on three out of four necessary conditions, it merits a less than *adequate* ranking, probably a *poor* ranking. The instrumental evaluation conclusion would thus be:

Special K is a poor cold cereal for a typical college student.

We now have the information necessary to develop our instrumental evaluation of these two cold cereals. What we need to do next is to structure this information into a valid argument. Typically, the main argument for an evaluation will have the form of a modus ponens argument. The conditional premise will lay out the conditions for the evaluation we are making, and the second premise will state that the item in question meets those conditions. In the case of an item that is receiving an adequate or better evaluation, your conditional premise will have to identify those features from the list of necessary and desirable features that make this item deserve its evaluation. Thus, in the case of Nabisco Shredded Wheat'n Bran, your conditional premise will have the form:

> If a cereal costs less than 20 cents/oz, has high fiber and low sugar content, has less than 20 mg sodium/oz, has less than 100 cal, and has an attractive taste, then it is a good cold cereal for the typical college student.

In setting out the conditional statement, we need to examine it carefully for truth. Recall the logic of the conditional. If it is true, the antecedent sets out conditions that, if fulfilled, are *sufficient* to insure the truth of the consequent. So one way to test the conditional is to consider various situations in which the antecedent is satisfied and see if the consequent is true in all of those situations. Can you imagine a cereal that has high fiber and low sugar content, has less than 20 mg sodium/oz, has less than 100 cal, and an attractive taste, but is not a good cold cereal for a college student? That shouldn't be too hard. Consider a hot cereal. You can certainly imagine a hot cereal that meets all of the conditions. If that is the case, clearly you need to amend the conditional:

> If a cold cereal costs less than 20 cents/oz, has high fiber and low sugar content, has less than 20 mg sodium/oz, has less than 100 cal, and has an attractive taste, then it is a good cold cereal for the typical college student.

In deciding whether the modification we have made is sufficient, you need to view the conditional as specifying a situation in which you make a promise. It says, *All you need to do to make a good cold cereal for the typical college student is provide the things specified. If you do so, I will agree that it is a good one.* Before making such a promise, you should consider carefully all the ways the other person might satisfy your conditions. If you are not prepared to decree that anything they might produce that meets your conditions is a good cold cereal for the typical college student, you need to modify your conditions.

In presenting this premise, note that we have not made mention of the desirable features that Nabisco Shredded Wheat'n Bran lacked. If we think it is important to take note of one or more of these features, then we could have done so by including it in an *even if* clause,[2] alerting the reader to the fact that this condition does not affect the overall argument in our premise:

> If a cold cereal costs less than 20 cents/oz, has high fiber and low sugar content, has less than 20 mg sodium/oz, has less than 100 cal, and has an attractive taste, then, even if it is only adequate in vitamin and mineral content (a desirable but not necessary feature), it is a good cold cereal for the typical college student.

Even if we don't spell out the criterion regarding vitamin and mineral content in the premise of our argument, we may want to take note in our essay that Nabisco Shredded Wheat'n Bran is only adequate in vitamin and mineral content, whereas it was desirable that it be high in both, and then explain why this shortcoming in a desirable feature does not disqualify it from being considered a good cold cereal for college students. (For example, we may note that most college students are likely to receive the needed vitamins and minerals through other foods they eat each day.)

Note that although failure to meet one or more of the desirable features does not jeopardize our attempt to show that an entity is instrumentally good, failure to satisfy even a single necessary feature does. In such a case we are required to argue that the item is not good, or poor. Our conditional premise will identify those necessary features on which the item is failing. Thus, our premise for Special K will have the following form:

> If a cold cereal does not cost less than 20 cents/oz, or does not have high fiber content, or has more than 20 mg sodium/oz, then it is a poor cold cereal for the typical college student.

Note that in this case what the antecedent specifies are only those necessary criteria on which Special K is failing. In this case we won't bother commenting on the necessary or desirable features Special K might possess because, given our criteria, it cannot be an adequate cereal. But some caution is still needed. The wording of the premise commits us to agreeing that any cereal that failed on *any* of these conditions would be a poor cold cereal for the typical college student. But perhaps that is not what we meant. If we meant only that the *collection* of these three qualities will disqualify the cereal, then we need to write the premise this way:

---

[2]An *even if* clause is not to be confused with an *if* statement. It is not the antecedent of a conditional. It simply signals the reader that we are prepared to stand behind the truth of our conditional statement whether or not the factor mentioned in the *even if* clause is true.

> If a cold cereal does not cost less than 20 cents/oz, and does not have high fiber content, and has more than 20 mg sodium/oz, then it is a poor cold cereal for the typical college student.

In the case of Special K, of course, it will fail to be a good cereal no matter which of these two premises we adopt. Nevertheless if we regard the criteria as being individually rather than collectively necessary, we should use the first of the two premises, because it draws attention to the fact that Special K fails on all three independent criteria, rather than on the collection of criteria.

Once we have determined what goes into this main premise, the structure of the main evaluative argument is now straightforward. The second premise states that the item satisfies or fails to satisfy the criteria we have set out, and the conclusion asserts our instrumental evaluation. Thus, in the case of Nabisco Shredded Wheat'n Bran, our argument has the following form:

> If a cold cereal costs less than 20 cents/oz, has high fiber and low sugar content, has less than 20 mg sodium/oz, has less than 100 cal, and has an attractive taste, then it is a good cold cereal for the typical college student.
> Nabisco Shredded Wheat'n Bran is a cold cereal that costs less than 20 cents/oz, has high fiber and low sugar content, has less than 20 mg sodium/oz, has less than 100 cal, and has an attractive taste.
> ∴ Nabisco Shredded Wheat'n Bran is a good cold cereal for the typical college student.

The Special K argument will also have modus ponens form:

> If a cold cereal does not cost less than 20 cents/oz, or does not have high fiber content, or has more than 20 mg sodium/oz, then it is a poor cold cereal for the typical college student.
> Special K does not cost less than 20 cents/oz, does not have high fiber content, and has more than 20 mg sodium/oz.
> ∴ Special K is a poor cold cereal for the typical college student.

What remains now is to construct our logical diagram around this argument, and then present our essay in good English prose. To create our logical diagram, we place the main argument at the bottom of a piece of paper. We now need to evaluate the two premises in our argument to determine which ones need support. In this case, most of the information for our second premise of each argument came directly from a reliable source, *Consumer Reports*. However, it is still worth examining how *Consumer Reports* procured this information. In some cases, sources like *Consumer Reports* do their own studies to determine how items fare on various criteria. In that case you might need to support the claims made in the second premise by developing arguments that review how the information was obtained and show that it is reliable. In this case, however, *Consumer Reports* took the information directly from the cereal boxes. This raises a good question: "Why should we trust this information, particularly in the case of cereals that received good ratings?" One answer is that the Federal Food and Drug Administration, which requires that such nutritional information be put on cereal boxes, also requires that the information be accurate. Another is that *Consumer Reports* did its own spot check of the information. So we could, if we desired, develop arguments supporting the various claims about the nutritional content of Nabisco Shredded Wheat'n Bran or Special K.

The first premise of an evaluative argument, however, almost always requires support. The first premise sets out the criteria, and you need to give justification for using these criteria. Consider again the first premise of the Nabisco Shredded Wheat'n Bran argument:

> If a cold cereal costs less than 20 cents/oz, has high fiber and low sugar content, has less than 20 mg sodium/oz, has less than 100 cal, and has an attractive taste, then it is a good cold cereal for the typical college student.

Five conditions are set out for being a good cold cereal. Why should possessing these factors make something a good cold cereal? Defending this conditional is actually a bit tricky. It won't be sufficient to note that each of the factors we have mentioned is itself a good thing for cereals to have. It may be true that each of the factors mentioned is a good thing, but it does not follow that having them is enough to make a particular cereal good, which is what you have claimed.

To approach defending this claim, ask yourself why you took these to be the relevant features to begin with. (Note: In one sense you simply borrowed some of these items from the analysis by *Consumer Reports*. But in using them in your own argument, you take on the burden of defending their use.) Presumably cost was pertinent because you realized that college students typically have restricted budgets. The next three factors were included because they make the food nutritious to eat. Taste is pertinent because humans tend to eat those things that taste better, and so will tend to favor a food that tastes good over other foods that are more nutritious but lacking in taste. Thus, these factors serve to make a cereal affordable, nutritious, and attractive. So what we can say is: *If a cereal has the features identified, it will be affordable, nutritious, and appealing*. Thus, we are in a position to construct a conditional syllogism for the first premise of our main argument:

> If a cold cereal costs less than 20 cents/oz, has high fiber and low sugar content, has less than 20 mg sodium/oz, has less than 100 cal, and has an attractive taste, then it will be affordable, nutritious, and appealing.
> If a cold cereal is affordable, nutritious, and appealing, it is a good cold cereal for the typical college student.
> ∴ If a cold cereal costs less than 20 cents/oz, has high fiber and low sugar content, has less than 20 mg sodium/oz, has less than 100 cal, and has an attractive taste, then it is a good cold cereal for the typical college student.

You will now have to ask whether these premises are both likely to be acceptable to your particular audience. Some audiences may need to know more. Some might question the second premise. They might ask: Why do you think it is enough for a cold cereal to be affordable, nutritious, and appealing? Others might question the first. For example, they might not see how these factors make something affordable. In fact it is just one of the factors, costing less than 20 cents/oz, which you take to make it affordable. To show why this is the case, you may need to construct an argument showing how 20 cents/oz. translates into a very modest expense for breakfast each morning. Or the person might not see how the factors cited make the cereal nutritious. Here three of the factors are what are relevant: Having high fiber and low sugar, having less than 20 mg sodium/oz, and having less than 100 cal. Now you need to construct an argument that shows why having these factors makes a cereal nutritious. Here you will need not only to point to the benefits each of these factors provides, but show they are the only ones relevant to judging the nutritiousness of cold cereal. This you might do by pointing out that, given other foods one will likely eat during the day, the main thing that is still needed is high fiber, and by showing how having more sugar, sodium, or calories, will be harmful.

CONSEQUENCE EVALUATIONS

We turn now to a second form of evaluation, one in which you evaluate an activity that an individual, a group, or a corporation might perform. As we have already indicated, activities are frequently evaluated in terms of whether they have good consequences or not and so we refer to them as *consequence evaluations*.

Before we proceed, we should note that a consequence evaluation of the sort we discuss here is not the only kind of evaluation you might make regarding actions. We often worry not just whether an action has good consequences for us, but whether the actions are *moral*. We might judge a particular course of action to be in our best interests but nevertheless think that it is immoral. For example, you might be considering the action of blackmailing competitors to get them not to compete with the new product you are about to release. This action could have very good consequences for you in terms of increased profits, but it is certainly morally questionable. A discussion of the basis for moral evaluations goes beyond the scope of this book, but we can take note of two of the most prominent theoretical frameworks used for making moral evaluations.

One approach, known as *utilitarianism*, is very similar to what we are referring to as *consequence evaluation* because it too focuses on the consequences of an action. But it argues that in evaluating an action morally we must consider the consequences of the action not just for the actor, but for *everyone*. The utilitarian claims that morally we are obliged to perform whichever action has the best overall consequences for all people. Thus, morally, blackmail would be wrong if others were harmed by this action, and there were another course of action (including doing nothing) that overall yielded more good or less harm than this action.

The second approach, known as the *deontological approach*, rejects consequences as a basis for moral evaluation and argues that certain kinds of actions are inherently right or wrong. An example in the Western tradition of a deontological moral view is found in the Ten Commandments, which require or proscribe certain actions not because of their consequences, but because they are deemed inherently right or wrong. Thus, one of the commandments proscribes adultery not because it produces bad consequences, but because it is inherently wrong, regardless of its consequences.

In discussing consequence evaluations, however, we abstract from moral evaluation. This is not to deny the relevance of moral evaluation; indeed, we assume that all of the action choices you are considering are morally defensible. Rather, the issues involved in moral evaluation are sufficiently complex that they require another course.

The claims made in consequence evaluations are different in significant ways from those made in instrumental evaluations. In consequence evaluations we do not require sortal terms. In instrumental evaluations it was largely by using sortal terms that we developed the criteria for evaluating the object, for the sortal terms provided us information about the use to which the object was to be put. In consequence evaluations, on the other hand, our determination of whether the consequences are good or bad depends on who is affected by the consequences. Most often we will be evaluating the consequences for the doer of the action. But we might choose to evaluate the action with respect to others who may be affected by the action. You should note that the evaluation of the very same action may be quite different depending on the person specified. Consider the following two consequence evaluation claims:

> *Taking your vacation next week will be good for you.*
> *Taking your vacation next week will be bad for your employer.*

We could easily imagine cases in which both of these statements were true. For example, if you are responsible for preparing the tax reports for your company, and next week is the last week before taxes are due, taking a vacation next week may have very good consequences for you (e.g., reduction in stress) but terrible consequences for your employer (e.g., fines if the tax reports are not filed or filed incorrectly). Thus, in stating your consequence evaluation it is essential that you specify the person or group for whom you are evaluating the consequences.

In arguing for a consequence evaluation there are two tasks you must perform: (a) determine what are the consequences of performing an action and (b) determine whether these consequences, taken together, are good or bad for the person(s) specified. In presenting the argument, one premise (the second) will specify what the consequences of a particular action are, whereas the other premise (the first) will state the judgment as to whether these consequences, taken together, are good or bad. Thus, an argument for a consequence evaluation might take the following form:

> If taking a course has the consequences that Cathy will be able to get the instructor she wants, will have completed a requirement for graduation, and will be prepared to take other courses that she wants to take the following quarter, then it is a good thing for her to do.
>
> Taking a statistics course next quarter has the consequences that Cathy will be able to get the instructor she wants, will have completed a requirement for graduation, and will be prepared to take other courses that she wants to take the following quarter.
>
> ∴ Taking a statistics course next quarter is a good thing for Cathy to do.

Note that these two premises perform very different functions in your evaluation. The first premise presents the claim that the consequences of taking a course would be good ones. It does not assert that a particular action will have these consequences. That is stated in the second premise.

The structure of a consequence evaluation is simple, but there is nonetheless a challenging component in developing a consequence evaluation. You need to make sure you have considered *all* of the consequences of a potential action. If you focus only on some, the action may appear to be good for the person, but when you consider all of its consequences, it may be bad. To continue with our example, consider some other possible consequences. It may be that the statistics course next quarter is scheduled at a time at which Cathy must frequently be at work and that she cannot get out of the work commitments without being fired. Thus, a consequence of taking the course next quarter is that she will either have to miss a number of classes, thus raising the prospect that she will not do well in the class, or she will get fired. There may also be other negative consequences of taking the course next quarter. For example, she may not have completed all of the math courses that would prepare her for doing well in the statistics course, thereby increasing the possibility that she will not do well. Moreover, there may be other courses that she needs to take next quarter in order to continue with her studies, and she is not able to take them and the statistics course.

These considerations count against the truth of the first premise of your argument, stated as follows:

> If taking a course next quarter has the consequences that Cathy will be able to get the instructor she wants, will have completed a requirement for graduation, and will be prepared to take other courses that she wants to take the following quarter, then it is a good thing for her to do.

This premise claims that as long as taking a course has these benefits, then no matter what else were true, taking it would be a good thing for Cathy. But these other considerations show that these consequences might be realized, and it still might not be a good thing. So, before you construct your first premise, you must thoroughly review all of the consequences of the proposed action that might in any way affect the judgment as to whether or not it is good. Some of them may make so little difference that they are not worth mentioning, but as you brainstorm the topic you should at least note them. Moreover, if all the consequences seem to be coming out on one side (e.g., pointing toward the action being good), then give extra attention to identifying possible consequences that might point in the opposite direction. It never hurts to consult with a friend, or an imaginary critic looking at your choice from hindsight (i.e., after you have done it). Ask: All of these considerations seem to point to this being a good action for X. Am I overlooking anything? Are there any consequences that point in the other direction?

In most cases, after you have carefully considered the matter, you will find some consequences that are good and others that are not so good. The first thing you must do is consider whether the good consequences outweigh the bad or vice versa. Sometimes this is relatively easy. Sometimes all of the major consequences are favorable, and there are only one or two unfavorable consequences that are easily compensated for by the favorable consequences. In other cases, however, you will need to weigh the consequences carefully to consider whether, overall, they point to the action being good or bad. A factor that makes this challenging is that not all consequences count equally. One way to approach this is to draw up a list of all of the consequences you have identified, and then give a numerical score to each (you might use a scale from -5 to +5). Continuing with the example of taking the statistics course, you might end up with the following list of consequences. Going down the list, you might assign scores that fairly rate the positive or negative nature of the consequence.

+2   Cathy will be able to get the instructor she wants.
+1   Cathy will have completed a requirement for graduation.
+2   Cathy will be prepared to take other courses she wants to take the following quarter.
+1   Cathy will be able to take the course with her friends.
- 4   Cathy will either have to miss a lot of classes and so not do well, or get fired from her job.
- 3   Cathy won't have completed all the preparatory courses, and so probably won't do as well in the course as she might.
- 3   Cathy won't be able to take the other courses she needs to take next quarter to continue with her program.

Note, there is no need to use the whole scale from -5 to +5. It is useful to save the maximum and minimum scores for the best and worst possible outcomes you can imagine. In the present example, when you total up the positive and negative scores, you end up with a score of -4, indicating that overall you find Cathy's consequences for taking the statistics course next quarter to be negative. If you had started out to defend the conclusion that taking the statistics course next quarter would be a good thing for Cathy, you will now need to revise your conclusion.

Once you have brainstormed to generate all the consequences that will affect your judgment, and have determined what conclusion they support, you need to put together your first premise. If there are consequences that point in the direction opposite to most other consequences, they should be acknowledged in the premises.

(You may, however, leave out consequences that have such a small impact that they seem rather unimportant. If, per the previous list, completing one more graduation requirement and taking a course with her friends are actually fairly minor benefits, you might leave them out.) You can acknowledge the consequences that go in the opposite direction in the following manner:

> If taking a class next quarter has the consequences that Cathy will either have to miss a lot of classes and so not do well or get fired from her job, and she won't do as well as she might due to not having completed all the preparatory courses, and she won't be able to take the other courses she needs to take to continue with her program, then, even if she would be able to get the instructor she wants and will be situated to take other courses that she wants to take the following quarter, taking that course next quarter is not good for Cathy.

To complete the valid argument, you must add a second premise stating that taking the statistics course will have these consequences, and draw the conclusion that taking the course is not good for Cathy.

Once you have set up the main argument for your evaluation, you need to consider what premises need support. Some of the consequences you claim will follow from the action will be obvious and will not need support. Others, however, will need to be demonstrated. Thus, in your logical outline you will prepare subordinate arguments showing that the action will have the specified consequences and draw an arrow from the conclusion of that argument to the premise in your main argument. Whether or not you have to demonstrate many of the claimed consequences, you almost certainly will have to support the conditional premise that embodies your evaluation of the consequences. If you have pointed to consequences that make the action good, you will often have to show that these are good consequences.

Special attention will have to be paid to situations in which there are some consequences that point in the opposite direction and are being acknowledged (e.g., in the *even if* clause in the previous example). You won't have to show that these do point in the opposite direction, but you must show that these are compensated for by the other consequences. You must show that the consequences of being able to get the instructor Cathy wants and being able to take other courses that require statistics are outweighed by the negative consequences indicated. Thus, you must show that getting fired or not doing well in the course, not doing as well as she might if she took the preparatory courses, and not taking other courses she must take to continue in her program outweigh the good consequences.

ABILITY EVALUATIONS

The final form of evaluation we examine is *ability evaluation*. You may have already had the experience of asking someone to write a letter of recommendation for you for a job or to get into college. What you were asking that person to do was evaluate your ability to perform in the job or at the school. This is a task you will often encounter yourself. In fact, in trying to convince someone to hire you or choose you for a position, you will often be required to make an ability evaluation of yourself. You will try to convince the employer that you have the abilities to do the job required extremely well. Moreover, if you supervise other employees, you will often be called on to evaluate your employees. For instance, you might be asked to evaluate whether one of your employees is suitable for promotion. You also make these evaluations frequently in civic life. Every time you vote you are evaluating which of several people is better suited to perform the position to which they are seeking to be elected. Although often you won't be called on to justify your vote (evaluation) with an argument, sometimes you might. The latter is especially true if you want to persuade others to vote for the same candidate.

Just as with instrumental evaluations, ability evaluations require a sortal. You must specify what the activity is at which you are evaluating someone. The reason for this is obvious. We can all think of people who have been good at one activity, but not at another. For example, many people will concur with the following evaluations:

> *Franklin Roosevelt was a skilled politician.*
> *Mohammed Ali was a talented boxer.*

But consider what happens if we switch the names of Roosevelt and Ali. Roosevelt may seem skilled as long as you are evaluating him in the category of politicians, but not when you are evaluating him as a boxer. In developing your evaluation you may want to take some care in determining which sortal you will use. Sometimes it will be useful to use a narrower sortal term, thereby narrowing the category in which you are evaluating someone's ability. Rather than evaluating someone as a great singer, for example, it may be appropriate to narrow the category and claim only that she is a great opera singer, or even just a great mezzo-soprano, or even just a great performer of the role of Brunhilde.

The sortal term plays a crucial role in your ability evaluation. It is from the sortal term that we will determine what attributes are needed to be good or bad at an activity. In fact, in brainstorming to develop your argument, you should temporarily turn your focus away from the particular person you are evaluating, and focus only on the category in which you are evaluating the person. What does it take to be good (or bad) at performing the activity in question? Let us take as our example evaluating someone as a good manager for a copy center. What skills does it take to be good at this task? Brainstorming this topic thoroughly will ensure that you have included all the necessary attributes that someone must have to be good at this activity as well as those beyond the necessary abilities that point to good performance. It may be helpful if you begin by considering what tasks the manager of a copy center is required to perform. One of the most obvious tasks is supervising other employees. But there are probably a number of other tasks that person is required to perform. These include intervening with customers if disputes arise, keeping the financial records for the center, ordering supplies, identifying peak load times and slack times (to determine staffing demands), designing or approving the layout of the center and its window displays, and designing or approving the advertising for the center. In addition, you may know that managers of small businesses usually must work long hours, and be able to substitute for employees who fail to show up. This characterization of the job gives you some guidance into drawing up the list of abilities a good copy center manager must have. You might end up with a list such as the following:

Must be able to motivate workers.

Must be able to set guidelines for other employees' behavior and enforce them.

Must be able to get along well with customers.

Must be good at resolving disputes without embarrassing either party.

Must be good at basic accounting.

Must be good at anticipating future needs.

Must be creative in designing layouts for the center or at least good at judging other people's designs.

Must be creative in designing advertising strategies or at least good at judging those proposed by others.

Must be able to solve problems.

Must be dedicated and able to work long hours.

Once you have a list of the attributes someone needs to be good at a task, you can examine the people you are evaluating to determine how well each satisfies these attributes. You may not be in a position to judge all of them. For now, focus on the ones that you can judge. If a person has exhibited each of these attributes, or shows promise of doing so, then you will be in a position to evaluate the person as a good manager for the copy center. However, the task gets trickier if the person exhibits one or more shortcomings. On some of these, that might be sufficient to rule the person out. For example, if the person is simply unwilling to work long hours, then typically that will be grounds for presenting a negative evaluation. Similarly, if the person is not effective in motivating employees or at enforcing guidelines on their behavior, that may be sufficient to show the person will not make a good manager. But there may be failings that can be overcome and result in the person being a good manager. For example, if the advertising for the copy center can be designed by a central office, then a person who is not good at designing or evaluating advertising strategies might still turn out to be a good manager if the person is able to identify the advertising needs for the center and communicate them to the central office.

Let us imagine we are evaluating a particular candidate, Shawn, who meets all of the criteria on our list except that of having talent in developing or evaluating advertising material. We have already decided that this is not a serious deficit, but probably one that should be mentioned. The conclusion of our argument is going to be:

Shawn would make a very good manager for the copy center.

In arguing for this claim, you must now set out the conditions for making a very good manager, and show that Shawn meets them. In structuring your main argument, though, you may not want to go through a long list of attributes that are pertinent to a particular job. One way to simplify matters is to cluster the attributes into three or four categories. For example, you might cluster the items in the previous list into three categories: interpersonal skills, business skills, and dedication to the job. Your main argument may then have the following form:

> If a person has the appropriate interpersonal and business skills, and is dedicated to the job, then the person will be a very good manager for the copy center.
> Shawn has the appropriate interpersonal skills.
> Shawn has the appropriate business skills.
> Shawn is dedicated to the job.
> ∴ Shawn would make a very good manager for the copy center.

You will now need to develop your logical outline to support the premises of this argument. In the course of doing so, you will need to expand on what counts as interpersonal skills and business skills. For this you can go back to your original list of attributes needed to be a good manager, and use those related to good interpersonal skills to show that Shawn has the appropriate interpersonal skills. Thus, you would construct an argument such as:

> If a person is able to motivate workers, is able to set guidelines for other employees' behavior and enforce them, is able to get along well with customers, and is good at resolving disputes without embarrassing either party, then the person has the appropriate interpersonal skills to be a good manager for a copy center.
> Shawn is able to motivate workers, is able to set guidelines for other employees' behavior and enforce them, is able to get along well with customers, and is good at resolving disputes without embarrassing either party.
> ∴ Shawn has the appropriate interpersonal skills to be a good manager for a copy center.

A similar argument can be used to establish that Shawn has the necessary business skills. In the course of this argument you will need to deal with Shawn's shortcoming in the area of advertising. This can be done by an *even if* clause such as those we have used in other arguments:

If a person is good at basic accounting and at anticipating future needs, is creative in designing layouts for the center, or good at judging other people's designs, and is able to solve problems effectively, then, even if the person is not so creative in designing advertising or in judging advertising proposed by others, the person has the appropriate business skills to be a good manager for a copy center.

Shawn is good at basic accounting.

Shawn is good at anticipating future needs.

Shawn is creative in designing layouts for the center or good at judging other people's designs.

Shawn is able to solve problems effectively.

∴ Shawn has the appropriate business skills to be a good manager for a copy center.

Each of these arguments has premises in need of support. In particular, you need to show that the interpersonal skills and business skills you have selected are pertinent for a copy center manager. In the case of the one identified skill that Shawn lacks, you will need also to show that there is a way to overcome this deficiency so it does not detract from Shawn having the appropriate business skills. You may also need to create subordinate arguments in which you present evidence showing that Shawn possesses each of the characteristics in question.

COMPARATIVE AND SUPERLATIVE EVALUATIONS

Throughout this chapter we have focused on noncomparative evaluations. But frequently we will want to compare different objects, activities, or people. We may want to know, for example, whether tennis or swimming is a better recreational activity for a busy professional. In developing a comparative evaluation, it is not sufficient to show that some particular object, activity, or person is good, for the other one may be better. Moreover, it is not necessary to show that any of the entities being compared is good. All may be poor, but you may still be able to show that one is better than the others. For example, all of the movies available in the rental store on a particular evening may be mediocre, but you may still be able to establish that one of them is better than certain others for you to rent.

There are also situations in which you will not only want to compare some of the available options, but to determine which of all of the available options is best. This involves a superlative evaluation. Essentially, however, a superlative evaluation is not significantly different from a comparative evaluation. What distinguishes it is that you must consider all of the alternatives. Thus, before you carry out the evaluation you must determine what is the population from which candidates can be chosen. For example, your supervisor may ask you to determine who is *best* qualified to manage the new branch. It is pertinent to know whom your supervisor wants you to consider. Should you be considering only those who have worked for you directly? Or are you to be evaluating all employees in the company? Or should you even go outside the company to consider people from other companies? There may be a group of individuals who have applied for the branch manager position, and this may specify the population: You are to evaluate who among the applicants is best qualified to be the new branch manager. Generally, it will be useful to specify the population being evaluated in your evaluative claim. Thus, you might conclude:

> *Of all of the candidates who have applied, Margaret Sampson is the best qualified to become the manager of the new branch.*

After you have settled on the population of candidates to be reviewed, a superlative evaluation reduces to a comparative evaluation. You simply must determine which of the individuals in the population is better than all the others.

The simplest case for doing a comparative evaluation is one in which one of the items being compared has all the positive characteristics of the competitors and more, or fewer of the negative characteristics of the competitors. For example, it would be very easy to compare the Nabisco Shredded Wheat'n Bran with Special K. The Nabisco meets all four of the criteria we identified as necessary for being a good cereal, whereas Special K is lacking in three of them. Given this, we can structure our comparative instrumental evaluation as follows:

> If a cold cereal costs less than 20 cents/oz, has less than 20 mg sodium, and has high fiber content, whereas another cold cereal does not meet these basic criteria, then the first is a better cold cereal than the second for the typical college student.
> Nabisco Shredded Wheat'n Bran costs less than 20 cents/oz, has less than 20 mg sodium, and has high fiber content, whereas Special K does not meet these basic criteria.
> ∴ Nabisco Shredded Wheat'n Bran is a better cold cereal than Special K for the typical college student.

The task of developing a comparative evaluation gets more difficult when one item is better on some criteria and another is better on others. For example, consider again the criteria we developed for being a good copy center manager. You might be considering two candidates, Carol and Jerry. Carol is better on some criteria, whereas Jerry is better on others. Who, then, is better overall?

There are several steps you can follow when you confront such a situation. First, eliminate from the list of criteria those on which all the competitors are equivalent. For example, if both Carol and Jerry are equally good (or bad) at motivating workers, basic accounting, and creativity in advertising, delete those from the list of criteria. Now focus on those abilities on which they differ. What you need to do now is determine both (a) how much better or worse one person is than the other on each criterion, and (b) how much each criterion matters. One way to do this is to set up a numerical system. Addressing the second issue first, go through the list of criteria and assign a score from 1 to 5 to indicate how much each criterion matters. Your list might look like this:

Importance	Criteria
5	Able to set guidelines for other employees' behavior and enforce them.
2	Able to get along well with customers.
3	Good at resolving disputes without embarrassing either party.
2	Good at anticipating future needs.
1	Creative at designing layouts for the center or good at judging other people's designs.
4	Able to solve problems.
4	Dedicated and able to work long hours.

The score for importance that you gave to a criterion now fixes the range of points you can assign to each person on that criterion. Thus, for setting guidelines and enforcing them you will rate Carol and Jerry on a scale of 0–5, whereas for ability to get along well with customers you will rate them on a scale of 0–2. We need now to go through and assign scores. The result could look like this:

Importance	Criteria	Carol	Jerry
5	Able to set guidelines for other employees' behavior and enforce them.	3	4
2	Able to get along well with customers.	2	1
3	Good at resolving disputes without embarrassing either party.	3	2
2	Good at anticipating future needs.	1	2
1	Creative at designing layouts for the center or good at judging other people's designs.	0	1
4	Able to solve problems.	4	2
4	Dedicated and able to work long hours.	4	2
TOTAL		17	14

The resulting score indicates that, given how you understand the criteria, Carol is better qualified to be the copy center manager than Jerry.

Once you have arrived at your comparative evaluation, you need to construct a valid argument for it. The form, as it has been throughout this chapter, will be modus ponens. In the first premise you need to identify the criteria that guided your comparative evaluation. You will focus on those criteria on which the items being compared differ. In the antecedent you will identify those criteria on which the person you judged overall to be better was superior. In the consequent you will include an *even if* clause that identifies those criteria on which the other person scores more highly, and a statement of your overall evaluation. Thus, for the aforementioned case, it will look like this:

> If one person is more qualified than another in terms of ability to get along with customers, being able to resolve disputes without embarrassing either party, ability to solve problems, and dedication and willingness to work long hours, then, even if the second person is slightly superior in terms of ability to set guidelines for employee behavior and enforce them, anticipating future needs, and being creative at layouts for the center, the first person is better qualified to be the new copy center manager.

The other premises will identify the criteria on which Carol is superior. You do not need to explicitly state that Jerry is in fact slightly superior on other criteria.

The key to this sort of comparative evaluation is the point scale you established. It need not actually appear in your essay. But because it established the importance of the various criteria, it has influenced the main premise. You now need to employ the considerations that led to assigning different levels of importance to different items to develop subordinate arguments to support the conditional premise. In particular, you must show why Carol's superiority on some items is sufficient to make her more qualified. In part this is due to the relative importance you assigned to the last two items, and how much better you judged Carol than Jerry on these items. You must also explain why Jerry's superiority to Carol on some items does not outweigh the ones on which she is superior. In part, this is because some of these items just were not very important, and in part this is because Jerry was not significantly stronger than Carol on these items. What you must do is develop arguments appealing to these factors to justify the conditional premise.

Comparative evaluations can sometimes be much more difficult to develop than noncomparative ones due to the fact that you must identify the particular criteria that differentiate the items you are comparing, and establish the degree of importance to be assigned to each. The challenge becomes even more demanding when you consider three or more competitors, each of which shows strengths on different criteria. There is, however, often no easy way out. You must simply do the preliminary work needed to develop the main conditional premise, and then proceed to defend its use.

7

Critiques:
The Essential Preparation

By now you have learned how to construct arguments of your own and how to use them to demonstrate conclusions in written prose. In this activity you are the originator of the argument. But sometimes you will be confronted with a demonstration developed by someone else. You must now decide whether to believe the conclusion of this demonstration. After careful examination, you might find that the argument is flawed: The premises given are insufficient to demonstrate the truth of the conclusion. You may also want to reply to the argument, showing how it is flawed so as to convince others (including, possibly, the author of the demonstration) that they should not believe the conclusion *based on that argument.* If so, you will be engaging in a second form of argumentation, which we call *critique.*

It is important to be clear about what a critique is supposed to accomplish. A critique is not the same as a demonstration that the conclusion of someone's argument is false. Imagine that someone has circulated a memorandum arguing that your company retain your current legal counsel. You, however, are convinced it is time for a change, and want to demonstrate that. You already know how to construct such a demonstration. It is important to note here that you can prepare such a demonstration without mentioning any of your colleague's arguments or rebutting them. A critique of your colleague's demonstration, in contrast, requires you to examine the arguments in the demonstration and show that they fail to establish the conclusion that the current legal counsel should be retained.

Just as a demonstration of a contrary claim does not do the work of a critique, a critique does not accomplish what a demonstration of the contrary claim accomplishes: A critique of your colleague's demonstration does not show that its conclusion is wrong. It only shows that the arguments advanced do not establish the conclusion it is claimed they do. In fact, there are occasions on which you may wish to critique an argument whose conclusion you accept. If you think that someone's argument for a conclusion you agree with fails to properly establish that conclusion, you may want to critique that demonstration as preparation for offering an alternative demonstration that makes the same claim. It is also a healthy activity to attempt to critique your own arguments. In our sample essay in chapter 1, for instance, we included two objections that might be raised against the arguments. This is often done as preparation for a *defense* of one's original demonstration.

Although a critique does not establish that the claim a person was arguing for is wrong, if your goal is to establish the opposite conclusion, it is often important that you include a critique of the arguments advanced for the original conclusion. The reason is that insofar as someone has advanced a demonstration, reasons have been presented for others to accept the person's conclusion. If those reasons are not sufficient, then that needs to be pointed out so as to neutralize their import.

In this and the next two chapters we limit our focus to the act of constructing a critique. Because a critique focuses on an argument that has been advanced, you will need to analyze that argument carefully so as to understand how it is supposed to work, and then identify the weaknesses in it. It is important that you become thoroughly conversant with the argument before you try to identify weaknesses in it. A common failing in developing a critique is to try to find faults too soon, before you have carefully analyzed the argument. You may then later discover that the faults you have found really do not undercut the demonstration and that it has escaped unscathed.

DIAGRAMMING THE ARGUMENT TO BE CRITIQUED

The best way to understand someone else's argument is to prepare a logical diagram of it. The difference between diagramming the argument of someone else and preparing a diagram for your own demonstration is that in diagramming someone else's argument you must figure out how that person *intended* to make the demonstration work. Thus, your task is to extract from the prose the logical structure of the argument the person intended. Your interest is simply in the logical structure of the argument, so you should eliminate all logically extraneous material such as rhetorical flourishes, repetitions, illustrations, asides, digressions, and connecting words. Locate the bare bones of the argument, that is, the various premises and conclusions.

Your first task in developing a logical diagram is to discover the overall structure of the argument. What is the main conclusion the person has tried to argue for? What are the arguments the author has offered that directly support that conclusion? Put these into a diagram just as if the argument were your own. That is, start from the bottom of the page. Put the conclusion at the center bottom with a line above it, and the premises of the arguments that have that as their conclusion directly above. If these premises are intended to comprise two or more arguments, put each into a separate column.

As you are doing this, concentrate on what you think the author meant. It is usually better to put the author's conclusion and premises into your own words. That way you will come to understand the meaning of what the person said. On the other hand, it is important not to put words into the arguer's mouth that were not intended, and not to distort the meaning of anything that was said. If, for example, the arguer argued that abortion is wrong except in cases of rape or incest, it would be a misrepresentation of this person's view to represent the conclusion as "Abortion is wrong." Similarly, if the conclusion was that reducing U.S. arms spending would probably help reduce the deficit, it would be unfair to the arguer to say that the arguer had tried to conclude that a reduction in arms spending would reduce the budget deficit. *Maybe* the arguer intended to say this as well, but so far as the argument in question goes, that is an inaccurate statement of the conclusion. Thus, be particularly attentive to qualifier words the other person has used.

After you have put the conclusion and the main argument into the diagram, work up the page to the supporting arguments. But leave yourself some extra space along the way, because the arguments the author put forward may well be enthymemes and you will need to add premises to make these arguments valid. (Sometimes it will be clear what premises need to be added as you go through the argument. If so, you can add them at that point.) Your task now is still one of identifying the main structure of the demonstration. Make it clear how each piece of the argument fits in. If a premise is supported, show the supporting argument, with an arrow going from the conclusion of the supporting argument to the appearance of the premise in a later argument. If there are multiple supporting arguments for a particular premise, show them in parallel columns.

Once you have captured the basic structure, review each argument in the diagram you have constructed. If the arguments are not themselves valid, ask yourself whether they are enthymemes that can be made valid by supplying additional premises or a conclusion. If so, supply the premises. To make it clear that you are supplying the premises, put these premises in parentheses. Here, as with paraphrasing the stated premises and conclusion, fairness is absolutely necessary. Fairness (as well as prudence) requires that you employ the *principle of charity* in reconstructing enthymemes. That is, you should give as sympathetic and plausible an interpretation as possible of what the person might have intended. If you supply premises or conclusions that the author cannot reasonably be assumed to have intended, the author will be able to defend easily against your critique by saying *I was misunderstood.* So when completing enthymemes you need to be careful in supplying the missing premise(s) or conclusion(s) so as to capture what the author probably intended.

Sometimes in attempting to complete an enthymeme you may discover that it can only be completed by supplying a premise that seems extremely dubious. You may recall from our discussion of enthymemes in chapter 2 that one of the reasons enthymemes are sometimes used is to hide problematic assertions. But if you are going to critique another person's argument for containing a problematic assertion, you need to be sure the assertion is the one required for the argument to be valid. If it is, you will be able to present a very powerful dilemma for the arguer—either the author's argument presupposes the (questionable) premise you have supplied, in which case it is unsound, or it presupposes another premise. Because the premise you have supplied is the only one that will render the argument valid, any other premise will make it invalid, and thus will also render it unsound. Thus the argument must be unsound.

Sometimes, however, it may appear impossible to supply a premise so as to make the argument valid. Whenever this is the case, it needs to be carefully noted. This piece of detective work on your part will form another important part of your critique.

In describing the process of constructing a logical diagram of the argument to be critiqued, we have emphasized the importance of the principle of charity and of giving a sympathetic rendering of what you are going to critique. The reason is that the most decisive critiques will be those grounded on a very sympathetic rendering of the argument. Such a critique will show that the argument in question is *inherently* flawed and cannot be patched up in some simple manner. In order to be as sympathetic as possible, pretend the argument is your own. Within the framework put forward in the original argument, make the argument as strong as possible. This does not require you to come up with additional arguments for the author's conclusions. (That would be to go outside of the framework of the original argument.) But it does require you to reconstruct what the author has said and complete enthymemes in the manner that makes the argument as strong as possible.

EXAMPLE ESSAY FOR CRITIQUE

In order to see better how this process works, consider an argument and see how we might go through the steps of preparing it for critique. We come back to this argument again in subsequent chapters and actually generate a critique of it. But at this juncture our goal is simply to construct the logical diagram that fairly captures the intent of the argument. Imagine this opinion piece appeared in the *Mytown Daily Defender* on August 6.

The Death Penalty: The Needed Deterrent to Murder
A. Common Citizen

The United States has one of the highest murder rates in the world, and every year it seems to rise. It is imperative that we do something about it now. The time has come to "fish or cut bait." In this case, what we must do is deter murder. And there is one sure way to do that: We must make sure that every convicted murderer faces the death penalty in short order. No more than 6 months should be allowed to pass from the handing down of the verdict to the implementation of capital punishment. If there are to be appeals, let them be conducted within this time span.

The crux of my argument is that we must choose between two options, and one of them is no longer viable. Our choices are to start using the death penalty for every convicted murderer within 6 months of conviction or to continue to show weakness in the face of crime. But we know the folly of the latter option. So, we have no choice but to start implementing the death penalty quickly.

Why is it so bad to show weakness in the face of crime? If we show such weakness, then nothing will deter people from using murder to solve whatever problem they face. And if nothing deters people from murder, society will simply get more dangerous. But who could want a more dangerous society? Probably only those gambling addicts who love living on the edge. Most people want to be protected. That is why we pay good money for police protection.

There are a number of other reasons for not showing weakness in the face of crime. First, the Bible instructs us how to deal with crime: "An eye for an eye and a tooth for a tooth." Second, if we show weakness in the face of crime, especially murder, we show no respect for human life. But clearly respect for human life is one of the most sacred values of any human society.

Some opponents of capital punishment argue that it does not deter crime. If it doesn't deter crime, they say we shouldn't use it. But the claim that capital punishment does not deter crime is nonsense. What could be a more effective deterrent to murder than the knowledge that when one is caught, one will suffer the same fate oneself? Assuming that the opponents of capital punishment are right in their other premise, then we should actually conclude that we should employ capital punishment, just as we have concluded from our other argument.

I have provided ample arguments for the expedient use of capital punishment on all people who have been convicted of murder. Given the choices, this seems to be the only sane option. I urge you to write to your congressional representatives, your governor, and your state legislators, urging them to make the necessary changes in law so that murderers will not be treated softly in the future, but reap their just desserts.

We begin constructing the logical outline of this essay by first identifying the conclusion. In this case the author has given us the conclusion in both the first and last paragraphs, and moreover, they seem to be consistent with each other. (If the conclusion seems to change in the course of a demonstration, that is something you should especially note.) The point the author is arguing for is that convicted murderers ought to be executed within 6 months of being convicted. In arguing for this conclusion, though, Citizen seems to be arguing for two changes in the current situation. The essay argues both that the death penalty should be the punishment for murder, and that it should be imposed within 6 months of conviction. We should word the conclusion in a way that makes this clear:

> All convicted murderers should be sentenced to death and have their punishment carried out within 6 months of conviction.

We put this at the bottom of our logical outline.

We now must determine the structure of the overall argument. The second paragraph presents what is clearly one of the main arguments for the conclusion. It has the form of an alternative syllogism:

> Either all convicted murderers should be sentenced to death and have their punishment carried out within 6 months of conviction, or we should continue to show weakness in the face of crime.
> <u>We should not show weakness in the face of crime.</u>
> ∴ All convicted murderers should be sentenced to death and have their punishment carried out within 6 months of conviction.

In this case we have continued to use Citizen's own words, *show weakness in the face of crime*, instead of paraphrasing them. A reason to do this here is that if we tried to paraphrase what Citizen means by *showing weakness* we may become very uncertain as to what is actually meant. Perhaps showing weakness refers to our current procedures in sentencing and punishing those convicted of murder. Or perhaps the author thinks any response other than capital punishment within 6 months is showing weakness. Because this is likely to be a very critical point when we begin to critique the argument, at this juncture we should retain Citizen's own words. However, we might do well to substitute *murder* for *crime* in this premise, because the author seems to be only addressing murder in this essay.

Are there any additional arguments that attempt to defend the main conclusion in this essay? The next two paragraphs present reasons for not continuing to be lax in the face of crime. So they do not argue directly for the conclusion. But the fifth paragraph seems to offer another argument. It begins by presenting an argument of the opponents of capital punishment. However, Citizen seems not to be primarily intent on presenting a critique of their argument, but rather seeks to use it to support a personal conclusion. Citizen rejects the first premise in the opponents' argument, but then puts the denial of that premise together with the second premise to argue for the use of capital punishment. Thus, Citizen seems to be arguing:

> If capital punishment does not deter crime, then we shouldn't employ it.
> Capital punishment does deter crime.
> ∴ Thus, we should employ capital punishment.

The problem is, however, that this argument does not have exactly the same conclusion as the other argument. Citizen clearly seems to take the argument to have the same conclusion, thus we should make the necessary modifications:

> If capital punishment does not deter crime, then it is not the case that all convicted murderers should be sentenced to death and have their punishment carried out within 6 months of conviction.
> Capital punishment does deter crime.
> ∴ All convicted murderers should be sentenced to death and have their punishment carried out within 6 months of conviction.

At this point we have covered all the arguments that have the main conclusion as their conclusion. Because these two arguments both have the same conclusion, and are presented as independent arguments, we should insert them into our logical diagram in parallel columns.

Next we turn to the remaining arguments, and see how they fit in. Citizen has already promised us that arguments will be provided for not showing weakness in the face of murder. In the third paragraph the following two premises appear:

> If we show weakness in the face of murder, then nothing will deter people from committing murders.
> If nothing deters people from committing murders, then society will get even more dangerous.

No conclusion is explicitly drawn from these premises. The remainder of the paragraph seems to go on to deny the consequence of the second conditional. But these two premises clearly have the form of a conditional syllogism. So let us tentatively supply a conclusion:

> If we show weakness in the face of murder, then nothing will deter people from committing murders.
> If nothing deters people from committing murders, then society will get even more dangerous.
> ∴ (If we show weakness in the face of murder, then society will get even more dangerous.)

The remainder of the paragraph now seems to support the claim that we should not let society get more dangerous. That together with the conclusion from the previous argument gives us a modus tollens argument for the claim that we should not show weakness in the face of murder:

> (If we show weakness in the face of murder, then society will get even more dangerous.)
> We should not let society get any more dangerous.
> ∴ We should not show weakness in the face of murder.

How does Citizen argue for the claim that we should not let society get any more dangerous? Citizen points to the fact that most people want to be protected, and as evidence for that points to the fact that we pay "good money" for police protection. We can construct from this a chain of valid modus ponens arguments:

> (If society is willing to pay police "good money" to protect people from murder, then most people want to be protected from murder.)
> Society is willing to pay police "good money" to protect people from murder.
> ∴ Most people want to be protected from murder.
>
> (If most people want to be protected from murder, then we should not let society get any more dangerous.)
> Most people want to be protected from murder.
> ∴ We should not let society get any more dangerous.

We have now teased out an argument for the claim that we should not show weakness in the face of murder. It has two premises, one of which is supported by a chain.

The fourth paragraph offers two more arguments for the claim that we should not show weakness in the face of murder. Each of these is put forward in a single sentence. The first refers to the biblical quotation, "An eye for an eye, a tooth for a tooth." Presumably the author is invoking the Bible here as authority as to how we should deal with murder. The easiest way to complete this argument is by supplying a conditional premise:

> (If the Bible prescribes "An eye for an eye, and a tooth for a tooth," then we should not show weakness in the face of murder.)
> The Bible prescribes "An eye for an eye, and a tooth for a tooth."
> ∴ We should not show weakness in the face of murder.

The other argument advances a conditional:

> If we show weakness in the face of murder, then we show no respect for human life.

It is clear that if the author wants this to support the claim that we should not show weakness in the face of murder; to do this a modus tollens argument is required:

> If we show weakness in the face of murder, then we show no respect for human life.
> (We should show respect for human life.)
> ∴ We should not show weakness in the face of murder.

Because these are offered as additional arguments for the claim *We should not show weakness in the face of murder*, we should represent them in parallel columns in our logical diagram.

The complete logical outline of "The Death Penalty: The Needed Deterrent to Murder" that we have now developed is shown in this logical diagram. In developing this figure we have not made any critiques of the argument, but have simply tried to understand it. Having a complete logical diagram is an essential prerequisite to developing a critique. When we critique an argument, we want to target specific points in it. With the logical diagram we can identify those points. In the next chapter we identify the tools at our disposal for critique; in chapter 9 we return to this essay and make specific objections in a critique.

(If society is willing to pay police "good money" to protect people from murder, then most people want to be protected from murder.)

If we show weakness in the face of murder, then nothing will deter people from committing murders.

Society is willing to pay police "good money" to protect people from murder.

∴ Most people want to be protected from murder.

If nothing deters people from committing murders, then society will get even more dangerous.

∴ If we show weakness in the face of murder, then society will get even more dangerous.

(If most people want to be protected from murder, then we should not let society get any more dangerous.)

Most people want to be protected from murder.

∴ We should not let society get any more dangerous.

(If knowing that if one is caught committing murder, one will die is an effective deterrent to murder, then capital punishment does deter crime.)

Knowing that if one is caught, one will die is an effective deterrent to murder.

If we show weakness in the face of murder, then society will get even more dangerous.

We should not let society get any more dangerous.

If the Bible prescribes "An eye for an eye, and a tooth for a tooth," then we should not show weakness in the face of murder.

The Bible prescribes "An eye for an eye, and a tooth for a tooth."

If we show weakness in the face of murder, then we show no respect for human life.

We should show respect for human life.

∴ Capital punishment does deter crime.

∴ We should not show weakness in the face of murder.

∴ Either all convicted murderers should be sentenced to death and have their punishment carried out within 6 months of conviction, or we should continue to show weakness in the face of murder.

We should not show weakness in the face of murder.

If capital punishment does not deter murder, then it is not the case that all convicted murderers should be sentenced to death and have their punishment carried out within 6 months of conviction.

Capital punishment does deter murder.

∴ All convicted murderers should be sentenced to death and have their punishment carried out within 6 months of conviction.

FIG. 7.1. Logical diagram—Death penalty.

8

Critiques:

Types of Objections

When you critique an argument, you are trying to show that the premises do not adequately support its conclusion. That is, you are trying to show that the argument is not sound. In chapter 2 we saw that logical soundness has two components: validity, which has to do with the logical *form* of an argument; and truthfulness, which has to do with the *premises* of an argument. These two ingredients of a sound argument provide you with two strategies you can employ to critique another person's argument: You can (a) challenge the form of the argument, or (b) challenge the truth of the premises. As a third possibility, you can combine these two and challenge both the form and the truth of the premises.

This chapter investigates each type of critique. We discuss the general strategy of assessing whether a flaw exists in either the form of the argument or in the truth of the premises and we identify a few well-known ways in which such flaws can arise. These are so well known that they have traditionally been assigned names and are referred to as *fallacies*. (A fallacy is simply a form of argument that is unsound.) It is worth familiarizing yourself with these named fallacies. They occur relatively frequently, and it is useful to be able both to detect them and to explain why they constitute fallacies.

CHALLENGING THE FORM OF AN ARGUMENT

To challenge the form of an argument, you must first determine what the form is. In developing a logical diagram of the argument to critique, you have exhibited the form. In chapter 3 we identified and assigned names to a number of different argument forms and determined their validity. Of each argument, you must now ask the question: Which of the logical forms does this argument exhibit, and is it a valid one? Does it affirm the consequent, or deny the antecedent? (Note, we might now speak of these invalid argument forms as fallacies.) Has the argument inferred from "All A are B" and "All C are B" that "All A are C"? Take particular note of those features that distinguished valid forms from closely related invalid ones. Have any of the arguments confused an *only if* statement with an *if statement*, or vice versa? Has the arguer inferred from "If A, then B," the premise "If not -A, then not -B"? If you are able to spot any logical flaws, you should note them carefully before going on to analyze the truth of the premises. Pointing out logical flaws will constitute a major part of your critique of the overall argument.

In many cases, the question of whether or not the logical form is valid will not arise, because you supplied the premises to make the arguments valid. There are occasions, however, when you will find that the author explicitly invokes a form you know to be invalid. For example, in Fig 7.1 we had the following argument:

> If capital punishment does not deter murder, then it is not the case that all convicted murderers should be sentenced to death and have their punishment carried out within 6 months of conviction.
> Capital punishment does deter murder.
>
> ∴ All convicted murderers should be sentenced to death and have their punishment carried out within 6 months of conviction.

As you should recall, this argument has the form of denying the antecedent, which is invalid. When you encounter a situation in which an author seems to be invoking an invalid form, you should be careful to manifest as much charity as possible. Did the author really intend the invalid argument, or did the author just slip and, for example, not appreciate the difference between *if* and *only if*? If you think the author intended a valid argument form, you might point out the error and then correct it, rather than making it the focus of your critique.

When you are addressing the validity of the argument, there are, in addition to the invalid forms we have already identified, two other fallacies for which you need to be on the lookout.

The Fallacy of Equivocation

We saw in chapter 3 that when you use hypothetical syllogisms you must be careful not to commit the fallacy of three terms. The *fallacy of equivocation* is just a very specialized form of that same fallacy, which occurs when only two terms are used, but one of them is used with two different *meanings*. Let's see how this might occur. Suppose someone presents us with this argument:

> Anyone who is a doctor can advise me as to where my appendix is located.
> Dr. Pangloss, an English professor, is a doctor.
>
> ∴ Dr. Pangloss can advise me as to where my appendix is located.

The argument seems, at first sight, to be of the general form:

> All A's are B's.
> x is an A.
>
> ∴ x is a B.

However, the word *doctor* is used here with two different meanings in the two premises. In the first it refers to a medical doctor, whereas in the second it refers to someone who holds a PhD. Thus, in fact, the argument is an example of this form:

All A's are B's.

x is an A'.

∴ x is a B.

This latter form, as we saw in chapter 3, is not valid. When a single term has been used in two different senses, we can speak of *equivocating* on it. Thus, the previous argument is unsound because it equivocates on the term *doctor*.

The fallacy of equivocation often occurs in fairly subtle forms. Abstract terms (such as *discrimination, freedom, liberty, right*) are very easy to use in different senses. Thus, the following example uses *discrimination* in two different ways:

> It is absurd to pass laws against discrimination, for discrimination is something that ought to be encouraged, not forbidden. People who are able to discriminate between good and bad music, good and bad cuisine, and good and bad art are people to be envied, not put into jail.

When you are in doubt as to whether this fallacy has occurred, a good strategy is the following: Write out the argument *without* using the word you suspect may be equivocated on. Instead, replace it the first time it occurs with a definition that fits the context. The second time that word is used in the argument, insert the same definition you wrote for its first use. If that premise then sounds strange, or even false, you have a pretty good indication that the word has been used in two different senses, and that you have an "A" and an "A'" instead of two "A's."

The Fallacy of Begging the Question

In a good argument, we rely on the premises to establish the conclusion. If this order of things is reversed, and the premises wind up depending on the conclusion, then the argument form is flawed. The special name given to this form of flawed argument is *begging the question*. This fallacy takes many forms, but two of them are of immediate relevance. They are called *begging the question by using equivalent expressions* and *begging the question by arguing in a circle*. Let us look first at the form of the fallacy that uses equivalent expressions. Consider the following argument:

Atlanta is the capital of Georgia.

∴ Atlanta is the capital of Georgia.

Notice that in this argument, the truth of the conclusion depends on the truth of the premise. That is to say, in order for the conclusion to be true, the premise must also be true. (If it is not, then the conclusion must be false.) And if the premise is true, then we can be sure that the conclusion must be true. But in this argument, the premise is also (and for the same reasons) dependent for its truth on the truth of the conclusion. It is this feature of the argument that makes it logically flawed. Although technically speaking, such an argument is valid, it leaves much to be desired as an argument form, because we normally think of giving evidence, or reasons for a conclusion as consisting of something other than merely repeating oneself. If assertion A is true, then that does guarantee that A is true, but it can hardly stand as evidence that A is true.

Presumably no one would ever be tempted to use this argument. Repeating oneself is just not an effective way of convincing people of the truth of a claim. But similar arguments get used quite often, even though they are no less logically flawed. Consider:

> This drug is soporific.
> ∴ This drug will cause me to fall asleep easily.

The only difference, logically speaking, between this argument and the previous one is that it uses a synonym for *soporific* in the conclusion, instead of repeating the very word. But this doesn't change the logical fact that one is still just repeating oneself in this *argument*, and so the fallacy of equivalent expressions is present here as well. Or consider a slightly more subtle example: "Beethoven's Fifth Symphony is better than his Fourth, because the Fourth is inferior to it." Again, in order for the premise ("The Fourth is inferior to it [the Fifth]") to be true, the conclusion that is supposed to be based on it ("Beethoven's Fifth Symphony is better than his Fourth.") must also be true. The premise and the conclusion are just equivalent expressions.

The second form of begging the question is called *arguing in a circle*. Here the premise and conclusion do not contain the same word, or even equivalent expressions, but the former still presupposes the truth of the latter. Consider the following argument for the existence of God:

> Jones: "That God exists is shown by the fact that the Holy Bible says so."
> Smith: "But how do you know that what the Bible says is true?"
> Jones: "I know that what the Bible says is true because it is the word of God."

Put into a logical diagram with the missing premise supplied, this argument reads:

> (If something is the word of God, then whatever it says is true.)
> The Bible is the word of God.
> ∴ Whatever the Bible says is true.
>
> Whatever the Bible says is true.
> The Bible says that God exists.
> ∴ It is true that God exists.

This argument (sometimes called the *argument from scripture*) is fundamentally flawed by the fact that what it concludes, namely, that there is a God, must be true in order for the second premise in the first argument to be true. For there must be a God (which is what the conclusion asserts to be true) in order for the Bible to be the word of God (which is what the premise asserts to be true). Arguments with this fatal flaw are said to argue in a circle, in much the same way that a dog might chase its own tail. Circular arguments are not always as easy to spot as this one, but you will receive some practice in doing so in the exercises. Whenever you do spot them in criticizing someone else's arguments you should take note of them, and add them to your list of whatever other logical flaws you have already discovered in the argument.

CHALLENGING THE PREMISES OF AN ARGUMENT

When you have finished analyzing the diagrammed argument for its validity, it is time to look at the premises themselves. Are the premises all true? If they are not, then even though the argument may be valid, it will still be unsound. Actually, when you are developing a critique of an argument, you don't have to demonstrate that a premise is false. The burden of proof is not on you, but on the person making the demonstration. All you must do is show that there are *plausible reasons to doubt its truth*. If the premise is false, or if the author has not demonstrated that the premise is true, and there are reasonable grounds for being suspicious of its truth, then the premise is flawed.

In reviewing an argument, you do not need to review all of the premises in your logical diagram. Those with arrows going into them are supported by other arguments. If the supporting arguments are sound, then these premises will be true. Hence, at the outset you can ignore those premises with arrows directed at them. If, however, those supporting arguments turn out to be unsound, you may have to return to the later premises themselves and ask whether they are true, independently of the poor argument that has been given on their behalf. If they are, then you won't direct your critique at them or their supporting arguments.

There are a host of ways in which premises can be false, not all of which we can cover. There are, however, some errors that are so prevalent that we give them special attention. We divide our discussion into three parts. We begin with a detailed looked at the fallacy of false generalization or false conditional, which is one of the most common sources of error in arguments. We then turn to a collection of traditional fallacies often named in logic books. Each of these also involves in some way a false premise. Finally, we discuss two types of objections that can be made in critiques that do not require you to show definitively that a particular premise is false.

False Generalization or False Conditional

One of the most common kinds of errors in an argument is a generalization or conditional statement that, although possibly true of many instances, is not true of all. Consider the following generalizations:

> All M.D.'s make over $60,000 per year.
> All seaports in the United States have drug problems.
> No U.S. states have fewer than two states bordering them.

These are true of many or even most instances. But each of them has exceptions. Thus, stated as general claims, they are simply false.

Generalizations are clearly used in categorical syllogisms such as the following:

> All A's are B's.
> X is an A.
> ∴ X is a B.

Hence, whenever you confront a categorical syllogism, you should inspect the premises to see if they constitute false generalizations. But you should also remember that in chapter 3 we established a relation between categorical statements of the form *All A's are B's* and conditional statements of the form *If something is an A, then it is a B*. Thus, the various forms of conditional syllogism, modus ponens, modus tollens, and conditional syllogism, frequently employ generalizations in disguised form. You encounter a conditional statement of the following form:

> If a person had as much money withheld from income as he or she paid in taxes last year, then the person does not have to pay a penalty on any additional tax owed this year.

Then ask yourself whether the following implicit generalization is a false generalization:

> Anyone who had as much money withheld from income as he or she paid in taxes last year does not have to pay a penalty on any additional tax owed this year.

If there are exceptions to this rule (as there may in fact be if there are additional requirements that must be satisfied), then it is a false generalization. If it is, then the conditional statement is false as well.

One common cause of false generalizations is inadequate experience. A person who commits a false generalization may just have stopped looking or thinking too soon. Someone who moves to a city and then experiences two rainy summers in a row may be tempted to conclude that the city always has rainy summers. But that may be because that person hasn't looked long enough. More experience might reveal that the city does not generally have rainy summers.

Another common cause of false generalizations is the psychological trap posed by *anecdotal thinking*. Anecdotes, or brief stories of actual incidents, can be very helpful when one wants to *illustrate* a generalization one has independently justified. This is particularly true if the story is striking or vivid. But in anecdotal thinking this process is reversed. The vividness of the incident is used to do logical work, and one leaps from a single striking incident to a generalization about a whole class of things. For instance, people may think of a welfare recipient they know, or have heard about, who cheats the government and drives two Cadillacs. Leaping from that shocking instance to a broad claim, the anecdotal thinkers then claim that all or even most welfare recipients are cheats who don't need the aid they receive. "Man who" kinds of statements frequently exhibit anecdotal thinking, and so are guilty of the fallacy of false generalization. Consider the following "man who" statement: "Why, I know a *man who* never wears a seatbelt, and when he had a wreck, the doctors told him that the only reason he was alive was because he was thrown out of the car." This incident may really have happened, but if one proceeds to conclude that seatbelts shouldn't be worn, one has been overimpressed by the vividness of an *exceptional* case. One has falsely generalized.

Although relying on the single, exceptional case can cause one to commit false generalizations, a single case is often sufficient to *refute* a false generalization. A general claim of the form "All A's are B's" is refuted by a single *counterexample*— an example of an A that is *not* a B. Similarly, "No A's are B's" is refuted by a single example of an A that *is* a B. Pointing out a single counterexample will render that premise untrue, and hence the argument that uses it unsound.

Notice that when a claim, such as "Most A's are B's" is made, it is not a counterexample to state, "There is an A that is not a B." This is because the first statement is perfectly compatible with the second. Because it did not say that *all* A's were B's, but only that *most* were, it allows for some A's not to be B's, and so it cannot be refuted by pointing out that some A's are not B's. Trying to refute statements beginning with such words as *most, some, almost all, many, a large percentage of*, and so on by pointing out examples of an A that is not a B, or even several A's that are not B's, can be called the *fallacy of false refutation by counterexample*. "Man who"-type statements are also used to commit this fallacy: "Welfare recipients are not on the whole chisellers or cheaters." "Yes, but I know a *man who* receives welfare and cheats the government and drives two Cadillacs, and so forth." The second statement does not refute the first, for by saying *on the whole*, the first statement allowed for the possibility of *some* cheaters. Because it is guarded in this way, the only way to refute it is to show that, on the whole (i.e., most), welfare recipients *are* chisellers or cheaters. The fallacy of false generalization or false conditional occurs very often when one presents an enthymeme rather than a complete valid argument and does not state the generalization or conditional statement that is intended to provide the first premise. The person may state other premises, each of which is viewed as offering evidence for the conclusion. But the argument will only be sound if one can add a true premise to the effect that *in all cases in which the premises are true the conclusion is also true*, or *if these claims are all true, then the conclusion is also true*. In many cases, however, you will discover that such a premise is a false generalization or conditional. We specifically identify three circumstances under which that might happen.

Stated Premises Are Incomplete.

In many instances in which people offer premises on behalf of a claim, but don't take care to insure that the argument is valid, the premises that they do present turn out to be *incomplete*. The premises presented may often be true as far as they go, but because of other factors that were not considered, the conclusion may not follow. For example, it may be true that certain studies that the arguer has quoted support the view that cigarette smoking is not causally linked with incidences of lung cancer. Were the arguer to attempt to construct a valid argument around the studies identified, the following premise would have to be added:

> If these studies show that smoking is not causally linked to incidences of lung cancer, then it is not.

But there may be other evidence that shows that smoking is causally connected with lung cancer. If this evidence is powerful enough, it undercuts the truthfulness of the conditional premise. When there is evidence pointing in both directions, one must take all evidence into account and not infer from the occurrence of studies that a certain conclusion follows. Of course, one may find that some of the evidence should be discounted. For example, if most studies show a causal link between smoking and incidences of lung cancer, then we may be in a position to discount those that don't (or vice versa). But to be complete, we should take these other studies into account in our argument. One way to do that is through the sort of *even if* statement we introduced in an earlier chapter:

> If most studies do show that smoking is causally linked to incidences of lung cancer, then, even if some do not, smoking is causally linked to lung cancer.

Once you have acknowledged the evidence that goes in the opposite direction, you need to show why it should be discounted. This is the job of the arguments that will support the conditional premise.

Consider another case in which stated premises are incomplete. Two eyewitnesses in a criminal trial have identified the person in the grocery store minutes before the robbery took place as being the same person as the defendant. As a defense attorney you may want to try to impeach that evidence, that is, to try to show that the eyewitnesses involved are unreliable, nearsighted, and so forth. But suppose you are unable to discredit those witnesses. Then there is another tack you might take. Without discrediting their testimony directly, you may be able to show that there is more evidence to be considered, that is, that the original evidence given is incomplete. If you are able to bring in other eyewitnesses who will testify that the defendant and the person in the grocery store are not the same person, you will have added to the amount of evidence that has been produced, and will have shown that more factors needed to be considered than just those produced by the prosecution. Again, the prosecutor's argument employed the assumed premise:

> If two eyewitnesses identified the person in the grocery store minutes before the robbery as the defendant, then that person is the defendant.

By presenting other evidence, you undercut the plausibility of this premise.

Looking for the incompleteness of existing premises often requires you to look at the situation more broadly than the original premises suggest. Suppose, for example, you are a comptroller of a corporation who has been asked to critique a sales pitch that has been written to your company by a car dealer. The dealer recommends that a certain kind of car be bought by the company. In particular, the dealer may argue that this car is inexpensive to maintain because it seldom needs repair. You may discover that the claim about seldom needing repairs is true. Before leaving the topic of repair, however, it might be useful to look at the question differently. If you are able to produce additional evidence that when the car does need repair, the parts cost several times what the parts of other, less reliable cars cost, then you will have shown the original premises to be incomplete. The strategy here is not so much to look for false premises, but to look for additional premises that will shed new light on the original ones.

The fallacies of half-truth and lifting out of context are two ways that unscrupulous arguers sometimes present premises that are incomplete. The *fallacy of half-truth* occurs whenever a person makes a true statement, but fails to mention relevant facts that materially affect the import of the statement. Without these additional facts, the statement originally made will usually create a false impression. Imagine a documentary filmmaker who wanted to "prove" that Atlanta was a filthy run-down city in which human misery abounded and disease and hunger were epidemic. By carefully selecting locations, and by pointing the camera only at certain scenes, and editing out those in conflict with this claim, it would no doubt be possible to produce a very effective documentary that showed exactly what was intended. Or imagine another filmmaker who wanted to prove exactly the opposite point. By carefully selecting shots, locations, and people to be interviewed, this person very likely could make Atlanta appear to be the land of hope and glory, where universal wealth, well-being, and happiness reign every hour of the day. The important point is that neither of these documentaries would have to fabricate a single bit of evidence. Not a single lie would have to be told. The problem with both of them would consist in the distortion that presenting only one side of the story brings. Leaving out the other half of the truth is often a very effective way of lying without telling a single lie.

Consider another, simpler example of half-truth. A television commercial informs the audience that in recently conducted tests at Utah's Bonneville Salt Flats, standardly available Mercuries—straight off the showroom floor—averaged over 44 miles per gallon. If the commercial then fails to mention that these tests were conducted with 25 mph tail winds, that the drivers were professionals selected for their ability to achieve high mileage ratings, and that the Salt Flats produce less friction on the cars' tires than ordinary roads produce, it will be guilty of the fallacy of half-truth. In these cases of half-truth, as in cases of incomplete premises generally, the problem lies not in what is said, but in the premise that must be added to make the argument valid. In order for the commercial to convince you that the standard Mercury gets high mileage, you must supply the following premise:

> If the Mercuries in the test got such mileage, then the Mercury under standard driving conditions will also get very high mileage.

But once we consider the circumstances of the test, we realize this premise is insupportable. Hence, the whole argument presented in the commercial is unsound.

The *fallacy of lifting out of context* is quite similar to that of half-truth. In this fallacy, written or spoken material is quoted, but without surrounding material that would make a difference in the meaning of the material. Consider the following original critic's review of a play:

> This has got to be one of the season's worst disasters. The most noteworthy thing about this play is the fact that it was ever produced at all. Plays such as this ought to be consigned to the rubbish bin long before this one will be. It deserves to suffer the fate of every tremendous flop!

By selectively lifting words from this review, the unscrupulous promoter may use it to advantage in an advertisement: "This has got to be one of the season's . . . most noteworthy . . . plays. . . . Tremendous!" Notice that in this example no word has been used in the advertisement that was not in the original. No lie there! And the ad even contains three dots every time material has been omitted. Apparently a scholarly dedication to exactness! The only problem is that the overall meaning and effect of the ad is quite different from that of the original review. More subtle examples of this fallacy can occur whenever whole sentences are lifted out of the context in which they have been presented. If a president, in the context of discussing sales of military tanker aircraft to a particular country, states that no more of those tankers should be sold, the context may clearly indicate that the president means "sold to that particular country." If this is so, then anyone who later quotes the president as saying that no more of those aircraft should be sold to anyone commits the fallacy of lifting out of context. Unfair trial attorneys often find it to their advantage to use this technique when interviewing witnesses. They may ask, "Didn't you say at the time of the accident that you wished you hadn't done it?" The witness may then try to answer, "Yes, but what I meant was that I wished I hadn't even left the house this morning, not that I wished I hadn't hit the other car." But unfair attorneys will interject immediately after the witness has uttered the first word of this testimony and abruptly say, "Thank you very much for your statement. Now, to move on to another matter. . . ." By not affording the witness an opportunity to clarify the meaning of the statement, the attorney has taken the statement out of context, and has thereby distorted its meaning.

Stated Premises Are Misleading.   Some premises, although stating the truth, use words that tend to imply more (or sometimes less) than the truth. Suppose you see an advertisement in a newspaper for a "gigantic sale" at a stereo shop with "all name brands included; discounts of up to 60%!" You are in the market for a new set of speakers, so you drive to the store, hoping to find the particular set you want for 60% off. But when you get there you find that only one set of speakers was discounted at 60%. That happens to be an "Exultation" brand, which you've never seen advertised or even heard of, and it has already been sold. Disappointed, and perhaps feeling deceived, you look at the ad again. What you find is that nothing about those speakers is in fact inconsistent with the ad. They are, after all, a "name" brand. It just happens to be one with which you're not familiar. And the fact that the remaining speakers in the store are discounted between 5% and 10% is not contradicted by the statement that there will be discounts of "up to" 60%. Ten percent is surely on the way up to 60%! The false hopes you had that made you drive to the store were created by the misleading language used in the ad. "Name brand" suggested to you that it was one you would have heard of, and "up to 60%" suggested that what you were looking for would be discounted 60%. By suggesting that certain things will be true that aren't, certain kinds of language can easily mislead. Again, the problem with this implied argument for going to the sale is with a premise that wasn't stated. To make the argument that you will find your speakers at the sale value, you supplied the premise:

> If a store has all name brands on sale and is offering discounts of up to 60%, then I will be able to find the particular speakers I want for 60% off.

The wording of the ad suggested this premise was true, but it turns out not to be. Hence, the argument was unsound due to a false conditional.

Using so-called *weasel words*, which suggest much, but promise little, is one way to produce misleading premises. Other examples of weasel words and phrases are: *as much as, can be, may include, virtually, helps to, works to, acts like, looks like, has the feel of, will remind you of*, and so on. As a logical critic, it is your job to be alert for such phrases, and to contrast what they seem to say, and what they actually guarantee. For example, suppose you spot the following advertisement for "cosmetic dentistry" inside a municipal bus: "Bonding uses composite resins and is not expensive. It can be performed in our office in just one or more visits." You might infer you should make an appointment, thereby assuming the premise *if the cosmetic dentistry can be performed in just one or more visits, I should make an appointment*. But ever alert for weasel words, you will want to note that whereas the ad seems to promise that few visits are necessary for this dentist's services, in fact it guarantees nothing of the kind. "Or more" is consistent not only with two or three, but also with a dozen or a hundred. Whereas an apparently relevant and strong reason seems to have been given for visiting this dentist's office, in fact it is hardly a reason at all, because it assures you of nothing with regard to the number of visits you will have to make.

Another kind of misleading language includes words with several meanings. Whereas the person using the language may have one of these in mind, the context often suggests another to the reader. *Average* is a good example of a word with an *ambiguous meaning*, because there are no less than three different ways to determine an average. Average can refer to the mean (which is determined by adding all the items and dividing by their total number), or to the median (which is determined by taking the item that has an equal number of items below and above it), or to the mode (which is determined by taking the item that occurs most frequently). Thus, in the set of items with values 10, 5, 3, 1, 1, the mean average is 4, the median average is 3, and the modal average is 1. Depending on the context, you may assume that mean average is being referred to by speakers, whereas they may be referring to the median, and so forth. Thus, if realtors tell you that the neighborhood in which they want to show you a house is well-off, because the average house in it is worth $150,000, you will probably be misled if the primary reason for this figure is one $550,000 house, surrounded by others with values of $60,000, $50,000, $40,000, and $30,000. Here the median might be more indicative of what you had in mind than the mean. As with other cases we are considering here, the problem presented by arguments using ambiguous language can be traced to the falsity of the premise that is not stated. Implicit in the realtor's argument that you should consider the neighborhood well-off was the premise:

> If the average house is worth $150,000, then the neighborhood is well-off.

This premise is true if we understand average as meaning median. But the claim the realtor actually made is only true when we understood average as meaning mean. Under this condition, the conditional statement is not true. Thus, the argument can never be sound.

Stated Premises Are Irrelevant.   Sometimes people put forward reasons on behalf of a conclusion, but these reasons are irrelevant to the conclusion, and hence offer no support for it. Such irrelevancy is found if, in the course of a criminal trial, defendants tell the jury that they should not be convicted of the crime because they are the sole supporter of a family of nine who would have no one else to care for them. Or consider the joke about the boy who killed his mother and father and pleaded for the court's mercy because he was an orphan. In both cases the reason given for the conclusion (i.e., that the defendant should not be convicted) is irrelevant. The future of the children has no bearing on the real question at hand, namely, whether the defendant is guilty or innocent of the charged crime.

Supplying the premise that is needed to make the argument into a valid instance of modus ponens is generally a sure way to detect the irrelevancy of the premises. To make the first example valid, one must add:

> If a person is the sole supporter of a family of nine who would have no one else to care for them, then that person did not commit the crime.

Once stated, you realize that this premise makes no sense. What does the person's role as supporter of a family have to do with not committing the crime? When a conditional premise makes no sense, that indicates that the reason given probably was not relevant to establishing the conclusion.

In criticizing irrelevant premises, it is always important not only to point out the irrelevancy of the premise to the conclusion, but then to return to the conclusion itself. Irrelevant premises tend to divert attention away from the conclusion, and it is therefore often necessary for the critic to force a return to the issue at hand. Often this can be done by saying something like, "That is another issue, but important as it may be, we must return to the issue at hand. The question here is X, not Y." In the previous example, this might amount to saying, "How these children should be cared for is itself an interesting question, but it has no bearing on the issue at hand, which is whether the person committed the crime. Let us return to a consideration of that issue."

Traditional Fallacies Involving False Premises

So far we have focused on generalizations or conditional premises, the falsity of which undercuts the soundness of an argument. We turn now to a brief discussion of 10 celebrated fallacies with which you should be familiar. Some of these also involve false generalizations or false conditionals, but in ways that are quite distinctive.

The Fallacy of False Alternative.   This occurs very frequently in an argument using the form alternative syllogism. It involves identifying fewer alternatives than in fact exist. Consider the following argument as an example:

> Susan must own either a record turntable or a CD player.
> Susan does not own a CD player.
> ∴ Susan owns a record turntable.

In terms of its logical form, this argument is a perfectly proper use of an alternative syllogism. But still it may have a false conclusion. The conclusion will be false just in case Susan owns neither a turntable nor a CD player. The reason for this, of course, is that the first premise failed to take that possibility into account. Because it did not, it states a *false alternative*.

Notice that although in this example, the premise stated that there were two alternatives when in fact there are three, *any* statement listing fewer than the actual number of alternatives is guilty of this fallacy. In setting up an alternative syllogism, the burden is on the person using the argument to make sure all possible options are considered. Look out for this fallacy any time someone employs an alternative syllogism.

The kind of thinking that generates false alternatives is often generated by questions that require choices between options. Someone asks, "Are you going to vote for the Democrat or Republican?" Often this question can tempt one into thinking that those are the only two choices. But in this case one might not choose to vote for either the Republican or the Democratic candidate, but for an Independent, a Socialist, or Libertarian candidate, just to mention a few of the alternatives.

The Fallacy of False Disjunct.   This fallacy is closely related to false alternative. In a false disjunct, someone lists some possibilities, but states falsely that no combination of them can occur. "You can't vote for both the Republicans and the Democrats" is simply false in some elections. Sometimes you can vote for a split ticket, casting a vote for a Democratic presidential candidate, for example, and a vote for a Republican senator.

Disjuncts are used in the form we called *disjunctive syllogism* and you should be on the lookout for this fallacy any time you encounter that argument form. The following argument employs that form:

> You can't be a citizen of two countries.
> Alice is a citizen of the United States.
> ∴ She isn't a citizen of Switzerland.

The argument is perfectly valid. But the conclusion may be false, because the first premise is. Under certain conditions, and with regard to certain countries, one can be a citizen of both the United States and another country. Furthermore, other countries are quite liberal in allowing dual citizenship for their citizens, and it is very easy for these people to be citizens of two countries.

The Fallacy of False Alternative-Disjuncts.   This fallacy occurs when someone states falsely that of a number of possibilities, they are all the possibilities there are, and that they cannot occur together. When a waiter asks whether you'd like sour cream or butter on your baked potato, the suggestion is that you have two choices: (a) sour cream and (b) butter. But in fact there are two more possible choices: (c) neither and (d) both. Book titles and professors' essay questions are often guilty of suggesting false alternative-disjuncts. The following are some suspect examples:

> Should the drinking age be raised to 21 or kept at 18?
> *Plato: Totalitarian or Democrat?*
> "The Abolitionists: Reformers or Fanatics?"
> "Jesus Christ: Benighted Fool or Savior of Mankind?"
> *Compulsive Arbitration: Menace or Promise?*
> "Is Decriminalizing Drug Use Desirable or Not?"

As with the baked potato example, each of these questions can be answered in one of four ways. For example, it may be that decriminalizing drug use is either (a) desirable or (b) undesirable, as the question suggests. But one might find that it is (c) both desirable and undesirable, insofar as it has many good elements that are equally counterbalanced by its bad elements. And one might find that decriminalizing drug use really wouldn't make any difference at all, and that hence it is (d) neither desirable nor undesirable.

The Fallacy of Composition.   Most things in nature are made out of parts. The parts and the whole usually exhibit different properties. The chair on which you are sitting, for example, is composed of small molecules moving at a high rate of speed relative to each other. But fortunately your chair is not moving at a high rate of speed relative to the objects around it. The *fallacy of composition* neglects this fact and assumes that a whole will retain the characteristics of the parts of which it is composed. Consider the following argument:

> The football team will be the best in the league this season, for it will have the best quarterback, the best receivers, and the best backfield in the league.

Unfortunately, the high quality of the parts of a sports team does not necessarily transfer to the team's performance as a whole. The team may not function together well as a whole. The argument relies on an unstated premise:

> If the individual players are the best, the team will be the best.

Such an assumption is frequently false. One has no guarantee that an automobile made of only the highest quality parts will be a good car. Assembled by incompetent or inexperienced factory workers, a car made of only high-quality parts may still turn out to be a lemon.

The Fallacy of Division.   This fallacy assumes exactly the opposite of what the fallacy of composition assumes. It commits the mistake of assuming that what is true of the whole will always be true of the parts. The New York Mets team that won the 1969 World Series was an outstanding example of a team that did not have a single "star" on it, yet it was an exceptional team. Here the high quality of the whole did not translate into the high quality of its parts. Only if one made the mistaken assumption that what is true of the whole is true of the parts of which it is composed would that inference be guaranteed. And that is precisely the mistaken assumption that characterizes the fallacy of division.

The Fallacy of Ad Hominem Argument.   This fallacy takes its (Latin) name from the fact that it introduces into an argument a premise about the man (i.e., person) advancing the argument. More specifically, it refers to the social, religious, political, or other views of the person, or to that person's character, personal background, or self-interest in order to discredit (or even support) a statement that the person has made. "You shouldn't listen to what she says, because she's a Communist (or an X or a Y or a Z, etc.)" is sometimes used to discredit a person's statement. But does it? Only if we assume that everything that a communist (or an X or a Y or a Z) says is false. But this is very unlikely to be the case. (Think, as before, of a single counterexample to show that it is false.) So when a person introduces such a premise into an argument, we need to think of what the missing premise is that is necessary to make the argument valid. The following argument is plainly unsound, because it assumes that racists can't possibly advance true views:

This new view about the causes of cancer must be false, because it has been advanced by a racist.

Spelled out in complete logical form, it is:

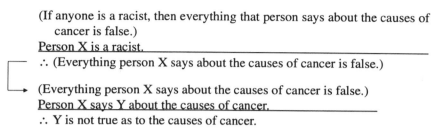

(If anyone is a racist, then everything that person says about the causes of cancer is false.)

Person X is a racist.

∴ (Everything person X says about the causes of cancer is false.)

(Everything person X says about the causes of cancer is false.)

Person X says Y about the causes of cancer.

∴ Y is not true as to the causes of cancer.

In this example, the false (and hidden) premise is the first one. The assumption behind it is that people's social views are directly related to their scientific views, such that if the former are objectionable, the latter are false.

One very tempting form of this fallacy is to assume that if the consequences of a view are in the self-interest of the person advancing the view, that the view must be false. Here is an example:

You can't believe a word of what Dr. X says about teachers' pay raises. Of course she's in favor of higher teachers' salaries. She's a professor, after all, and she stands to benefit from raises.

Dr. X may very well stand to benefit from the view she advocates, but that by itself does not render that view false. Whether teachers' pay raises are a good idea is an issue that is independent of the self-interest of the person arguing for the idea. It is false that someone whose self-interest is involved cannot speak the truth or have the correct view about an issue. Insofar as it is assumed that this is true, the *ad hominem* fallacy has been committed.

The Fallacy of Appeal to Tradition.   People sometimes think that because something has been in existence a long time, that guarantees that it is good or desirable. A German beer advertises that it has been brewed since the 14th century, or a tailor advertises that he has been in business for over 40 years. In order to make a valid argument from these claims, however, we must supply the missing premise:

Whatever is old is good.

But this premise is false. Often what is old has become outmoded, and needs to be changed. Perhaps the beer *has* been brewed for over 600 years. There are still many ways of accounting for its continued existence other than its age. The company may still be in existence because, although it has been brewing an inferior product, it has been able to convince people through its advertising that it is superior. Or perhaps it has always been the least expensive beer on the market, and that is why it still exists. Or perhaps it has a higher alcoholic content than its competitors, and that is why people have continued to buy it, despite its noxious taste.

In short, "We've been doing it this way for years" should never *by itself* be decisive in deciding whether a product, service, or practice should be desired or retained. Racial segregation, apartheid, and sexist practices all have long histories. But that doesn't make them legitimate. This is not to say that we should just ignore traditions. Sometimes traditional things are good and sometimes their endurance is testimony to their virtue. But we must do more than note that something is traditional. We must determine why it has been accepted for so long, and see if that makes it correct.

The Fallacy of Appeal to Novelty.   This fallacy is one of the favorites of the advertising industry. We can all recall advertisements and labels on products that read *New improved X.* This fallacy is the exact opposite of the appeal to tradition, but suffers from the same problems. The claim that something is the newest thing must be combined with a premise that says:

> Whatever is newest is good.

It is false that what is new is therefore good or desirable. "The New Coke" may just be the worst Coke, and the latest tax shelter may be just the one that loses you the most money. Newness by itself is no guarantee of quality, but the belief that it is has misled many people. Rather, we have to carefully examine what distinguishes the new from the old, and see whether those features are in fact improvements.

The Fallacy of Appeal to a Saying.   This is a variation on the appeal to tradition, in which a saying or adage is supposed to embody the wisdom of the tradition, for example: "You can't teach an old dog new tricks, so we won't bother to buy a computer for the residents of the retirement home." This is an example of an argument that relies on a well-known saying to justify a decision. This time, however, the problem lies not in the extra premise that must be added to make the argument valid, but in the saying itself. The saying, "You can't teach an old dog new tricks," at least in its metaphorical application, is false. There are many cases of people learning new things as they grow older. The fact that this falsehood is put into the form of a saying somehow seems to make what is otherwise obviously false appear to be true. It's as if sayings, because of their age—the fact that they've supposedly been around a long time—together with the feeling that they come out of some misty accumulation of ancient wisdom, must be true.

One sure sign of the falsehood of such sayings is the fact that almost all *ancient* sayings have as their counterparts other sayings to exactly the opposite effect. "You can't teach an old dog new tricks," but "With age comes wisdom." "You can't judge a book by its cover," but "Clothes make the man." "Haste makes waste," but "The early bird gets the worm." Fortunately, none of these contradictory sayings is entirely true. Nonetheless, many authors like to support their position by appeal to such sayings. Their use accounts for a great many false premises in arguments. As a perceptive critic, you will want to keep your eyes open for such sayings in arguments.

The Fallacy of Bandwagon.   The fact that large numbers of humans adopt a belief or practice is sometimes cited as evidence for the truth or wisdom of that belief or practice. But it isn't. "Millions of people believe there is a God" does not by itself prove that there is a God. The only way it would do this would be if the following missing premise were true:

> Whatever millions of people believe is true.

This, however, is a generalization we have great reason to doubt. Millions of people also believed that the earth was flat or that some people were possessed by demons. Truth is not determined by a head count: The fact that large numbers of people believe something does not show that it is true, any more than the fact that small numbers of people believe it shows that it is false. Nor does the fact that large numbers of people engage in a practice show that the practice is desirable or good.

Advertisers often invoke the bandwagon fallacy: "Millions of Americans are switching to our product. Shouldn't you?" This is an advertising technique that should appeal more to sheep than to humans. The response to such a claim ought to be: "Why should I?" In fact no good reason for switching has yet been given in such an advertisement. There may be a good reason people are switching, but that reason, not the fact that they are switching, would be the reason for you to switch. Children seem to have a special fondness for this fallacy. Teenagers who argue that they ought to be allowed to have premarital sex because all of their friends are doing so assume the same false premise as the person who thinks that because millions of Americans have switched products, that is a good reason to do so. Carried to the extreme, this fallacy need not even involve large numbers of people. When little Johnny argues that he ought to be allowed to go swimming without a life vest because Tommy's parents allow him to do so, this may still be regarded as an example of this fallacy. Johnny is arguing that an example has been set, but his argument would be no less unsound if he were to produce examples of dozens of friends whose parents allow them to go swimming without life vests. The false premise would still be present—the belief that what others are doing has anything to do with the truth or rightness of what they are doing.

Objecting to Premises When You Cannot Show Them to Be False

As we have noted, when developing a critique of an argument, you don't have to demonstrate that a particular premise is false. It is often sufficient to raise doubts about the truth of the premises without determining precisely where a falsehood has arisen. There are two prominent ways of doing this.

Inconsistency of Premises.   Sometimes you won't know which premise is false, but you will know that one must be. This happens when there is an *inconsistency*. Inconsistency arises when two premises, or a premise and a conclusion, make claims that cannot both be true. As we have seen from one of the rules of immediate inference, if a statement is true, its denial must be false. If it is true that Graham Swift is the author of *Waterland*, then it must be false that Graham Swift is not the author of *Waterland*. Hence any argument in which it is asserted at one point that Graham Swift is the author of *Waterland*, and at another point that he is not, contains inconsistent premises.

Here is an argument with inconsistent premises:

> If she had won the lottery, she would now be in Europe.
> If she had not won the lottery, she would now be in the United States.
> <u>She's not in either Europe or the United States.</u>
> ∴ She must be in Asia or Africa or Australia.

Because we know that the person referred to here either did or did not win the lottery, we can infer by using Premises 1 and 2 of this argument that she's either in Europe or the United States. But that contradicts the third premise, which says she isn't in either Europe or the United States. So something has to go. The set of Premises 1 through 3 is inconsistent with each other, so one of them must be false.

Notice that as yet, you don't know which of them is false. But as a critic you need not know that. Your job is to detect falsity in the premises, and when you have found an inconsistency, you are certain that this argument must contain some. Your recommendation should be that this argument be sent back to the drawing boards. It just won't work, any more than a blueprint that on one page shows a new building to be 32 stories tall and on another shows it to be 30 stories tall. There's just no way to construct such a building, and there's no way to construct a sound argument out of inconsistent premises.

You won't often find inconsistencies in the bald form that we have seen them here. Most people won't actually say, in the course of a few sentences, both that Graham Swift wrote *Waterland* and that he didn't. But sometimes inconsistencies will be lurking just beneath the surface. If we assume there was just one author for *Waterland*, an inconsistency will exist if the person asserts at one stage that Graham Swift wrote it, but in another part of the argument, attributes it to someone else. Even when inconsistencies are not glaringly obvious, you can sometimes discover them through careful examination and paraphrasing of an argument.

Stated Premises Are Inadequate.   Sometimes you will find that an argument contains a premise and you simply do not know whether it is true or false. This may, by itself, suffice for mounting a critique. It was the author's responsibility to provide adequate support for all premises that the intended audience would not already know to be true. When you critique other people's arguments for having inadequate premises, you are claiming that what they thought they could *assume* as a premise cannot be assumed, but must be argued for. For example, someone might argue that because a high rate of inflation will be guaranteed by a proposed tax bill, and because a high rate of inflation is highly undesirable, that proposed bill should be defeated. One critique of this argument might be that, although the conclusion does follow logically from the premises, it still needs to be shown that a high rate of inflation *will* be guaranteed by the proposed tax bill. Notice that in criticizing the argument in this way, you are not stating that the premises are false, but only that they require *more argument*.

To make a critique based on inadequately supported premises compelling, you generally have to do more than assert that you are not convinced. What you need to do is show that there are *plausible* grounds for thinking that the premise is false. To do this, it is often helpful to use your imagination and portray a scenario under which the premise is false. If this scenario is reasonably plausible given all that the author said and you know to be true, then you have motivated doubt in the truth of the premise. For example, you might describe a possible scenario in which the tax bill is passed but a high rate of inflation does not follow. For example, the tax bill might lead to reduction in the deficit as well as in consumer borrowing, thus reducing interest rates and thereby reducing, not increasing inflation. As long as you can motivate doubts, you have shown that the premises have not been adequately supported and hence the argument is not yet compelling.

In this chapter we have noted a number of problems that can arise with arguments. Some of these are so well known that people will often refer to them by name. Hence, it is useful to learn the names. But that is not the primary goal. It is more important for you to be able to find problems yourself. To do this, you should bear in mind the central point that there are two ways in which arguments can fail to be sound or good: They can be invalid or they can have false premises. Once you have learned to identify arguments in other people's writing, you must be prepared to tease out such flaws. As with learning to construct arguments, the best way to master the skill of critiquing an argument is to practice. When you see someone make an argument, examine it carefully to see if it is valid (or can be made valid) and whether its premises are true.

9

Critiques: Presenting Objections

In previous chapters you have learned how to prepare an argument for critique and learned the points on which you can critique an argument. In this chapter we focus on actually developing your critiques and presenting them in written form.

DEVELOPING CRITIQUES

To develop your critiques you must utilize the tools developed in the previous chapter as you work through the logical outline of the demonstration you are going to critique. It is best to begin your review from the bottom of the logical diagram and work up. We take as our demonstration to critique the essay "The Death Penalty: The Needed Deterrent to Murder," which we diagrammed in chapter 7. In this section we work through each of the arguments, looking for possible weaknesses. In the following section we draw on these to formulate our critical essay.

The demonstration has two main arguments for its conclusion, each of which we must examine in turn. The first main argument takes the form of an alternative syllogism:

> Either all convicted murderers should be sentenced to death and have their punishment carried out within 6 months of conviction, or we should continue to show weakness in the face of murder.
> We should not show weakness in the face of murder.
> ∴ All convicted murderers should be sentenced to death and have their punishment carried out within 6 months of conviction.

This is a valid form, so we won't fault this argument for validity. In the previous chapter we advised that any time you encounter an alternative syllogism, you need to investigate carefully whether the alternative statement has presented all of the alternatives. Does the alternative statement in this argument present all the alternatives? That depends critically on what the author means by *continuing to show weakness in the face of murder.* Does that mean *continue to treat convicted murderers in the way they are now*? Or does any other action than sentencing convicted murderers to death and carrying out their sentence within 6 months constitute showing weakness in the face of murder? If the former statement is meant, then the author seems clearly to be guilty of the fallacy of false alternative. But if the latter interpretation is correct, than the alternative has covered all of the options, because anything other than what the author proposes would fall under the category of showing weakness in the face of murder.

Can we determine definitively which meaning of the phrase *show weakness in the face of murder* the author intended? Probably not. Hence, we have to consider both interpretations. If the author means by *show weakness in the face of murder* treating convicted murderers as they are treated now, then we can object to the argument for including a false alternative, and proceed to show how there are other options that have not been excluded. If the author intends for us to interpret *show weakness in the face of murder* as including anything other than the author's recommendation, then we have to see if the arguments advanced for not showing weakness in the face of murder support that claim. If they do not, then this argument will fail for having an unsupported second premise.

What we are doing by proposing alternative interpretations of *show weakness in the face of murder* is preparing a dilemma. We offer two choices. We then show that whichever choice is made, the argument will still turn out to be unsound. If the first option is chosen, then the first premise will be false. If the second option is chosen, the second premise will either be false or insufficiently demonstrated. But before we pounce on this dilemma, let us see how the second premise is defended.

The logical diagram presents three arguments for the claim that we should not show weakness in the face of murder. The first is:

> (If we show weakness in the face of murder, then society will get even more
>   dangerous.)
> We should not let society get any more dangerous.
> ∴ We should not show weakness in the face of murder.

This argument is an instance of modus tollens and so is valid. What about its premises? Both are themselves supported by arguments, so we need to look at those arguments. The argument for the first premise was the following:

> (If we show weakness in the face of murder, then nothing will deter people
>   from committing murders.)
> If nothing deters people from committing murders, then society will get
>   even more dangerous.
> ∴ If we show weakness in the face of murder, then society will get even
>   more dangerous.)

Again, this argument is valid: It has the form conditional syllogism. So let us consider its premises. The second premise seems plausible enough, although we might question how many people, beyond those who now commit murders, have any desire to murder. If everyone who desires to commit murders already does so, then the lack of deterrence is not likely to make society more dangerous than it is now.

The critical premise in the previous argument seems to be the first one:

> If we show weakness in the face of murder, then nothing will deter people from committing murders.

Note first that this premise seems to support the weaker interpretation of *show weakness in the face of murder*, for it suggests that showing weakness consists in offering no or little deterrence to murder. If there are other ways to deter murder than capital punishment, then the alternative statement we considered earlier will be false. But let us see whether this premise could be true if we take the other interpretation of *show weakness in the face of murder* according to which using anything other than capital punishment is to show weakness. Is it the case that nothing other than capital punishment will deter people from committing murders? In questioning the truth of this claim we might begin by noting that as things stand, many people do not commit murders. Some people might, on occasion, find themselves provoked to kill someone, but be deterred by something other than the threat of punishment. For example, they might be deterred by their conscience, or they might be repulsed by the very idea of taking a human life. This might suggest to us that there are alternative ways to deter murder than through the use of punishment. We might be able to do it by developing a program of moral education that inculcates in everyone a respect for the value of human life. Even focusing on punishment, and granting, as the author seems to believe, that current punishment does not deter murder, we should ask whether there are alternative punishments that might deter murder better than current systems of punishment. Perhaps a punishment of life in prison without parole would be effective. The author hasn't shown us that it wouldn't. And for now that is sufficient for us to target this as a point at which to object to the argument.

The author's second argument for not showing weakness in the face of murder appealed to the biblical injunction:

> (If the Bible prescribes "An eye for an eye, and a tooth for a tooth," then we should not show weakness in the face of murder.)
> The Bible prescribes "An eye for an eye, and a tooth for a tooth."
> ∴ We should not show weakness in the face of murder.

The passage quoted certainly does seem to advocate a tough, not weak, stand in the face of all crimes, including murder. But is this a good argument? In the previous chapter we introduced the fallacy of appeal to a saying. One problem we noted with most sayings is that there are other sayings that directly contradict them. Even within the Bible there are plenty of passages that seem to point in the opposite direction. One thinks of the passage, "Judge not that ye not be judged," and other passages emphasizing mercy. We will leave the topic of proper biblical interpretation to others, but we should simply note the mistake of pointing to individual passages when other passages point in the opposite direction.

Perhaps a more serious problem with this argument concerns whether the Bible should be accepted as final authority on such topics. Certainly some people do accept the Bible as the moral arbiter of their lives. If the Bible had a clear position on showing weakness in the face of murder that would be decisive for them. But not everyone is Jewish or Christian, and even among those who are, there is tremendous divergence in the authority to be given to biblical text. Some see it as an historical text that can provide important guidance in formulating their own moral and religious positions, but not as final authority. For anyone who does not give ultimate authority to the Bible, a quotation from the Bible will not settle the matter. A justification for accepting the Bible's authority is required.

The essay offers one last argument for not showing weakness in the face of murder:

> If we show weakness in the face of murder, then we show no respect for human life.
> We should show respect for human life.
> ∴ We should not show weakness in the face of murder.

Although few would dissent from the statement *We should show respect for human life*, many would interpret this statement in very different ways. Some people argue that allowing the terminally ill to end their life (euthanasia) when the conditions of life get too bad (e.g., from crippling illness) shows respect for human life, but others insist that respect for human life requires that one preserve life at all costs. Perhaps the author of this passage intends a fairly strong reading of this passage: Showing respect for human life prohibits the taking of life. If so, however, the author is demonstrating inconsistency, for the punishment for murder being advocated involves the taking of human life and thus the denial of respect for human life. If this is what is meant, then, we will critique it on the grounds of inconsistency.

But perhaps the author meant something less by *show respect for human life*. The author might intend it to mean only recognizing the gravity of acts that take human lives and responding to them appropriately. If so, then we need to question the truth of the first premise. Recalling our uncertainty as to how to interpret *show weakness in the face of murder*, we need to consider this premise interpreted both ways. One meaning was that showing weakness consisted of continuing to treat murderers as they are now. Let us substitute the alternative wording for both clauses into the premise:

> If we continue to treat murderers as we do now, we fail to recognize the gravity of acts that take human life.

For some people this premise will seem very plausible, whereas others would argue that we do treat convicted murderers in a very severe way that recognizes the gravity of what they have done. However, there is a more serious difficulty with this interpretation. If we use this interpretation of *show weakness in the face of murder*, we have already seen that the subsequent alternative syllogism will exhibit a false alternative. So consider the alternative reading, according to which *show weakness in the face of murder* means doing anything other than imposing the death penalty within 6 months of conviction. The premise now becomes:

> If we do not impose the death penalty on convicted murders within 6 months of conviction, then we fail to recognize the gravity of acts that take human life.

This premise is certainly suspect. At least it requires further argument, for many people can conceive of alternative modes of imposing punishment on convicted murderers (life sentences without parole) that would insure we recognize the gravity of murder.

At this point we have completed our survey of the arguments on the left side of the logical diagram. The main argument on that side consisted of an alternative syllogism. In order for the first premise of that argument to avoid committing the fallacy of false alternative, it was necessary to interpret the phrase *show weakness in the face of murder* to mean doing anything other than imposing the death penalty on convicted murderers within 6 months of conviction. Is there any support for the second premise, interpreted in this manner? Two of the three supporting arguments have the potential for being sound only when we employ the other, weaker interpretation. Hence, they offer no support. The second supporting argument exhibits the fallacy of appealing to a saying and of resting on an authority that is not universally recognized as determining what action should be done. So the argument on the left side seems quite suspect.

On the right side of the diagram we have the following main argument:

> If capital punishment does not deter crime, then all convicted murderers shouldn't be sentenced to death and have their punishment carried out within 6 months of conviction.
> <u>Capital punishment does deter crime.</u>
> ∴ All convicted murderers should be sentenced to death and have their punishment carried out within 6 months of conviction.

The first thing to note about this argument is that it has the form of denying the antecedent, and hence is invalid. But let us not jump too hastily. Perhaps the author intended a different conditional premise. If we simply left the word *not* out on both sides of the conditional, the argument would have the form of modus ponens. Trying to be charitable, let us consider this possibility. (If, in the attempt to be charitable, we modify the author's premise in such a dramatic manner, we need to explicitly note that fact.) The first premise now becomes:

> If capital punishment does deter crime, then all convicted murderers should be sentenced to death and have their punishment carried out within 6 months of conviction.

We must now see what support there is for this premise. In support of the original premise the author appealed to the opponents of capital punishment and thus avoided arguing for the premise. But because taking out the word *not* from both sides changes the meaning, the author can no longer appeal to the opponents for this premise. But no other support is offered. So we must simply consider whether this premise is plausible. Basically, the premise seems to be simply an instance of the general claim:

> If any policy deters crime, then it should be employed.

This is a general claim, so we need to ask whether we can think of any counterexamples to it. If it could be established that they would deter crime, presumably any punishment less than capital punishment (e.g., life in prison without parole) would be equally supported by this principle. Thus, the principle is insufficient to support capital punishment. This already provides us with one way to challenge the author's argument, for it does not offer us any reason to prefer capital punishment over other effective forms of punishment.

But we can go even further in raising objections to this premise. Are there actions that would deter crime but we do not think should be employed? Probably we can all think of forms of punishment that might be sufficiently gruesome to deter anyone from committing a crime that might result in receiving such punishment. But avoiding the gruesome, consider a policy of rewarding people handsomely for every month in which they do not commit a murder. That might be just as effective as capital punishment, and by this principle ought to be adopted. Of course, there are reasons for not adopting it (it might require prohibitively high taxes in order to fund it), but that simply leads us to question whether there might not also be reasons for rejecting capital punishment even if it does deter murder. Opponents of capital punishment can offer plenty of reasons, not the least of which is that quick imposition of capital punishment may lead to the execution of many people subsequently discovered to be innocent. Because these have not been answered, this premise at best seems unsupported.

This argument also contained the premise that capital punishment does deter crime, and in fact offers support for it. There is a supporting argument, and that is where we should look:

> If the use of capital punishment will instill the knowledge that committing murder will bring the same fate upon oneself, then capital punishment deters crime.
> The use of capital punishment will instill the knowledge that committing murder will bring the same fate on oneself.
> ∴ Capital punishment does deter crime.

Both of these premises are at least dubious, and support is offered for neither. The first premise is particularly suspect. We know that many murders are committed on impulse. Murderers may feel sufficiently angry that even the knowledge that they are likely to be killed as well will not stop them from murder. The second premise is also doubtful. Many people who commit murder presumably assume that they will not get caught. As a result, the use of capital punishment will not instill in them such knowledge.

SELECTING AMONG YOUR OBJECTIONS

We have now completed our review of the logical diagram for "The Death Penalty: The Needed Deterrent to Murder." We have found problems with nearly every argument in the diagram. Thus, we have plenty of ammunition for our critique. However, we do not want to use all of it. Dissecting every single flaw of an argument in an essay is overkill, and is likely to turn off our audience. You need to carry out the exercise to determine the weakest points in the argument, but now you need to be selective. Pick out those parts of the argument against which you can make the most effective objections.

The most effective points of critique are not necessarily those at which you think the author is most in error. The biggest errors may arise at relatively inconsequential points in the author's argument, and if you direct all of your objections there, the author may be able to respond: *Well, I grant I was wrong there, but that does not affect my main argument.* What you need to do, therefore, is find the flawed points in the argument that are most critical to the author's case, and direct your attention there. If these points are sufficiently critical to the case, then the author will not be able to make such a retort. If the author is not able to defend those points in the argument, surrender will be the only option. In general, this means you want to direct your arguments to points as close to the bottom of the logical diagram as possible. If you can show that a main argument is seriously flawed, or if you can show briefly that supporting arguments fail to demonstrate the correctness of premises in the main argument, then you will have effectively demolished the line of argument.

Reviewing our critiques of "The Death Penalty: The Needed Deterrent to Murder," note that we have found something problematic with both main arguments. The one on the left side of our diagram potentially contained a false alternative. For that to be avoided, the supporting arguments would have to show that we should not do anything other than sentence convicted murders to death and carry out their sentence within 6 months. But two of the supporting arguments fail to support that claim, and the third (the one referring to the biblical passage) exhibited flaws of its own. Here, then, we have a good focus for critique. The argument on the right-hand side was formally invalid as it was presented. That is an effective point of critique, especially if we also show that to make it valid will introduce an unsupported and quite questionable premise. This offers a second point of attack in our critique. In the next section we proceed to construct an essay that exposes these weaknesses in the original essay.

PUTTING YOUR CRITIQUE INTO PROSE

We turn now to the task of putting your critique into coherent prose. This is a somewhat more demanding task than that of putting your own demonstration into prose. At various points in your critique you will be reconstructing the arguments of the essay you are critiquing. You will try to present these as sympathetically and as compellingly as possible. You will also be showing where the weaknesses exist in the argument under critique and how those weaknesses undercut the claim to have demonstrated the conclusion. You need to make it clear at all times which of these tasks you are performing. You don't want your reader to become confused and think the argument you are reconstructing is the one you are advocating, or that in raising objections you are characterizing the position of the person you are critiquing. Thus, you will have to be sure to provide clear guideposts indicating what you are doing at each step in the argument.

The following provides a schematic outline for a critical essay that is frequently very useful:

Introduction
       Background and context of the original argument
          The five *W*'s—*Who, What, Why, Where, When*
       Statement of critique and overview

Body
       Re-presentation of logical structure of original argument
          Explicit premises and conclusions
          Implicit (enthymematic) premises or conclusions
       Objections to inferences
       Objections to premises

Summary
       Statement of overall soundness of original argument

A typical critique essay has the same three main parts as a typical demonstration: an introduction, a body, and a summary. But there are considerable differences in terms of what goes into each section. We take each section in turn.

Introduction

As with a demonstration, you must establish the context for the essay so as to orient the reader to what you are trying to accomplish. It is important to let your audience know what it is that you will object to in the critique, and to give it a sense of the importance of the original argument. Hence in your introduction you need to cover the five *W*'s: who, what, why, where, when:

Who made the original argument
What the conclusion is
Why it is important
Where it was made, including the context
When it was made

Specifying who, why, and when lets the audience know something of the background of the original argument, and may give it a sense of its importance. Identifying the author of the argument is particularly important in this regard. If the argument against abortion that you're going to critique is simply a slogan you once heard at an anti-abortionist picket line, then critiquing it may not be a terribly important activity, but if it was stated by the president of the United States, it may be of more importance to your audience. (Again, notice the importance of knowing your audience.) It might also be of much greater importance to show its failing because the president is likely to be very influential in shaping the opinions of others. Identifying where and when the original demonstration appeared serves to document that the argument was actually made and also helps establish its significance. Was this argument one that appeared in the Letters to the Editor section of the Boondocks *Telegraph*? If so, its importance (though not its soundness) may be less than if the secretary of state offered it on national television as the principal justification for an official government action.

Perhaps the most important of the *W*'s is what. You must establish what the argument you will critique purported to establish. It is often useful to give a brief characterization of the nature of the argument (without, however, detailing every premise), but it is absolutely essential that you let your audience know what conclusion the argument advanced. Letters to the editor of newspapers and magazines often fail at this very point. The opening sentence will be something like, "I couldn't disagree more with your editorial the other day," and then plunge right into raising objections to it: "You need to realize that what you've advocated will destroy this country, and so on." Without some sense of what claim the original editorial was trying to demonstrate, the reader has no idea what the writers are talking about, much less whether they are objecting to a claim for which an argument was offered. In some cases, the essay that you are critiquing may contain several arguments, and you may choose only to critique one of them. If so, you should also make that clear. Of course, if the original authors had multiple arguments for the conclusion, undercutting one of them may not undercut their whole case. However, if you have picked out the one that seems to be the strongest, or one which, for other reasons, it is essential to set straight, then your critique may still be important. In this case, you should tell your reader your reasons for focusing on just one of the arguments.

Lastly, you should tell your audience why the argument is important. Understanding demonstrations and critiques of them is difficult work. If the issue is important to them, then readers may make the effort necessary to determine whether your objections to the original argument are correct. Typically you will choose to critique an argument because you think it raises significant issues and that it is important for your audience not to take a position for the wrong reasons. Convey this importance to your audience.

In addition to informing your reader regarding the original argument, you need to make it clear what you are going to do in your essay. First of all, that means informing your audience that you intend to critique the original essay. Unless you intend to combine your critique with a demonstration of the opposite conclusion, *you will not be arguing that the conclusion is wrong.* Rather, you will be showing that the arguments offered do not establish the conclusion. Beyond indicating that you will critique the original argument, you should give the reader a brief overview of how you will carry out that critique. You might state, for example, that the author's argument rested on two assumptions, both of which you will show to be unjustified. Or you might let your audience know that you will next restate the critical argument(s) before focusing on the point(s) at which mistakes are made.

Body

In the body of a critique, you will first want to re-present the original argument, emphasizing those parts that will be the focus of your critique. If you end up objecting to a premise or the validity of an argument, it should be clear to your reader how that was used by the original authors to establish their conclusion. Often presenting the argument that you will critique will require restructuring it. This is particularly true if it wasn't originally presented in a logically coherent way. Missing premises may need to be filled in, and misplaced premises linked clearly with the conclusions they are intended to support. Often rewording will be helpful in making the argument cohere. Let the logical outline of the diagram that you constructed be your guide in presenting the argument.

In restructuring and re-presenting another person's argument you need to be especially careful not to let your objections intrude. Your reader needs to know exactly what the argument was so as to be convinced that you have identified its flaws. Abusive, unflattering, critical, or any kind of evaluative language should be strictly omitted at this point. "Smith made the idiotic remark that. . ." is not a fair report of a premise that someone has used in an argument. If the remark is idiotic, and is germane to the argument, then present it as objectively and charitably as you can and let the reader judge the idiocy. (Of course, when you turn to presenting your objections, you may show what is wrong with the statement, but it is still best not to use pejorative language. If you have exposed the error, the audience members can decide that the original argument was idiotic without your telling them.)

We must emphasize again the importance of being accurate and charitable in presenting the argument to be critiqued. Many people try to make a business out of critiquing arguments no one has made. This commits the *fallacy of the straw person.* Like a person made of straw, such arguments are easy to knock down, but doing so does not advance the discussion. Be careful, therefore, not to establish a straw person that appears silly at the outset, but to give as plausible and fair a reconstruction as possible. Not only does accuracy demonstrate fairness on your part; it also has the advantage of making the argument seem plausible. The more plausible you make the argument that you're going to critique, the more your audience will be interested in your critique. One sure check on whether your re-presented argument is fair is to ask yourself, "Is this reconstruction something that the original arguer would be content with?" If the answer is "No," then you need to rewrite it until it is.

Having re-presented the original argument fairly, you can then turn to presenting your objections to it. At this point you will already have reviewed your diagram of the original argument to have determined a number of flaws in that argument. You need now to select those that are most telling against the original argument and present them clearly and precisely. As we have already discussed, you will either challenge the validity of one or more arguments, or the truth of premises in these arguments. These will be arguments or premises whose role in the original argument are made clear in your re-presentation of that argument.

In cases in which you decide to challenge the validity of an argument, you will need to take some care in presenting your objection. Most readers will not be familiar with the vocabulary for describing arguments we have used in this book; consequently, you will need to explain how and why invalid arguments are flawed, and not just assign names to them. To avoid sounding like a teacher giving lessons in logic, you may find it helpful to use analogies. Instead of explaining the details of what the fallacy of affirming the consequence is, and how it has been committed in the argument before you, you can draw a parallel between what the arguer has said and a more obviously flawed example. If someone offers the following premises as a support for the claim that the debt ceiling must have been raised, then you can make up a more obviously faulty example using the same form:

Whenever the debt ceiling is raised, the M1 will fall.
The M1 has fallen.

"This is like saying," you might say, "that if you eat too much lasagna you'll get fat, and then concluding of fat people from China that they must have eaten too much lasagna." You will then need to explain that because the arguments are parallel in their form, the author's own argument offers no more support for its conclusion than the one you have offered.

Although the task for the body of your essay is clear, there is no simple rule for how to organize it. In some cases, especially those in which the essay being critiqued contains only a few main arguments, you might re-present the whole original argument before identifying the points at which objections will be raised and presenting these objections. But if the re-presentation gets at all complex, and your critiques are going to focus at different points in the re-presented argument, it may be better to interweave the two. Show how one line of argument goes, explain why it is flawed, then proceed to the next. In each case, though, it should be very clear when you are re-presenting the argument, and when you are critiquing it.

Summary

Here you will want to provide your reader a final assessment of your reading of the argument that draws together the various objections you have made in the body of your paper. If, for example, the original argument contained three main arguments, and you have shown that two of them rest on unjustified premises, and that the third is not logically valid, remind your reader of this fact. Make it clear that what you have shown is that the original authors have not established their conclusion. As in a demonstration, you may also find it appropriate at this point to clarify and point out the limits of your critique. Perhaps you agree with the original conclusion, but simply think the argument in question is a bad one for it, or perhaps you will want to point out that your critique was not directed, say, toward zoning laws in general, but only toward this particular one, and the arguments given for it. Warding off misunderstanding and misinterpretation of what you have said is good defensively, even when you are critiquing.

Let us now put together our critiques of "The Death Penalty: The Needed Deterrent to Murder."

A Critical Response to "The Death Penalty: The Needed Deterrent to Murder"

In the August 6 edition of the *Mytown Daily Defender*, A. Common Citizen presented two arguments for sentencing convicted murderers to death and carrying out the sentence within 6 months of conviction. The questions of whether or not to employ capital punishment, and of how long a period to allow for appeals before implementing the punishment, are critical ones confronting our society and demand careful consideration by all citizens. I am not here going to take a stand on the death penalty. Rather, I am simply going to show that Citizen's arguments are flawed. In what follows I examine each argument and show a critical flaw in each.

Citizen's first argument presents us with an alternative: Either we must sentence all convicted murderers to death and impose the penalty within 6 months, or "continue to show weakness in the face of crime." The author then presents three reasons against the second option. Before turning to Citizen's arguments against this option, let us consider what might be meant by "continue to show weakness in the face of crime." Although various interpretations might be considered, two seem particularly likely. The first is to continue treating convicted murderers as we do now. Although Citizen does not state what the current treatment is, it includes assigning prison sentences to many, and sentencing some to death, albeit with long delays before the sentence is imposed as a result of various appeals. Whereas many might find the current situation to be one that *shows weakness in the face of crime*, if this is the interpretation we should assign to Citizen's second alternative, Citizen has clearly ignored other options. We might require lifelong prison sentences without parole. In arguing against one option, Citizen has failed to consider all of the options, and hence has not established a case for rapid implementation of capital punishment on all convicted murderers.

However, Citizen might view anything short of rapid execution of all convicted murderers to be to *show weakness in the face of crime*. If so, then there are no alternatives to consider. But then we must ask, if life-time sentences without parole count as showing weakness in the face of crime, what is wrong with being weak? Citizen offers three arguments showing why we should not be weak in the face of crime. The first focuses on deterrence. The core of the argument is the claim that if we do not deter people from murder, then more people will murder, and we shouldn't let that happen. We might question whether the claim that failure to deter people from murder will lead to more murder is true, but it is sufficient to note this argument only addresses deterrence in general, and cannot demonstrate the folly of anything short of rapid execution of all convicted murders. A second argument focuses on respect for human life. Citizen claims that if we show weakness in the face of murder, then we fail to respect human life, and argues that because we ought to respect human life, we must not show weakness in the face of murder. Whereas one might wonder how capital punishment respects human life, the main problem with this argument as well as the preceding one is that it does not establish that we should not be weak in the face of murder, when anything short of rapid execution of all convicted murderers is interpreted as showing weakness. Life-time sentences without parole for convicted murderers would seem to recognize the heinous nature of the crime and show proper respect of human life.

Citizen offers a final argument for not showing weakness in the face of crime. Citizen appeals to the biblical injunction "An eye for an eye, and a tooth for a tooth." This argument might indeed support the claim that anything short of capital punishment is weakness in the face of murder, for the injunction suggests that one should pay for a life with a life. There are two problems with this argument. First, not all members of our society accept the Bible as the authority on how we should run civic life. We need some argument as to why we should accept biblical authority in this sphere. Second, the Bible does not offer unequivocal testimony on this score. Much of the Bible emphasizes forgiveness and mercy.

Thus, none of Citizen's arguments establish that there is something wrong with weakness in the face of murder when anything short of rapid execution of the convicted murderer (i.e., life in prison) is counted as weakness. Because this alternative has not been eliminated, we lack a reason for accepting Citizen's conclusion.

Citizen offers a second argument, one that is borrowed in part from opponents of capital punishment. They maintain that if capital punishment does not deter crime, then we should not employ it. But Citizen insists that it does deter crime, therefore we should employ it. We don't need to settle whether capital punishment deters crime in order to see that this argument fails to establish the conclusion. Even if we accept the claim that capital punishment deters crime, it and the premise "if capital punishment does not deter crime, then we should not employ it" do not establish that we should use capital punishment. This argument is comparable to the following argument: If higher taxes will not reduce the deficit, then we should not have higher taxes. But higher taxes will reduce the deficit, so therefore we should have higher taxes. In this argument one may believe both premises and reject the conclusion. The same is true of Citizen's argument. The premise Citizen requires to make the argument is: If capital punishment deters crime, then we should employ it. But Citizen offers no argument for this, and many people would reject this premise. One reason is that not all means of deterring crime are acceptable. For example, continuous police surveillance of all citizens might deter crime, but we would find that unacceptable. Similarly, many people find capital punishment unacceptable even if it would deter crime. Before we can be convinced to accept Citizen's argument, we must be given a reason to believe this premise.

I have reviewed both of Citizen's arguments for the contention that all murderers should be sentenced to die and that this punishment should be effected within 6 months of conviction, and have found both of them wanting. One of them rests on a premise that is either false, or unproven, depending on how you interpret Citizen's phrase "show weakness in the face of crime." The other is logically invalid, for even if we accept the premises, the conclusion might still be false. This does not mean that his conclusion is false. But Citizen has not proven it, and those of us concerned about the correctness of the death penalty must investigate this matter further.

Let us recap our discussion of presenting critiques by noting what this model critique has done. First, it identified the who, what, why, where, and when of the original argument in the first paragraph. Second, in that paragraph it announced the intention of critiquing the argument without proving the conclusion to be either true or false and foreshadowed how it would do so. Third, in the body of the critique both of Citizen's arguments were re-presented sufficiently to show the points at which the objections were made. Fourth, the soundness of both arguments was challenged. In the first case, two readings of the crucial phrase show weakness in the face of crime were identified, and both were shown to lead either to a false premise, or an unproven one. In the second case, the argument was shown to be invalid, and a modification that would make the argument valid was shown to involve an unsupported premise. Fifth, the objections were summarized in the final paragraph. Finally, it was reiterated that the critique had not shown the conclusion to be false, only that it had not been adequately demonstrated.

10

Defending Against a Critique

Just as you might critique the arguments of others, you may on occasion find that an argument of yours has been critiqued by someone else. You may also discover that an argument by someone else that you took to be relatively good has become the object of a critique. If you do not find the critique to be convincing, you may want to respond to it. This involves defending the original argument. In logic, as in sports, the best defense is usually a good offense. If you have been careful to use only unflawed argument forms, and only unflawed premises, then your argument will be hard to critique and your defense may be relatively easy. As we consider later in this chapter, it is often a good strategy to anticipate how a critique might be developed in presenting your original demonstration, and to defuse that critique at that point. But no matter how good an argument you construct, and how well you have tried to anticipate a critique, you will often find that a critique has been made of your argument, and you will find yourself in a position of having to defend your argument.

There are times at which a defense is inappropriate. The critic may have truly found a weakness in your argument. There is no point or merit in "stonewalling it" when you have been caught with false premises or an invalid argument, and so admitting error is always the first order of business in responding to a criticism. Notice, however, that admitting to a logical or factual flaw in your argument need not commit you to abandoning the conclusion(s) you originally argued for, for as we have already seen, the most a critique can ever show is that either the validity or premises *of the argument that you used* is flawed. Having admitted your logical or factual error(s), it is still open to you to construct another demonstration for your original conclusion. If the flaws only undercut one of two or more multiple arguments you offered for your conclusion, you can grant that the argument in question fails, and direct your audience to the other arguments that you think still adequately demonstrate the truth of your conclusion. However, it may turn out that the critique has convinced you that there is *no* good demonstration for your original conclusion. In that case you ought to abandon it forthwith.

In this chapter, we assume that you have not been convinced by the critique. You remain convinced both of the truth of your original conclusion and that your argument was basically a sound way of demonstrating its truth. So we now focus on how you might mount a defense.

When we get to the point at which authors are defending their argument against a critique, we have reached a pretty complex stage of back and forth argumentation. Obviously this is a process that can be repeated indefinitely, with parties continuing to respond to the new claims put forward by each other. One of the challenges at this stage is simply to keep track of what has been said by whom, and for what purpose. In order to respond effectively to such a confrontation of arguments, you need to make sure you know how each part of the dialogue fits into the overall process of argumentation, and to convey this understanding to your audience before proceeding to add your contribution to the argument.

To provide a focus for our discussion, suppose you had written the following essay:

Mars by 2010

In a joint project with other countries, the United States should make a commitment to land humans on Mars by 2010. The program is feasible, would likely lead to many scientific breakthroughs, and would provide an objective that would draw people together so as to reduce conflicts and tensions. Anything that satisfies these three criteria would be extremely worthwhile and something we should commit to. So I will show that the program to land humans on Mars is feasible, would likely generate new scientific breakthroughs, and would draw people of different countries together.

First, such a program is feasible. Both Russia and the United States have well-developed space programs, and the Europeans, Japanese, and Chinese are developing theirs. Already today we can send space probes to Mars without humans on board. There are some obstacles to sending humans, for it will be necessary to outfit the capsule for a year-long trip in each direction. But these obstacles are less major than those the United States had to overcome in landing humans on the moon in the 1960s and are ones we can easily anticipate overcoming with 20 years of cooperative research.

Second, such a program would likely lead to many scientific breakthroughs. Two reasons in particular point to this conclusion. There is historical precedent for anticipating such breakthroughs. Many of the scientific breakthroughs in technology and health care whose fruits we are enjoying today came from the space program. Moreover, the problems that must be overcome for such a mission are very comparable to ones we face on planet Earth. Solutions will have to be found for recycling the waste produced in the capsule, for generating energy from solar sources, and for ensuring the health of the astronauts. Hence, the solutions are likely to be translatable into solutions for problems here on earth.

Finally, such an ambitious program would provide a rallying point for the world's population. It won't overcome all differences, but it will provide a clear example of how we can work together despite differences. The main reason to believe this is once again the example of the U.S. space program in the 1960s. When President Kennedy put forward the goal of going to the moon, it provided a focus for the nation. Even though there were many conflicts in the decade, for example over the Vietnam War and race relations, the space program was a common point for U.S. pride and kept our divisions from destroying us. The world is similarly divided today. Since the late 1980s, nationalism and ethnic strife has been on the rise on many continents. The common objective of travel to Mars could help keep these divisions in perspective by showing what we can do when we cooperate.

I have shown that an international effort to land humans on Mars by 2010 meets the criteria of being feasible, of likely offering major contributions to science, and of helping unify the world's peoples. It is thus a goal to which the United States should commit itself.

Let us consider how you might defend against possible critiques.

The first step in responding to a purported critique is to make sure it *is* a critique. Many arguments become needlessly protracted because the arguers fail to realize they were not responding to each other's arguments but were "talking past one other." This is an interesting but often frustrating social phenomenon, and it should be avoided in arguing logically. The most frequent way for two people to talk past one another is for the first to present a demonstration and for the second to assume the role of critic, but in fact to offer a demonstration of the opposite conclusion (we might call this a *counterdemonstration*). If Person 1 says "A, for Reasons Q and R," then it is a counterdemonstration, not a critique of that argument, for Person 2 to say, "A is false, for reasons S and T." One of them is affirming A, and the other denying it, but the second is not responding critically to what the first said. So far, all a third observer would be able to tell is that there are reasons for believing A and reasons against believing it. Which are better, or whether any are very good, has simply not yet been discussed. And that is the job of the critic—to show that the reasons the original arguer has presented are in some way flawed.

The following paragraph would constitute a counterargument to your argument for travel to Mars, not a critique.

Travel of humans to Mars is not a goal the United States should pursue. The reasons are simple. It would divert too many resources away from problems we face here on earth. For example, we need to overcome the endemic poverty that is holding a significant portion of our population in check, and we need to improve our educational system so that we will have citizens prepared to live in the high-tech and multinational society of the 21st century. Moreover, sending humans on such missions is unnecessarily risky. Almost everything we could learn from going to Mars could be secured through missions that don't have humans on board. The use of humans on such flights is a bit of theatrics, not a useful contribution to science.

This argument does not address the argument you made, and so is not a critique of it.

Should you find yourself in a situation in which someone has offered a counterdemonstration to one you advanced, you should not mount a defense. Rather, you need to develop a critique of the counterdemonstration. Diagram the counterdemonstration argument that is being put forward, and then examine it either for false premises or invalid arguments. In presenting your critique you might note that this argument had been put forward to demonstrate the opposite of a position for which you had already argued. But you also need to make it clear that your argument has not yet been challenged, and that what you are doing is challenging the argument for the opposite position. Of course, if you find the argument for the opposite position compelling (that is, you find the arguments to have true premises and to be valid), then you will need to reconsider your own argument. Because you would have then accepted that your conclusion was false, you will need to figure out why your argument was unsound. Did it have false premises or was it invalid? In any case, you will need to withdraw your argument in this circumstance.

Let us assume, however, that you are confronted with a genuine critique. Someone has faulted your original argument either for having false premises or for being invalid. In mounting your defense of your argument there are two basic strategies you can use: First you can buttress your argument to show that your argument does not have the flaw or flaws that the critique claimed. Second, you can critique the critics and show that in making their objections to your arguments they employed invalid arguments or false premises. We consider each of these in turn.

BUTTRESSING YOUR ARGUMENT

In challenging your argument, your critic has alleged that your argument has certain weaknesses. The first strategy is to show that the weaknesses do not exist. This will most often occur when your argument has been misunderstood by the critic or when the critic attacks a premise that you can demonstrate to be true. In such cases you will buttress your argument by showing how the argument should be understood and by providing the needed support for your premise.

When confronting a critique, one of the first items to consider is whether the critic correctly understood your argument. As we noted in previous chapters, one of the most common failures of critics is to misrepresent the argument they are about to criticize. In presenting their critique, the critics should have demonstrated how they understood your argument. If so, you can read that reconstruction and see if it accords with your intention. If not, you may have to figure out from the objections the critics offer what they took your argument to be. There are at least two ways in which your position might be misunderstood. The critics might have misunderstood something you explicitly said. Or the critics may have supplied a premise that you did not explicitly state, but which they claimed to be necessary for your argument.

Let us first consider a case in which a premise you explicitly stated was misunderstood. In offering a critique of the aforementioned argument, someone might attribute to you the premise that the Mars project will definitively bring new scientific breakthroughs, and then proceed to point out that scientific breakthroughs can never be guaranteed. In responding to such a critique, it is necessary for you to note how you *qualified* your premise. You only contended that it was *likely* to produce such breakthroughs. Thus, you can respond to your critics as follows:

> I grant that it is possible that no new scientific breakthroughs will actually occur, but I did not claim that such breakthroughs are guaranteed, nor does my argument require that. I claimed that such breakthroughs were *likely* on the basis of what has happened in the past. That is all that we generally require in order to decide to pursue an action.

Someone might also have misconstrued the basic structure of your argument, thinking, for example, that you were offering three separate arguments for pursuing the Mars project. For example, the critic might focus on your claim that the Mars project was feasible, and proceed to say:

> The author seems to assume that if something is feasible, we ought to do it. But there are many things that are feasible which we don't do. It might be feasible, for example, to build a permanent space station on the moon, but we haven't chosen to do so. Moreover, it is presumably feasible to paint all the houses in the United States blue, but that is not a good reason for doing so. Just because it is feasible doesn't mean we should plan a mission to Mars.

To answer such a critique you need to point out that your argument depended on three criteria being satisfied: The project had to be feasible, promise scientific breakthroughs, and provide a goal to draw people of different countries together. If so, you might state your response as follows:

> My critic attributes to me the claim that if something is feasible, we should do it. I agree with the critic that this would be a bad claim from which to argue for the Mars project, but it was not, in fact, the claim I made. Being feasible was only one of three conditions I set down for pursuing the Mars project. My claim was that if the project was feasible, would likely generate scientific breakthroughs, and would provide an objective that would unify people from different nations, then it ought to be pursued. I then showed that all three conditions were satisfied.

The other case involves a critic attributing to you something you did not explicitly say, but that the critic contends is needed for your argument to be valid. The critic might object to your claim that the Mars mission will produce scientific breakthroughs by developing solutions to recycling waste by claiming you must be assuming all solutions that work in space can be applied directly to problems on earth. The critic may then argue that this is an unreasonable assumption by pointing out the differences between the amount of waste generated on a 2-year space voyage by a few people and that generated by billions of residents on earth. In this case, you can respond by showing that the assumption supplied by the critic is not the one your argument requires:

> My critic has attributed to me the assumption that if a scientific breakthrough solves a problem in space, it will thereby solve the problem on earth. But I do not need to

assume this. What I was assuming, and what seems reasonable, is that a solution to a problem in space may provide important insights that will help us solve the comparable problem on earth. The tools used to recycle waste in a space capsule may not be applicable to all the waste problems on earth, but they may well provide useful ideas that will help us solve some of the waste recycling problems we face here.

It is relatively easy to parry the assault when you have been misunderstood. But the case is more challenging when the critic understood your original argument correctly but in your judgment did not succeed in undercutting your argument. Now you must show that your original argument is strong enough to support your conclusion. It is very unlikely that your critic both understood your original argument and objected to its being invalid if it was really valid. If that does happen, for instance because the critic misunderstood the logic of an *only if* statement, you will need to offer a very brief lesson in logic, in which you explain how the error you are accused of did not in fact occur. The more likely situation in which you will find yourself is one in which the critic has objected to a premise you still believe is true. The critic might object either because the premise was dubious, or because it could be shown to be false. In either case, what you must do now is try to show that the premise is in fact true. (If the critic claims to have shown that your premise is false, then you will probably also want to criticize that demonstration. We discuss how to do that in the following section.)

In response to your demonstration that the United States should commit itself to a multinational mission to Mars, a critic might challenge a premise as follows:

> The author has tried to show that a Mars mission is feasible by claiming that the obstacles confronting a trip to Mars are less severe then those confronting the Moon program in the 1960s and that we can easily anticipate overcoming them with 20 years of research. But are they really less severe and are they really surmountable? The author acknowledges that the trip will take approximately a year in each direction. Think of some of the problems this will present. A 2-year supply of food will need to be transported, and some of it must be kept fresh if the crew is not to confront deficiency diseases much like those that confronted seafaring people before the 20th century. Further, the astronauts will have to maintain their physical conditioning during 2 years of travel in weightless conditions. Are these really less severe than the problems of going to the moon, which only took a couple of days? The author hasn't shown us that they are.

In this case the critic has focused on a premise you asserted but never demonstrated. The critic has not shown that the premise is false, but has raised some serious doubts about its truthfulness. Realizing now that the premise in question was not accepted by your audience without support, you need to supply the necessary support. You will now offer an argument to show that the obstacles are less significant than those facing the moon program and that they can be expected to be overcome:

> My critic has raised doubts about my claims that the obstacles facing a Mars mission are less severe than those facing the moon mission in the 1960s and that they may

ultimately not be overcome. These obstacles may seem greater than those facing the moon program, but our perspective may be tainted by the fact that the moon program is in our past. Once a problem has been solved it is hard to appreciate how major it must have seemed before the solution was in hand. But before humans had gone to the moon, the problems confronting that mission were great indeed. In the pre-moon days humans had always flown in earth orbit, and spaceships could be brought down within a couple of hours if problems arose. The moon mission required ships that could be maintained in space because the missions could not be aborted. Moreover, the space capsules required totally different navigational systems than were required for earth orbit. Finally, scientists had to design a capsule capable of taking off from a foreign surface. These and other problems seemed gigantic at the time, but have diminished in significance because they were all solved.

Now consider the problems the critic has put forward. They are indeed significant, and I cannot prove that they will be overcome because that would require knowing the solution. But we can at least envisage the type of solution. Most food can be dehydrated, and resynthesized using water that is recycled on board the spaceship. The requirements for fresh food are not what they were in the day of naval exploration when people did die of deficiency diseases. Vitamin pills that prevent these diseases are readily available at most stores. Moreover, one can envisage ways of overcoming the exercise problem. One can create artificial gravitational fields in isolated chambers in which astronauts could exercise. Or techniques could be developed to stimulate muscles electrically, which would maintain muscle tone. When I said such a mission was feasible, I did not say there would be no obstacles. Rather, I contended that the obstacles could be solved, and I have shown how thosed pointed to by the critic might be overcome.

Essentially, in developing a defense of this sort, you are offered a second chance to defend the weak premises of your argument. Ideally you should have anticipated which premises the critic would not have found acceptable and offered support for them at the outset. But now you have an opportunity to make good on that deficiency. In planning your defense, it is useful to construct a diagram of the crucial part of your argument, and offer arguments for the premise in question. Your task here is no different than it was in the original demonstration except that you must make clear how you are answering the critic's objections.

CRITIQUING THE CRITIQUE

The second way of responding to a critique is to show that the objections made in the critique are themselves flawed. Instead of providing the evidence for your original position, you now try to undercut the critic's attempt to raise doubts or to disprove your premise. Thus, you are now yourself cast in the role of a critic as you attempt to show that what your critic says is flawed. To do this you need to make use of the skills we developed in the previous chapters. The most common situation in which you will want to critique your critic's argument is when the critic has tried to show that one of your premises is false. If the critic has done this, but you are sure that your premise is true, diagram the critic's argument, and then determine where the flaw in the argument is. (If you know the conclusion is false, then the argument must fail either for being invalid, or for having an untrue premise.) Once you have found the error, you will proceed to show that your critic made this error and how the criticism fails without this claim.

Imagine that the critic had responded as follows to your contention that a joint Mars mission would provide a focus for unifying people from different nationalities:

> Far from providing a rallying point that would unify people, the proposed Mars mission would cause further disharmony. The major split of the next 20 years is likely to be that between rich and poor countries. If the rich industrialized countries devote themselves to a space mission, that will reduce the resources that can be devoted to helping poorer nations and so further exacerbate conflict in the world.

Because the critic has not only challenged one of your premises, but provided an argument designed to show that it is false, you need not only show that the premise is true, but you also need to undercut the critic's argument that attempts to show that it is false. You might reconstruct and diagram the crucial part of the critic's argument as follows:

> If the Mars mission will reduce resources devoted to helping poorer countries, then it will further exacerbate conflict in the world and not offer a rallying point that will unify people.
> The Mars mission will reduce resources devoted to helping poorer countries.
> _____
> ∴ The Mars mission will further exacerbate conflict in the world and not offer a rallying point that will unify people.

In responding to this argument, you won't fault its validity because you have made it valid. Rather, you must focus on the premises. The first premise seems quite plausible; thus, you might decide to grant it and focus instead on the second premise. You must now at least raise sufficient doubts about this premise to undercut the critic's argument. To do so, you might point out how the resources in question are not of fixed quantity and that the pursuit of the Mars mission might actually increase the stock of resources that will be devoted to the poorer countries.

In critiquing the critique, you can avail yourself of the full range of resources we discussed in chapter 8. In particular, you should pay close attention to whether the critic has committed any of the informal fallacies we discussed. Begging the question is a frequent mistake that critics make, and you should be especially on the alert for it. But half-truths, false alternatives, misleading statements, and inadequate evidence against what you said are also to be found in critiques.

USING CRITIQUES AND DEFENSES AS PARTS OF DEMONSTRATIONS

So far we have treated constructing critiques and defenses as separate activities from developing demonstrations. But many times you will find it useful to construct a critique and defend against it in the course of a demonstration. If you consider the example essay presented in chapter 1, you will see this strategy exemplified. In arguing that Mytown ought to develop a program of voluntary curbside recycling, the author not only presented an argument for the conclusion, but considered some possible objections. The author not only presented the possible objections, but then defended against them. This can be a very useful strategy when you can anticipate certain objections. By explicitly developing the likely critique and showing how it can be answered, you preempt the objection.

One advantage of considering critiques and responding to them in the course of developing a demonstration is that it encourages you, as the author of the demonstration, to think about the issue from the opposite point of view and to identify what are likely to be the most serious weaknesses with the argument you are constructing. It is not necessary, however, to present all of the objections you consider as possible critiques in the course of your demonstration. Once you have identified the potential objection, you may be able to preempt it without ever mentioning it. You simply develop a strong enough argument in the course of the demonstration so that the objection will not arise. Whether you mention a possible critique explicitly and then respond to it, or only ensure that the demonstration itself already presents the answer to the objection, is often a matter of style. It is not a good idea to clutter a paper up with too many interruptions in which you consider and answer objections. Rather, the device of explicitly raising and responding to objections ought to be used selectively to deal with objections you have reason to think someone is likely to raise.

In addition to the strategy employed in the example in chapter 1, there are two other approaches you might use to integrate criticisms into the process of developing demonstrations. These do not, per se, involve the construction of a defense, but they are ways to counter objections at the outset that may obviate the need for a defense. The first of these approaches requires that the arguers not only demonstrate their conclusion, but also formulate the very best demonstration of the opposite conclusion possible. In effect, they are required to become a devil's advocate for the exact opposite of their own conclusion. The point of presenting the argument for the opposite conclusion is then to critique that argument, thereby increasing the plausibility of one's own conclusion. We call this argumentative strategy that of the *devil's advocate*. It is perhaps easiest to picture this strategy unfolding vertically.

Demonstration of A
Demonstration of -A
Critique of demonstration of -A
Conclusion = A

This diagram indicates that first the arguers present their argument(s) for the conclusion in which they believe, here represented as A. Then the arguers formulate the best argument(s) possible for the exact opposite conclusion. If they argue in the first demonstration that, say, the best diagnosis for a patient is cholera, then as a second argumentative step the arguers will present the case for the best diagnosis not being cholera. As a third step, this strategy requires that the arguers then critique this second demonstration as well as possible. If that critique is successful, then the original demonstration stands, and the conclusion that follows is the original one, A.

Why, you might wonder, would anyone ever want to engage in what may appear to be logical gymnastics? The answer is that this strategy is useful in two ways. As a method for discovering the truth of a matter, it is often extremely helpful in warding off the intellectual malady called "tunnel vision." This is the tendency we all have to stick to our first view of a matter, failing to recognize contrary evidence as it comes in, and thus failing to revise our view to be consistent with it. In extreme cases of tunnel vision contrary evidence to one's original view may even be noticed, but be treated as confirming the original view. Requiring medical students who believe the patient has cholera to present the best case against this diagnosis will often cause them to rethink the case they had originally made. The conclusion in the end may still be the same as the original diagnosis—cholera—but now it will be a conclusion that has taken other options seriously.

The devil's advocate strategy has much to recommend in terms of its persuasiveness. Having demonstrated to your audience that you are aware of a case to be made against A, but that that case must fail, you will be perceived as having been extremely open-minded in your considerations. And you *will* have been open-minded, provided that you do not hedge in your demonstration of -A. You are not being a true devil's advocate if your demonstration of -A is so weak that it is easily criticized in the third step. It is very tempting to hedge your demonstration of -A in this way, but also dangerous, for it invites your audience to point out that there is a better case against A than the one you have presented.

It is not necessary to refer to a devil's advocate when you use this strategy. Having presented your demonstration, you can say something like, "But some would disagree with this conclusion, A. They would say that -A is true, for the following reasons:. . . . My response to their argument is that. . . ." By using linguistic devices such as "some would say" you avoid attributing the second demonstration to anyone, including yourself. This often has its advantages, insofar as it directs the audience's attention away from you, the original arguer, and toward the strength of that demonstration. When you then say, "My response to their argument is. . . ," you redirect the attention to you. This can help to keep it clear in your audience's mind that it is A you wish to defend. Otherwise someone is likely to think when they hear you defend -A that this is the position you believe in.

The second alternative approach that you may find useful is referred to as the *dialectical strategy*. It too involves a demonstration of a conclusion and a demonstration of its opposite, but the final conclusion differs from the original one. Visually, it might be represented in this way:

Demonstration of A   Demonstration of -A
Criticism of demonstration of A   Criticism of demonstration of -A

Conclusion = A'

Arguers who use this strategy first give a demonstration of A, and then the best demonstration they can of its opposite, -A. But instead of only offering a critique of the demonstration of -A, they go on to critique the demonstration of A as well. Assuming that both criticisms are partly successful, they then conclude that a modified version of A, here listed as A', must be true. Notice that if the critique of the demonstration is not at all successful, then we have the strategy of the devils' advocate, in which A is the final as well as the original conclusion. But when both critiques are partly successful, we are forced to conclude something other than the original conclusion, A. (If both critiques are completely successful, then we have no conclusion.)

This strategy represents what very often happens in the give-and-take of argument—we set out to demonstrate one thing, but find there is something to be said for its opposite, and so modify our original conclusion, possibly by qualifying it, or restricting its range of application. For example, someone might begin by arguing that abortions should never be legally permitted. Considering the arguments against this, however, they may in the end conclude, not the other extreme—that they should always be legally permitted—but that they should not be permitted except in the cases of rape, incest, or severe danger to the mother's life. Here both extremes have been rejected, and a modified version of the original conclusion accepted.

It is not always the case that the truth lies between two extremes, but when it does, this macrostrategy will be helpful in uncovering it, and then in presenting it in argumentative form to an audience.

11

Authority

Consider the following conversations:

Person A: "I wonder how long it will take us to drive from Buffalo to Chicago."
Person B: "About 9 or 10 hrs, because I just called the AAA office, and they said that it's 552 miles."

Person C: "What's that white star over there near the moon?"
Person D: "That's not a star. That's the planet Jupiter."
Person C: "What makes you so sure?"
Person D: "Because the planetarium said in its monthly star-gazer's guide that that's where Jupiter would be tonight."

Person E: "Twenty-five years ago, 1 out of every 10 American married women had never had a child. Today that ratio has grown to one 1 out of every 4."
Person F: "How do you know that?"
Person E: "*Newsweek* said so in a recent article."

Person G: "My next canoe paddle is going to be a Kruger."
Person H: "Why?"
Person G: "Because it has a Kevlar blade, and a 50-inch paddle only weighs 18 ounces."
Person H: "How do you know that?"
Person G: "Because that's what the ad in *Canoe* magazine says."

Attorney I: "Who was the person who sold the tractor to your husband?"
Witness J: "Irving J. Fledermaus."
Attorney I: "And how do you know that it was Mr. Fledermaus?"
Witness J: "Because my husband told me so before he died in the tractor accident."

Each of these conversations contains at least one argument. In each of them, a person claims to know a fact—that Buffalo to Chicago is 552 miles, that the white star is Jupiter, that the childbearing rate among married women has decreased, that a Kruger paddle is made of Kevlar and is lightweight, and that Fledermaus was the seller of the tractor. When asked for evidence that will support these knowledge claims, each person then gives a reason. The reason that each gives is of the same kind. Because none of them have ascertained the fact themselves (B has not driven the mileage and determined that it was 552 miles, D does not have any way of telling that it is Jupiter, E has not personally done the statistical sampling, G has neither done the fiber analysis to determine that the blade is made of Kevlar nor weighed it, and witness J was not the one to whom Fledermaus sold the tractor), each relies on someone else to tell them the truth. The reason they believe what they believe, and the reason they give to the person challenging their knowledge claim, is that someone else told them so. Each, therefore, is making an *appeal to an authority*. That is, they are relying for their facts on someone else in whom they place some degree of confidence. Notice that as we are using the term here, an "authority" is not necessarily an academic or a governmental official or anyone in a position of power or control or even esteem, but simply any person on whom another person relies for information. If I ask a professional musicologist what's the best edition of the Mahler 10th Symphony, or if I ask a 3-year-old where I left the car keys, then I am appealing to each of them as an authority for information.

Clearly relying on authorities for our facts is a familiar process that we all engage in many times a day. When we look on the label of a soup can to see whether to add water, when we follow a fellow hiker's directions to get to a waterfall, when we believe that aliens recently visited a farm family in Idaho because of an article in the *National Enquirer*, when we turn on the radio at 10 o'clock because we want to hear a concert that the station has said will be broadcast then, and when on a machine we push the button labeled "Power On" in order to start it, we are relying on authorities for our beliefs and often our actions. Relying on authority is not only an ordinary part of our lives, it is essential. If we could not do it, our lives would be radically different from what they are. We simply do not have the time or ability to check out each piece of information that we rely on throughout our daily lives for ourselves.

Even though relying on authority is essential to our lives, it is a practice that raises problems. Not all authorities are equally reliable. In fact, no human authorities are perfectly reliable, such that we can assume everything they have said is true. But some are far less reliable than others. A physician who has treated many patients who exhibit a particular set of symptoms may be a reasonably good authority on the disease diagnosis for a patient who manifests those symptoms and on the success and effects of different ways of treating the disease. The physician may make an occasional error, or not know of side effects that a particular treatment will produce in a specific patient, but on the whole it may be quite reasonable to trust the physician's information. On the other hand, your friend who has had no health care training but who has talked to friends who have exhibited these symptoms and learned some of the new therapies they have tried is a far less reliable authority and is more likely to be wrong.

What is at stake here is the *level of credibility* of different authorities. Once we recognize that not all of them are equally worthy of our belief, the question we must address is how to determine who is a reliable authority. This issue arises not just with people, but also with published material. Not everything that is published is equally credible. Often the place of publication matters greatly. Even though the *New York Times* makes mistakes, an article in it that reports a plane crash is probably quite worthy of our belief, whereas an article in a supermarket newspaper that reports that a human mother in India gave birth to a poodle with two heads is not. Likewise, a magazine advertisement by the car's manufacturer that says a new car is the best car on the road is not as credible as a test review of the car in *Consumer Reports*.

When we cite an authority in the course of an argument, we are implicitly making a supporting argument. Thus, if in the course of an argument we cite the *Encyclopedia Britannica* as a source for the claim that the Sun is a star in the Milky Way Galaxy, we are making an argument of the form:

> The *Encyclopedia Britannica* says that the Sun is a star in the Milky Way Galaxy.
> ∴ The Sun is a star in the Milky Way Galaxy.

On the other hand, if we cited the *Star* (a supermarket tabloid) for the claim that an alien creature visited central Idaho last week, our argument would have the form:

> The *Star* says that an alien creature visited central Idaho last week.
> ∴ An alien creature visited central Idaho last week.

Clearly these are both enthymematic arguments, and the obvious premise that we need to add to make them valid is "If the *Star* (*Encyclopedia Britannica*) says something, then it is true." The question about the credibility of an authority now becomes a question about the plausibility of such a premise. Because any authority, even the *Encyclopedia Britannica*, can make mistakes, the premise stated in the categorical form "If somebody says it, then it is true" will always be false. It must be qualified. What is at issue is how much the premise must be qualified before we accept it as true. In the case of the *Star,* we might have to qualify the premise by stating, "If the *Star* says it, then it is only somewhat likely to be true," whereas we might only need to qualify the *Encyclopedia Britannica* premise to read, "If the *Encyclopedia Britannica* says something, then it is quite likely to be true."

Authorities are not something that are simply given to us. Rather, any time we rely on an authority, we make a judgment that the authority in question is reliable. If the authority is not reliable, then we exercised poor judgment in deciding to accept the authority. For example, if you rely on acquaintances who tell you that they have a gut feeling that a particular stock will do very well in the next month and you invest all of your assets in that stock and it crashes, you are the one responsible for your downfall. You choose to rely on your acquaintances. The same is true if you rely on what someone else says for a premise in an argument. If what the person said is not true, *you* have produced the unsound argument. The responsibility rests on you in either case to check out the purported authority to determine if that person should be relied on. If you fail to establish the credibility of the authority but cite the authority anyway, then if the authority turns out not to be credible, your argument is undercut. Moreover, if you are in the habit of relying on authorities whose credibility you have not established, then others will soon realize that your own arguments are not credible.

In this chapter we explore the question of how we can evaluate the credibility of authorities that either we might want to use in arguments or that might be used by others in arguments we wish to critique. We examine a number of criteria we can use to assess the credibility of the information we get from authorities and thus to assign qualifiers in the implicit premises that arise in the appeal to authorities. We begin with cases in which particular factual claims about what events have transpired are in question. Then we consider more complex cases of reliance on authority, such as relying on experts in a field for determination as to what is the best theory to trust.

AUTHORITIES ABOUT FACTUAL EVENTS

Levels of Authority

We generally feel most certain about what transpired in a particular situation when we witness it for ourselves. But we are each able to witness directly only a small percentage of the events in the universe—only those occurring in the part of the universe where we happen to be during the years we happen to be alive. We cannot, for example, directly witness our own birth, and so we must rely on others to tell us who our parents are. The need to rely on others to tell us about what events have transpired is, therefore, widespread. But we know that different people often give different reports about events, and it may be important for us to determine which version of the events to believe. When you learn you have just lost a major client, for example, it might be important for you to know what transpired in a meeting between your assistant and the client. The client may tell you something different from what your assistant has reported. Or if you are on a jury in which someone is being charged with inciting a riot, you must determine whether the accused carried out the alleged actions in the way the prosecutor says. Many people may offer their testimony as to what happened, and you must determine who should be believed.

To determine the criteria needed to assess information provided to us by authorities, we need first to distinguish between various levels of authority. These levels are determined by the degree of access an authority has to information. There is, on the one hand, information that is obtained *directly* by the people reporting it. By directly we mean that the people did not obtain it from any other person, but witnessed or observed it themselves. In contrast to direct, or what we may call *first-hand information*, there is second-hand, third-hand, and so forth, information. Juan did not see John entering the building, but was told by Jean that she saw John entering the building. Jean has direct, or first-hand information, Juan has second-hand information, and Johann, to whom Juan reports that John entered the building, has third-hand information.

There is also information that is obtained *immediately*. By immediately we mean that the people who witnessed it did not infer it from something else that they (or anyone else) witnessed. If Jennifer, for example, sees another person entering a building, and is able to identify that person as her friend John Doe, then Jennifer may be said to have immediate, or noninferential information that the person is John Doe. (Because she did not obtain the information from another, it is also first-hand or direct.) But if Samuel infers it is John Doe from the coat he sees the person wearing (a coat Samuel knows to belong to John Doe), then we shall say that Samuel has inferential, or nonimmediate information that it is John Doe. Because Samuel has seen the coat himself, it is first-hand information, albeit not immediate. Virginia, who is told by someone who saw the coat that it was of a kind the person knows to belong to John Doe, and who infers that it was John Doe based on this information, has neither first-hand nor immediate information. Rather, she has second-hand and inferential information. Calvin, who is simply told about the event by another person who directly observed John entering the building, possesses second-hand, noninferential information.

Each step in the transmission of information as well as each inference someone has to make increases the risk that the information in the end will not be accurate. To see the errors that can enter when information is passed from one person to the next, start a rumor going. After a few cycles, someone will probably report the rumor back to you, but in a form that is somewhat distorted from your original. To see how inferential errors arise, leave out a few important details when you begin the rumor. Later you will see how people filled in the rumor through inference. (If you attempt this experiment, be sure to make your rumor innocuous so as not to hurt anyone!)

Because the ability of humans to report accurately what they have been told by others is notoriously low, the possibility of error is increased with less direct information. We can put this more positively, and formulate our first criterion for assessing the credibility of information based on an authority: Other things being equal, the more direct the original source of information, the more credible it is. First-hand information is better than second-hand, and second-hand better than third-hand, and so on. Our second criterion stems from the immediate-inferential distinction we drew earlier. It is that other things being equal, immediate information is more credible than inferential information. There is more room for error when Jean infers that it was John from having observed a person with John's coat than there is when Jean sees John's face. Not many people have his face, but others could be wearing his coat, or one like it.

Combining these two criteria, we can say that, all other things being equal, information that is both direct and noninferential is the most credible kind. We refer to this kind of information as eyewitness information. What this amounts to saying is that if we can find out from the person who is in charge of calculating the Dow-Jones average what it was at a certain time, that information is more credible than the information as presented in a newspaper report. And both of these kinds of information are better, other things being equal, than relying on someone who has read the newspaper account and reports what it said. Depending on the kind of inferring that has been done, inferential information based on eyewitness information may be more or less credible than immediate second-hand information, but again, all things being equal, immediate second-hand information is more credible than inferential second-hand information.

We have said that eyewitness information is the most credible kind, *ceteris paribus*. But this does not mean that it is all true, or that it is all equally credible. Let us look at some of the factors that determine its degrees of credibility. We then turn to some of the additional factors that make the various kinds of second- and third-hand information more or less credible. When an eyewitness observes an event and then presents information about it to us in the form of a report (whether oral or written), the credibility of the report is a function of two factors: the possibility of *deception* and the possibility of *error*. Authorities on whom we rely for information may lie, or they may make mistakes, and the credibility we attach to any report needs to take account of both of these possibilities. Because the criteria we develop for the credibility of a report with respect to deception are much simpler than those for error, we discuss them first. We then turn to the criteria with respect to error.

Criteria with Respect to Deception

Lies, unlike mistakes, require intent. Therefore proving that something is a lie is not always an easy job. It requires showing that (a) the information is false and (b) the liar knew it to be false. The first of these tasks is often not easy, but the second is notoriously difficult. Our goal, however, is not to be able to prove whether someone is lying, but to be able to detect when it is reasonable to suspect someone of lying. If you have reason to suspect that a person is lying about an event, then that is sufficient reason for you not to give much credence to that person. There are two reasons in general for suspecting someone of telling us a lie. These are that: (a) the person has a reason for telling us a lie, and (b) the person is known to be a liar.

Because lies imply intent, and because intentional actions are actions done for a reason, lies are told for a reason. The most frequent reason people tell lies is that they stand to benefit in some way by doing so. The truth will in some way hurt (or at least not benefit) them, and so they experience a conflict of interest between telling the truth and telling a lie. Whether they tell a lie or the truth then depends on how strong their commitment to truth is, versus how well their self-interest will be served by lying.

Self-interest lies behind most lies,[1] so we need to take the self-interest of the authorities into account when assessing the credibility of their report. *Nemo judex in sua causa*, Roman jurists used to say—"No one should judge his [or her] own cause." The maxim is too strong to apply directly to reports. "No people should report on what is in their self-interest" would rule out too many helpful sources of information. But we can take the point and express it in degrees of self-interest. When we do, we invoke the criterion that the degree of credibility of a report is proportional to the degree of self-interest in the reporter. This avoids our having to ignore any report given by a self-interested reporter, and it certainly does not suggest that everyone who has any personal interest at stake will always lie to us rather than tell the truth. It does commit us, however, to relying less on what a used car dealer says about the condition of a particular car than what an independent mechanic can tell us, to searching for more reports than those given by the two opposing parties in a lawsuit, and to at least thinking twice before believing everything we read in advertisements.

Our next criterion for assessing credibility says that it is a function of the "track record" of our sources of information. Again, the Roman jurists had a wise, if strong, attitude toward liars: *Falsus in uno falsus in omnibus*. "Once a liar always a liar" is a motto we adapt to assess the credibility of someone who has lied to us in the past. That is to say, we assign no credibility at all to a person in whom we have placed our trust for accurate information but who has abused it so severely. The degree of credibility of a report of a person who has lied is, with regard to the sort of information lied about, zero. Notice again that this does not mean that a liar can never tell the truth. What it says is that because we cannot trust the liars' word, we should neither believe that what they say is true nor believe that it is false. We should simply ignore it. As becomes evident in the next section, the possibility of mistaken testimony requires a somewhat less stringent policy.

Criteria with Respect to Error

Lying requires an intent to deceive, but people may provide erroneous reports without any intent. They may think they are telling the truth. Their reports, however, may still be in error. In assessing the credibility of a report, then, we must not only assess the intent of the person giving us the report, but also the possibility that the person was in error. The more ways in which a particular report of an event could be subject to error, the less credibility we should assign to the report, and vice versa. There are three temporal stages at which error may enter into an authority's report. The first is at the time of the observation(s) on which the report is based, the second is in the time between the observation and the report, and the third is at the time of the report. Using the language of computers, cognitive psychologists sometimes call these the stages of *acquisition*, *storage*, and *retrieval*. They are also referred to

---

[1] We are excluding from consideration here those cases in which someone lies to us for our own good, and those cases of pathological lying, in which lying itself becomes the end, rather than any other interest the liar may have.

as the stages of *perception, retention*, and *recall*. Let us consider each of these stages in turn, and note the various mechanisms that can produce error. Taking these mechanisms into account, we can then formulate criteria for assessing credibility with respect to error.

Perception.   The first stage, *perception*, occurs at the time of the observation and involves the processes by which people determine what they are observing. This is the process by which eyewitnesses acquire whatever information they will acquire about an event. A naive view of human perception regards it as analogous to what happens to a piece of film in a camera when it is exposed to the light from a visual scene. Just as the film simply records, passively, "what is there," so our perception of an event may be seen as a passive activity in which we record what happens. However this view misrepresents what both cameras and humans do. What the camera records depends on where it is pointed; what kind of film is in it; what lens is on it; what the lighting sources and conditions are in the scene; how open or closed the lens aperture is; how fast the motion is in the scene; how fast the shutter speed is set on the camera; how steadily the camera is held by the photographer; how well the camera is focused; and the camera's angle, distance, and overall placement in relation to the scene. Almost all of these factors have analogues in human perception, but there are even more factors to be taken into account. The possibilities of bias and error in human perception are numerous enough to occupy an entire course in the philosophy and psychology of perception, but here we can scan only a few of the more salient ones that philosophers and cognitive psychologists have identified.

In assessing the credibility of any eyewitness report, we need first to ask about the physical conditions that existed at the time of the perception. More specifically, we need to ask about the physical condition of both the eyewitnesses and their surroundings. Certain physical conditions of the environment favor accurate perceptions, whereas others tend to distort. Rain and fog and low levels of light make visual perception less accurate than clear and well-lighted conditions. Noise affects one's ability to hear clearly, and conflicting smells and tastes can affect those senses. Wine-tasters, for example, never taste one wine immediately after another, but interpose the tastes with a more neutral taste, such as a soda cracker. In addition, the distance between the observer and the event or object being observed can affect the observation, as can obstructions between the observer and what is being observed. "I saw, as I drove past him going in opposite directions on the expressway at night, that he was wearing a diamond ring on the little finger of his right hand, and that his belt buckle had his initials engraved in it" is just not very credible, given ordinary conditions of visual perception. Yet testimony such as this is sometimes given by eyewitnesses in courts of law. A witness in the famous Sacco and Vanzetti trial, for example, testified that she had observed Sacco in a car that passed 60 to 80 ft from her; that she noticed he weighed between 140 and 145 lbs; that his left hand, which was placed on the back of the front seat, was "a hand that denoted strength"; that he was wearing a grayish shirt; that his face was clean-cut and narrow; that his forehead was high; that his complexion looked greenish; that he had dark eyebrows, and his hair, which was brushed back, was from 2 to 2½ inches long. Unfortunately, this was part of the testimony used to convict Sacco. The witness who gave it had earlier identified another man, but changed her identification when he had a perfect alibi.[2]

The amount of time that the event occupies, as well as the amount of time in which the observation takes place, can influence observations. For example, a victim of an assault usually has a longer time to observe the culprit, if the person is visible at all, than a victim of a purse-snatching. In contrast, nuclear physicists have virtually no time in which to make their observations concerning collisions among subatomic particles, and so must rely on photographs. Whenever possible, repeated observations are preferable to single ones. The reporter who has interviewed subjects several times is in a better position to tell us about the kind of people they are than a reporter who has only interviewed them once.

Conditions in the environment also determine the context in which perception occurs, and this can affect what a person sees. Seen in a context of men over 6'6", a man 6'2" will not appear very tall, but next to people under, say, 5'8", he will. Similarly, what is perceived as high, low, large, small, broad, narrow, smooth, rough, handsome, ugly, cold, warm, dark, bright, abnormal, normal, outstanding, dull, loud, soft, straight, crooked, fast, slow, too much, too little, appetizing, disgusting, long, short, restrained, outgoing, near, far, clear, opaque, and so on, can all depend on the context in which the observation takes place. To take an example, there is no speed that is simply slow. Whether a snail is slow depends on whether it is being compared to other snails it just defeated in a snail race or to a 747 jet. Words such as those in the previous list—actually a rather short list, to which you can probably add a dozen more words without thinking very hard—are said to be context-dependent. In any report in which such words are used, it is important to specify the context in which the observation was made. Otherwise they can easily mislead.

In addition to the physical conditions of the environment and the context in which the event or object appears, the physical and emotional condition of the eyewitness are also germane to the issue of credibility. Obviously a drunken eyewitness is not as credible as one who is sober. But other physical states, such as exhaustion, dehydration, extreme hunger, extreme heat and cold, illness, and stress or fear can affect one's perceptions. The person with a fever of 105°F who reports that bats flew over his bed during the night is simply not to be taken as seriously as someone with a normal temperature. Nor is the person under severe stress or emotional upheaval to be relied on as much as a person who is not. The effects of stress can be seen in the heat of battle, when soldiers often forget the most elementary lessons they have learned. During the battle of Gettysburg, for example, over 200 muzzle-loading rifles were loaded five or more times without ever being fired. One that had never been fired had been loaded 21 times.[3] Psychologists have

---

[2] Quoted in Patrick M. Wall, *Eyewitness Identification in Criminal Cases* (Springfield, IL: Charles C. Thomas, 1965), 20, 101.

3 Quoted in Elizabeth F. Loftus, *Eyewitness Testimony* (Cambridge, MA: Harvard University Press, 1979), 33.

formulated a law—the Yerkes Dodson law—to describe the effects of stress on perception. Roughly stated, it says that a mild level of emotional arousal increases the ability to perceive events accurately. But beyond that level, stress, fear, and apprehension inhibit one's ability to sense clearly what is happening around one. Incredibly enough, some appellate courts in the United States have actually held that severe stress, such as that experienced by a couple who were tortured and wounded, *contributes* to clear and accurate perceptions.[4] Psychological studies have not borne this out, nor does common experience. Imagine trying to play a game of chess immediately after you have been involved in an automobile accident. Your powers of concentration and attention are just not equivalent to what they may be in a calm and thoughtful moment.

Much of what we perceive is also influenced by the psychological phenomenon called closure. Consider our ability to read a stenciled sign. When we look at a stenciled "stop" sign, the *o* and the *p* have lines connecting the inside of the circles to the outside. It is our ability to overlook those lines, and to "close" the circles that allows us to say we saw the word "stop," rather than the letters *s* and *t*, followed by two strange symbols. Closure is a phenomenon that proofreaders must fight agaist at every turn. Many of us tend to "close" the misspelled word "against" in the previous sentence by supplying the missing "n," but proofreaders try to avoid the tendency.

As the examples of "stop" signs and missing letters show, closure can sometimes be benign, and at other times something we want to avoid. If we did not close the letters in the "stop" sign, we could not read it, but by closing the letters in "against" we fail to detect a mistake. Closing on the wrong things can have much more serious consequences than this, however. Passersby may hear gunshots coming from a store, then see two people exit the store, running. If they then see a gun and a knife on the floor of the store, they may actually think they saw the individuals holding the gun and the knife when they exited the store. What is in fact an inference from several observations is experienced by the witnesses as an observation itself. Bogus perceptions such as this have been demonstrated many times to occur in staged experiments in which simulated "crimes" were committed. And it is often not easy to convince the witnesses that they did not see what they thought they saw, short of showing them a film or a videotape of the events as they actually occurred.

Another factor affecting our perceptions is *background experience*. What we *can* see or hear is to a large extent determined by what we are prepared to see or hear. One observer sees a train go by. Another, a train buff, sees an express freight made up of gondolas, tank cars, and high rise cubes, pulled by four locomotives and headed by a U30B. It is not that the first observer has "seen" these things, but just doesn't know the names for them. Not prepared to see them, the person does not see them at all. Preparation, training, and experience can make a great deal of difference in what we can observe. "Experts," after all, are nothing other than people with "experience." Trained food and beverage tasters can detect and distinguish tastes that ordinary people can't, and trained musicians can hear what

---

[4] See Wall, *Eyewitness Identification*, 16–17, for a list and discussion of several such cases.

others can't. There is a story that the famous orchestra conductor Toscanini once stopped the orchestra in the middle of a rehearsal as they played a very dissonant chord in a contemporary piece of music. "Eh, *terzo corno!* Third horn! *Re!* I didn't hear!" Unable to see the third hornist because of bad vision, he had heard that the musician had *not* played the note that was written for him, having been engaged in cleaning his instrument at the time.[5] (Perhaps even more remarkable than his hearing, this story also points out Toscanini's phenomenal memory. He was rehearsing the piece without a score, from memory, and so had *remembered* the sound of the chord he should have heard at that point!) In addition to not being able to experience certain events or objects at all because of a lack of background experience, this lack can also cause people to *misperceive* objects or events. A pistol shot, to one unaccustomed to firearms, may be heard as a tremendous blast. Reporters who have not covered many riots or civil disturbances may find their first one much larger and more serious than it is. And medical students cutting into the human body cavity for the first time may fail to recognize the smells they experience as ordinary.

What we observe is not only a function of what we are able to observe, but what we focus our attention on. Our focus of attention can be either conscious or unconscious. The person who is looking for the hidden animals in a picture puzzle is more likely to see them than one who has no idea the picture contains them. On the other hand, by focusing one's attention on certain aspects of a situation, we may become oblivious to others. As a member of a pit crew of a sports car racing team in the days before radio communication was allowed, it was once the job of one of the authors to communicate with the driver by writing coded messages on a chalkboard and flashing them as the driver passed by the pits. Once, intent on looking for the driver's "thumbs up" sign to show that the driver understood the message sent, he returned to the pits to see the rest of the crew in horror. They had seen that the entire rear end of the car was on fire—a part of the scene he had not observed. One's attention can also be focused for one by features of the event or object. *Salience* or *vividness* are terms psychologists[6] use to describe the tendency of events or objects to "grab" one's attention. What is salient about an event or object may of course vary from person to person and culture to culture. Most men's foci of attention in viewing pictures of nude bodies are different from most women's. *Weapon focus* is a term used to describe the tendency that most victims of crime have to focus their attention on any weapon the criminal may be carrying. Insofar as this leads them not to notice other features of the scene, the ability to identify the criminal's face is thereby diminished.

Our *expectations* also influence what we perceive. Expecting to see only green Granny Smith apples in our refrigerator, we fail to see the (red) McIntosh that our spouse has put in there, and report that there are no apples in the refrigerator.

---

[5] Quoted from B. H. Haggin, "The Toscanini Musicians Knew," in Ulric Neisser, ed., *Memory Observed: Remembering in Natural Contexts* (San Francisco, W. H. Freeman, 1982), 416.

6 Loftus, *Eyewitness Testimony*, p. 25 et seq., uses "salience," and Richard Nisbett and Lee Ross, *Human Inference: Strategies and Shortcomings of Social Judgment* (Englewood Cliffs, NJ: Prentice-Hall, 1980), chap. 3, use "vividness."

Temporary biases in perception can be brought about by expectations caused by a series of recent perceptions. Experiments have shown that the perception of so-called ambiguous figures, that is, shapes that can be seen in one of two different ways, can be influenced by a preceding series of shapes. When a drawing that can be seen either as the face of a man wearing glasses or as a mouse, with its tail curled under its body, is preceded by a series of animal pictures, most people, expecting to see another animal, see the drawing as that of a mouse. And when it is preceded by a series of human faces, it is most often seen as the face of the man. What we see is influenced not only by what we expect to see, but at times by what we are accustomed to seeing, as well as by what we want to see. An experiment conducted in the late 1940s shows the extent to which expectations we have as the result of personal or cultural *stereotypes* can influence our perceptions. Groups of subjects were asked to view a drawing of a scene aboard a subway train. Several people in the picture were seated, but two were standing, facing each other. One, a Black man wearing a three-piece suit and tie, had one hand in his pocket and the other outstretched, open and with an empty palm. The other person standing was a White man, wearing a shirt open at the collar, without a coat. He was carrying an open razor in one hand. The subjects were asked to view the scene, then give a verbal report of it to a second subject, who then reported the account to a third subject, and so on, through six or seven subjects. Over 40 groups of these subjects were used, including children and adults and Blacks and Whites. Over half of the final subjects reported that they had been told that the scene showed the Black man rather than the White man holding the razor.[7]

Such cultural stereotypes can easily bias what we perceive, but so can individual, personal stereotypes. The person who believes that mountain people are untrustworthy is very likely to perceive a social situation among mountain people differently than someone without such a prejudice. And such a perception can be the start of a vicious circle. Prepared to view mountain people as untrustworthy, a person may see a situation as revealing a mountain person as untrustworthy. This perception will often be taken as confirming evidence of the stereotype, which then becomes strengthened, so that when the observers confront the next situation, they are prepared more than ever to "discover" the untrustworthiness of a person living in the mountains.

Psychologists have given the name *halo effect* to a perceptual bias closely related to the one we have just discussed. Believing in the overall goodness of an individual, a person may then tend to see only the good traits and deeds that that person performs, overlooking the bad ones and even perceiving some bad ones as good. Many parents notoriously display the halo effect toward their children, seeing what others view as misbehavior as "cuteness." The opposite of this might be called the *devil effect*, in which a person originally seen as bad can, as we say, "do no good" in the eyes of that observer. Only the persons' bad acts are noticed, with no allowance that at least occasionally they are good, and even some good acts are seen as bad. One experiment that demonstrates the halo effect quite well was

---

[7] Cited in Loftus, *Eyewitness Testimony*, 38.

conducted using two groups and an audience. The first group was known to be very much disliked by the audience; the second group was well liked. Both groups were asked to perform calisthenic exercises in front of the audience. Unknown to the audience, the first group was coached to be perfect in their performance, and the second group was trained to make deliberate mistakes. As you might expect, the first group was perceived as the one making all the mistakes.[8] Most of the discussion of the halo effect has centered on its occurrence when people observe other people, but it is clear that it and the devil effect can occur in larger contexts, not necessarily involving people. Someone who has been "pre-sold" on an automobile, for instance, may take it on a test drive and notice only its good features, overlooking the bad. And much of the propaganda that national governments disseminate about their enemies can be seen to have this effect on their citizens. Predisposed to see the former Soviet Union as an "evil empire," it was very difficult for many Americans to see anything of value in that country or its government or its citizens. On the other hand, anti-American sentiments can be very powerful too, so that nothing Americans can do when visiting some foreign lands will count as evidence of their being anything other than "ugly Americans" or "Yankee imperialists."

Another pair of perceptual biases are those of *wishful thinking* and its opposite, which might be called *aversive thinking.* Earlier, in discussing the role of self-interest with respect to deception, we said that self-interest is one of the chief causes of lies. But self-interest can also enter into one's perceptions. Hoping that the home team will make a first down, some football fans may actually perceive it as doing so when it hasn't. On the other hand, it is sometimes very difficult for a fan to see how the referee could possibly have counted the other team's lengthy pass reception as being in-bounds. Wishes and desires, both positive and negative, can cloud our perceptions of various kinds of events, and usually in unconscious ways. Scientists who call a halt to an experiment the instant they have gotten the data they want, without letting it run on to see whether conflicting data might also result in the long run are probably more guilty of this bias than of deliberate fraud. This bias can be particularly dangerous when it occurs among people in positions of authority or power. Wanting to hear evidence that the company is prospering, and being averse to evidence that it is not doing well, a manager or officer of a company will often convey this quite unconsciously to the employees. Picking up this message, they will then tell the manager only the good news, giving in effect what the manager wanted all along. When the company folds because proper protective measures were not taken, it is then difficult to decide how to assign responsibility. The fairy tale of the Emperor's New Clothes is a perfect illustration of this phenomenon.

Referees, then, should not be chosen from among the supporters of opposing sports teams. The reason for this is not merely that they might lie or cheat, but that the very process of perception can be clouded by self-interest. Similarly, the credibility of the observations of scientists who study the effects of smoking on

---

[8] Quoted in Edward B. Arnolds, William K. Carroll, Melvin B. Lewis, and Michael P. Seng, *Eyewitness Testimony: Strategies and Tactics* (New York: McGraw-Hill, 1984), 51.

health under the sponsorship of the Tobacco Institute, a trade organization of the tobacco industry, should be questioned, not just because such scientists may lie, but because quite unconsciously they may not observe what is there to be observed. Similarly, newspapers that endorse certain political candidates before elections are probably not the most credible sources of information on those candidates or their opponents.

Another criterion for assessing credibility with respect to error also relates to something we discussed in the section on lies. There we said that the "track record" of the source of the information is relevant to its credibility. With respect to error the same maxim applies. Rather than refusing to listen to them altogether, as we do with liars, we should take what people who have made mistakes in the past say with the proverbial "grain of salt." Likewise, people who are known to exaggerate or underestimate events should be listened to with that fact in mind. People who never experience rain in less than "torrents," or whose pains are never less than "agonizing," or who regard all movies that they see as "tremendous," or for whom all people over 6 ft in height are "at least 7 ft tall" should be listened to, but warily.

Because mistakes in perception can occur even when sources are not prey to the various perceptual liabilities we have described in this section, a final check on credibility is to use as many sources as possible. *Corroboration* is the term used to describe the process of checking one's sources against each other. When two or more independent sources agree, then their credibility is increased. When they disagree, the credibility of each is diminished. Of course it is important to make sure they are independent—that one is not using the other as a source, or they are not using the same ultimate source. Corroboration is useless when two sources of information have conferred or had access to the information of the other, because then the problem of *conformity* can influence the report. It is one thing for a source consciously to rely on another source for information, but it is another, and often quite insidious, thing for a source unconsciously to conform to what another person reports as having observed. There is often social pressure not to differ from others in what we observe, particularly when the others are numerous and unanimous. In a famous experiment conducted in the 1950s, sets of seven subjects were shown two lines, one clearly longer than the others, and asked to report which was the longer. The first six subjects in each set were coached beforehand to say that the shorter line was the longer. The majority of the uncoached seventh subjects reported as well that the shorter line was the longer, in the face of obvious contradicting evidence.[9] Another experiment tested individual versus group reports of a staged incident. Individual reports tended to be less thorough, though more accurate than the group reports, suggesting again the social power that numbers of people can exert, even when in error.[10]

Retention.   In seeking to develop criteria of credibility for information provided to us by authorities, we have so far looked at the difficulties, psychological

---

[9] Reported in Robert Buckhout, "Eyewitness Testimony," in Ulric Neisser, ed., *Memory Observed: Remembering in Natural Contexts* (San Francisco, W. H. Freeman, 1982), 122.

[10] Ibid.

and otherwise, that first-hand observers can experience at the time they make their observations. Most authorities on whom we rely for our facts do not, however, report the facts to us at the same time they make the observations. News reporters do not write their reports at the scene of the event they are witnessing, but back at the typewriter (or word processor) in the office or studio. Scientists do not write the articles they publish in journals the same day or even hour they make their experimental observations, and even the person to whom Fledermaus sold the tractor probably did not tell his wife at exactly the time he bought it whom he bought it from. The gap between the time of the original observation(s) and the time it is reported (which is often different from the time we read or hear the report) is called the *retention interval.*

The most important point about the retention interval, for our purposes, is the *length* of the interval. It is a well-known phenomenon, which you can no doubt verify from your own experience, that the longer we are required to remember something, the more we forget. The so-called forgetting curve, which plots the amount of material remembered against the time of retention, varies of course from person to person and event to event and detail of event to detail of event. It is also a function of many of the factors we considered in the last section. Details that were observed but not focused on as strongly as others will usually not be remembered as long, and details for which there was wishful thinking will in general be remembered longer than those for which there was not.

One way to "shorten" the time span between the time of observation and the time of the report is to take notes on the observation at the time it occurs. Then when it is time to report the observation, a written record rather than memory can be relied on. Even this is not foolproof, of course, because there is always the possibility of misremembering or forgetting what the notes mean. However, no scientists or reporters could be regarded as even minimally credible who did not take notes of their observations at the time they were made, and even the widow at the beginning of the chapter would probably be given more credence by the court if she had a written record of her husband telling her that the seller was Fledermaus. Many lawyers wisely advise their clients who foresee a lawsuit developing to keep a written record of all they observe. At the time of trial, that can be relied on by the clients when they testify, and even (in some jurisdictions) introduced as evidence. Students who take notes when they are studying or attending class usually do better on exams even when they are not allowed to consult them during the exams—a fact you have no doubt heard recited by professors and teachers. ("Highlighting" or underlining a text that you are reading is not nearly as effective. The reason for this is not hard to imagine—when you remember it, what you remember is merely someone else's words, and not the thoughts and context surrounding the words in the notes you should have taken.)

The interval between the observation and its report is highly relevant to the credibility of an authority, but other factors during the period of retention should be taken into account as well. What is called *postevent information* can influence a person's memory of what occurred. This is information introduced during the time of the period of retention. It may be in conflict with what was originally observed, or it may merely supplement it, but there is little doubt that it usually influences what is remembered. For example, suppose two witnesses observe an automobile accident involving a green car and a red car, and the cause of the accident is the green car running a stop sign. Suppose also that after the cars are towed away another witness says to the first two, "How fast do you think the blue car was going when it ran the stop sign?" When the first witnesses are later asked by the police for their description of the accident, the postevent information they have received (in the form of the question about the blue car) is likely to affect the answer. One set of studies has shown that observers are likely either to report the green car as being blue, or else to have what is called a *compromise memory,* in which they report it as being bluish-green.[11] Other studies have even shown that postevent information can cause people not merely to misremember what they observed, but to "remember" objects and details of events they never observed at all. One study involved witnesses to a staged theft of an object out of a bag. In fact, although they could not see it, the actor playing the thief took nothing out of the bag. The witnesses heard the "victim" say immediately after the event that a tape recorder had been stolen from the bag. When they were interviewed over a week later, over half the witnesses "remembered" seeing the tape recorder stolen, even describing it in some detail as having or not having an antenna, being black or grey, and as being in a case or not.[12]

An interesting variation on the phenomenon of postevent information is that of *unconscious transference.* This is the tendency to transfer information gathered in one observation to that of another. It is not uncommon for students of Shakespeare, for example, to remember events in one of his plays as occurring in another. Or an old telephone number—636–2781, say—is confused with the new—831–4482, and a person dials a combination—636–4482. The result in this example is harmless enough, but the results of unconscious transference can be quite serious when, for example, a railway agent held up at gunpoint misidentifies the criminal as someone who was nowhere near the scene of the crime at the time, but who had purchased tickets from the agent earlier.[13] In a case in which this happened, the person who had been misidentified fortunately had an airtight alibi and was not convicted, but in any situation where we rely on an authority who has made a first-hand observation, the problem of unconscious transference always needs to be taken into account.

Recall.   So far we have seen some of the ways error can enter into both people's observations and their retention of that information. When the time comes for them to remember the event or object, many of these factors can distort the facts. For example, aversive thinking may not have entered into the perception itself, but can enter at the point the event is remembered, to the extent that the observers may not be able to remember anything at all, or may remember only what

[11] Cf. Loftus, *Eyewitness Testimony,* 57–58.

[12] Loftus, *Eyewitness Testimony,* 61–62

[13] Cited in Wall, *Eyewitness Identification,* 119–120..

it suits them to remember. The time of the death of a parent, for example, may be remembered as closer to the present than it really was, whereas an extremely embarrassing event may be remembered as happening longer ago than it did. And events that tend to support one's present point of view tend to be remembered more easily than those that conflict with it. One study, for example, showed that when favorable information about Russia was presented to two groups, the group that was known to have unfavorable attitudes toward Russia did not remember the information as well as the group that had favorable attitudes toward Russia.[14] Closure as well may fail to occur at the time of the event, but then occur at the time of recall, with the observers filling in, without ever realizing it, parts of an event that would "logically" fit in, but that they actually do not remember. Similarly, expectations can distort memory just as easily as they can perception. It is particularly easy to project one's own feelings into others, and "remember" that another person in a situation experienced it the way one would have had one been in that situation.

In addition to the processes we have already studied, there are processes peculiar to memory that can cause mistakes at the time an event is remembered. One factor in recall that can lead to error is called the *law of recency*. It states that more recent events tend to replace more distant ones. Thus, if an object has been observed at different times, and a change has occurred in the object between the first and last times, the observer is more likely to remember it as being constituted the last way than the first. The law of recency apparently also applies to memories themselves, with serious results for the possibility of error. That is, as between the original observation and a memory of it, there is a tendency to remember the memory rather than the observation, even when the observation was accurate and the memory inaccurate. This phenomenon, called the *freezing effect*,[15] is illustrated in a series of experiments in which short prose passages were read to subjects, who were asked to reproduce them 5 minutes later. They were then shown the passage again, and asked to reproduce it 5 minutes later. This procedure was repeated several times, over several months, with the same subjects and the same passages. One of the passages had included the phrase "the whole stock," but one subject reproduced that originally as "the entire stock," and continued to reproduce it this way every time, despite being shown the correct version. At one point in one of the passages "several large firms in Oklahoma City" were referred to, as well as a "police raiding squad." One subject persisted in referring to the "Oklahoma City Police Vice Squad," whereas another continually referred to the "F.B.I. officials." Another referred to it throughout his reports as the "police riot squad." These examples of the freezing effect[16] are particularly notable because the situation in which they occurred included a presentation of the *correct* material before the reproduction was made each time.

---

[14] Reported in Arnolds et al., *Eyewitness Testimony*, 70.

[15] Cf. Loftus, *Eyewitness Testimony*, 84–86.

[16] Ibid.

Combined with the phenomena of *closure* or *expectation*, the freezing effect can lead to gross errors in reporting. In the dead of winter, witnesses may observe someone who is not wearing a coat enter a building from the street. When they first remember the event, the witnesses may remember the snow on the ground, and fill in the memory with the fact that the person was wearing a coat—perhaps, if the witness knows the person, a particular coat they remember the person as wearing on previous occasions. When the witnesses remember the incident later on, the coat is very likely to be remembered—that is, remembered from the previous memory. If the incident is then remembered several more times, it is very likely that the presence of the coat will always be remembered. And this in turn can produce another phenomenon—*certainty* that the coat was there.

Witness certainty (also known as *witness confidence*) refers to the degree of strength with which a witness holds a belief. Asked how certain she is that her husband said that Fledermaus sold him the tractor, Witness J may say, "Well, I think he did," or she may say, "Well, I'm pretty sure he did," or she may say, "I'm absolutely positive he did." Many people believe that witness certainty is a reliable indicator of the credibility of a witness's report. People who say they are "positive" about something are thought to be more likely to be telling the truth than those who merely say that they only "think" it is true. Many people, including a majority of the U. S. Supreme Court, believe this. In an important case decided in 1972,[17] the Court held that "the level of certainty demonstrated by the witness" is a factor that needs to be considered by the jury when "evaluating the likelihood of misidentification." In fact, however, many studies have shown that there is a poor correspondence between witness certainty and accuracy.[18] Some experiments, involving postevent information, have even detected an *inverse* relationship between the two.[19] One recent overview of these studies concludes that "the eyewitness accuracy-confidence relationship is weak under good laboratory conditions and functionally useless in forensically representative settings."[20] The best policy to adopt in evaluating the credibility of reports seems to be to ignore the degree of certainty expressed by the authority giving the report.

Another factor that seems to affect the accuracy of recall is the *kind of event or object* being remembered. Memories of the passage of time are particularly prone to error; for example, violent and unpleasant situations are often remembered as taking longer than they did. Years elapsed are usually underestimated, and unequal

[17] *Neil v. Biggers*, 409 U. S. 199 (1972). Cf. also the "Model Special Instructions on Identification" issued by a U. S. District Court. Judges are instructed to ask jurors whether they are satisfied that an eyewitness' identification "was the product of his own recollection." They are then told that they may "take into account. . .the strength of the identification." *United States v. Telfaire*, 469 F 2d 555 (1972), at 558.

[18] Cf. for example, Loftus, *Eyewitness Testimony*, 100–101; Arnolds, et al., *Eyewitness Testimony*, 73–74; A. Daniel Yarmey, *The Psychology of Eyewitness Testimony* (New York: Free Press, 1979), 150–151; and Gary L. Wells and Donna M. Murray, "Eyewitness Confidence," in Gary L. Wells and Elizabeth F. Loftus, (eds.), *Eyewitness Testimony: Psychological Perspectives* (Cambridge: Cambridge University Press, 1984), 155–170.

[19] Cf. Loftus, *Eyewitness Testimony*, 101.

[20] Wells and Murray, "Eyewitness Confidence," 165.

intervals of time are often equated.[21] One study suggests that when a sentence from a book is being remembered, the topic of the sentence can have a bearing on how well it is remembered. This study asked members of a Sherlock Holmes fan club to give the name of the story that contained certain sentences, and to tell the context in which the selected sentence appeared. *Description* sentences, such as "His tall, gaunt, craggy figure has a suggestion of hunger and rapacity" were seldom remembered, either as to story or context. *Isolated abstract* sentences, such as "To let the brain work without sufficient material is like racing an engine," were remembered slightly more often, and *isolated concrete* sentences, such as "My eyes tell me that on the inside of your left shoe. . .the leather has been scored by six almost parallel cuts," were remembered only slightly more often (a 70% failure rate for the title and 35% as to context). By far the most remembered sentences, however, were *relevant concrete* sentences—specific observations integrally related to the story or the solution, such as "Were it mixed with any ordinary dish, the eater would undoubtedly detect it, and would probably eat no more." The title was recalled over 70% of the time for this kind of sentence, and the context almost 90% of the time. What this study suggests (but, because it is one-of-a-kind, does not prove) is that the kinds of things about an event most easily remembered are those most concrete details that the person finds relevant to the gist of the event. In examining the testimony of John Dean before the Watergate Committee, and comparing it with the tapes that were discovered of his conversations with President Nixon, a researcher found that was exactly what was happening with his memory. Dean was fairly accurate with regard to the gist of what was said, but often wrong about isolated episodes and language.[22]

Perhaps the greatest source of error in recall occurs when observers are *asked* about what they observed. For in asking someone something, the possibility of *suggestion* is always present. We saw earlier how postevent information can influence a person's recall of an event, but now we are concerned with a question right at the time of the recall. Questions that influence or bias the answer that is given are called *leading questions*, and they are particularly apt to influence memories. The judicial system we use in this country makes extensive use of questions to obtain information from witnesses, and so some care has been taken to develop rules to limit the kinds of leading questions lawyers can ask in court. But even so the rules are not always followed. Outside of the legal setting, moreover, there are no rules restricting the way in which observers might be asked about events, and hence little check on the consequences of using leading questions. We talk about the biasing influence of questions later when we discuss the use of polls; the point is a general one applicable to any context in which a person's memory is being probed by questions. Ultimately, therefore, all of the processes involved in authoritative reports of events—perception, retention, and recall—are

---

[21] Cf. Arnolds et al., *Eyewitness Testimony*, 80–82.

[22] The first study is reported in Ulric Neisser and John A. Hupcey, "A Sherlockian Experiment," 293–299, and the second in Ulric Neisser, "John Dean's Memory: A Case Study," 139–161. Both appear in Ulric Neisser, ed., *Memory Observed: Remembering in Natural Contexts* (San Francisco: W. H. Freeman, 1982).

TABLE 11.1

Criteria of Credibility for Information Based on an Authority

All other things being equal, the greater the extent to which a report of an authority approximates the following standards, the more credible it is:

1. Its information is direct (first-hand rather than second-hand, etc.) (i.e., the authority making the report is the same person who made any observations on which the report is based.)
2. Its information is immediate (noninferential).
3. The observer making the report has not lied in the past.
4. Any observation(s) on which the report is based are not biased by a conflict of interest.
5. Any observation(s) on which the report is based were made under optimal physical conditions.
6. The report specifies the context for any context-dependent words it contains.
7. Any observation(s) on which the report is based were made with adequate time to observe the event or object.
8. The physical condition of the observer is not relevantly impaired at the time of any observation on which the report is based, or at the time of making the report.
9. The observer was not functioning under conditions of stress, fear, or apprehension at the time of any observations on which the report is based.
10. Any observation(s) on which the report is based were not biased by closure.
11. Any observation(s) on which the report is based were made by an observer whose background experience was appropriate to the observation.
12. Any observation(s) on which the report is based were not biased by inappropriate focus of attention.
13. Any observation(s) on which the report is based were not biased by expectations.
14. Any observation(s) on which the report is based were not biased by individual or cultural stereotypes, including the halo or devil effects.
15. Any observation(s) on which the report is based were not biased by wishful or aversive thinking.
16. Any observation(s) on which the report is based were not biased by a desire to conform to others' observations.
17. The report is corroborated by other independent reports.
18. The report is not contradicted by other reports.
19. Any observation(s) on which the report is based were repeated.
20. Observers have not made mistakes, exaggerated, or underestimated facts in their reports in the past.
21. The interval between the observation and the report is not long.
22. Notes were taken at the time of the observation, and the report was constructed relying on those notes.
23. Any observation(s) on which the report is based were not biased by postevent information, including unconscious transference, a compromise memory, the law of recency, or the freezing effect.
24. Any observation(s) on which the report is based are not biased by leading questions.

Finally, it is a condition of assessing the credibility of a report that witness confidence not be used as a criterion for assessing credibility.

fallible processes. In reporting on events, even those we have personally observed, we are quite unlike a video recorder. This is true even when the authority strives to be totally honest. Many of the factors that influence our perception, retention, and recall of events are unconscious and beyond our control. In relying on ourselves or others as authoritative sources regarding events that have transpired, therefore, we must simply be aware of the factors that can introduce error into the reporting process, and evaluate the trust we place in the authorities accordingly.

Table 11.1 summarizes the points we have made in this section.

AUTHORITIES ABOUT PUBLIC ATTITUDES

Although reliance on authorities to tell us what events occurred is a particularly salient use of authority, there are other uses of authority that are extremely important in our society. In a capitalistic democracy, one of the most important sorts of information concerns what people in the population think or feel about an issue or product. This information is needed by a host of different groups in our society. Two of the most obvious consumers of such information are corporations and politicians. For corporations, the main need is to know whether their products will be bought by the public. However, they also need to know such additional information as how their public image may be affected by a decision they might make. Politicians need to know not just how many people will vote for them in an upcoming election, but also how a particular action on their part might be perceived by their constituency. These are not the only groups, however, that need to know how the public thinks about an issue. Health workers often need to know what the public understands about a health risk and how successful various ways of educating the public will be. For example, when people continue to smoke or to engage in promiscuous sexual activity when the health risks of these activities have been widely discussed, health workers need to find out whether the public understands the risks and what their reasons are for continuing to engage in the risky activity.

To get information about what a group of people thinks on a topic one needs to *poll* them. Often the group one is interested in is too large to poll everyone. Hence, one must use the results of polling a relatively small group to make a determination of what the whole group believes. Given the increasing reliance on polling data, it is important that you be aware of the factors that determine whether polls are reliable. We focus on three such factors. The first is the questions that the poll uses. It becomes obvious that the way a question is asked can significantly bias the results of a poll and there are numerous pitfalls to avoid. Second is the choice of the population to be sampled and the method of contact. The final factor is the way in which the results of the poll are analyzed.

It is important to know how to assess polls because they are becoming increasingly popular in our society. In addition to their usefulness in providing information about what people think, they have become popular because they are relatively easy to do. Thus, newspapers increasingly are publishing polling data as *the news*. Some of these polls are well conducted and could give you reliable information about what the populace thinks. Others, however, are poorly done and provide very unreliable authority. If you are to be discriminating in your reliance on such authorities, it is important for you to appreciate what is required for a poll to be a good authority.

Polling Questions

The beliefs people have about a subject matter are often very complex. This means the way in which the question is asked may critically affect the answer given. Notice the difference between the following closely related questions:

> Do you think the accused committed the crime?
> Do you think the accused should be found guilty of the crime?
> Do you think the accused will be found guilty of the crime?
> Do you think the accused should be punished for the crime?

People's attitudes about the accused may be quite complex. They may in fact think that the accused has committed the crime, but not think that the accused should be found guilty. Perhaps they do not think there is enough evidence to meet legal standards. Or their reason might be that what the accused did should not be considered a crime. Or their reason might be that what the accused did was a crime, but in this instance the act was justified and not deserving of punishment, and the only way to present this view is to say that the accused should not be found guilty. On the other hand, someone could think that the accused should be found guilty, but not think the person will in fact be found guilty. And someone may think that the accused committed the crime and should be found guilty, but not be punished. Thus, one could get very different patterns of answers to these four questions. And, if only one question were asked, we would only get one part of the picture about how people thought about the accused.

It requires much practice to be able to develop polling questions that produce the information that is sought. In fact, good polling firms often put a great deal of effort into developing good questions. Often they will test a batch of questions on a group of people before using them in an actual poll. They may ask people a number of questions that they think ask the same thing, and see whether people in fact answer them the same. If they don't, they will then look for the subtle differences in the question that may be responsible for the differences in response. They may also interview people after they have completed the questions to determine how they understood the question and the basis for their answers. In this way they can determine whether the questions are producing answers reflective of the part of the person's beliefs that are relevant. We cannot here teach you how to develop good questions. However, we can alert you to some common errors in constructing polling questions. These are ways of constructing questions that bias the results of the poll, and thus undercut its authority. They do so by leading the person being polled to answer in a particular manner. We identify six such ways of developing leading questions.

The first way of asking a leading question is to *invite a "yes" or "no" answer* by use of phrases such as "You agree, don't you?" or "Don't you agree?". "You didn't look at your watch when this happened, did you?" suggests an answer in the way it is phrased. By putting the question in the negative, the questioner invites a "No" answer. Similarly, the following questions all suggest that the questioner expects to hear a "No" answer, and so they bias the answer:

> You're not saying that. . . , are you?
> Surely you don't mean to imply that. . .?
> It isn't true that. . . , is it?

Notice the differences in nuance and suggestion in the following questions that someone might ask a hardware store employee:

> "You don't have any brown double-gang wall switch plates, do you?"
> "Do you have any brown double-gang wall switch plates?"
> "Where are the brown double-gang wall switch plates?"

Each of these asks for the same kind of information, but facilitates a different answer by the employee. The first version makes it easier than the others for the employee to say "No," insofar as it presents the assumption that the company won't have any of the switch plates in stock. The third version does exactly the opposite, by presenting the assumption that the company will have them. The real question, it tends to suggest, is not whether the company has them, but where they are. The second question is the least suggestive.

In general, one should be particularly leery of a poll question that begins with "Do you agree. . ." or "Don't you agree. . . ." Audiences tend to want to cooperate with the person asking the question and to avoid controversy. Unless the issue is extremely important to them, and they are willing to engage in controversy, people are likely to simply give poll takers the answer they seem to want and be done with it. Thus, when asked "Don't you agree that this box will make our product more attractive to shoppers?" most people will simply say "Yes" and go on. If you really want to know how people think about the new box, you need to ask a nonleading question such as, "Do you think that this box will make our product more attractive to shoppers?"

A second way a question can "lead" the answerer to give a biased answer is by *putting limited options forward.* "Do you usually bathe once, or twice a day?" biases the answer that will be given in two directions. In suggesting that one or two times daily is the "norm" for bathing, it makes it difficult for people who average three or four or more baths a day to answer, as well as for the person who bathes less than once a day. Similarly, a poll that asks whether you intend to vote for the Republican or the Democratic presidential candidate suggests that those two choices are the norm, and makes it awkward for the respondent to name a third-party candidate. That different ranges of alternatives offered in a question can influence the answer was demonstrated in an experiment in which two groups of randomly selected people were asked how many different kinds of headache remedies they had tried. One group was asked whether they had tried 1, 2, or 3 products other than the one they currently used. Another group was asked whether they had tried 1, 5, or 10 other products. The first group's answers averaged 3.3 other products, and the second group's answers averaged 5.2 other products.[23] Clearly, a much less biased way of asking the question is not to limit answerers to any number of options, but to let them state the number themselves.

A third kind of leading question *forces the answerer to answer two questions in the same way.* "Are you in favor of convicting and hanging the defendant" suggests that if people are in favor of a conviction, they will also be in favor of capital punishment. If a person is in favor of the first, but not the second, then the only way to answer the two questions is to reject the original question and insist that it be divided. Likewise, "Did you enjoy the class and the professor?" and "Was the professor well prepared and punctual?" each need to be divided into two questions.

A fourth way of biasing an answer is to *put a statement into the question.* "When you use a mouthwash, do you use product X or Y?" assumes that you do use a mouthwash, and thereby makes it difficult for the person who does not use a mouthwash to answer. (This question also puts limited options forward.) A district attorney who asks a defendant, "When you killed the victim, did you use a butcher knife or a paring knife?" is probably trying to trap the defendant into accepting the statement that is built into his question, namely, that the defendant did kill the victim. This is an example of a leading question that would certainly be disallowed in any U.S. court. The use of statements in polling questions can be just as biasing when they occur before the question. Consider the following poll item:

> The Japanese are already more affluent than Americans and the gap is increasing. In light of this, do you think the United States should continue to provide for the military defense of Japan?

The opening statement is intended to make you think about the question of paying for Japan's military defense in one way. Its role in biasing the question can be appreciated by considering how a different statement can bias the question in an opposite way:

> Given that it is in the interest of the United States to restrict Japan's military power in light of its use of that power in World War II, do you think the United States should continue to provide for the military defense of Japan?

A fifth way to construct a leading question is to *put biasing words into the question.* "Did you watch the insanely stupid segment of the evening news last night?" is probably too obviously biased to be used by any poll-taker. But there are more subtle ways of inserting biasing words into a question. "How long was the movie you saw?" is a very different question from "How short was the movie you

---

[23] Cf. Elizabeth F. Loftus, "Leading Questions and the Eyewitness Report," *Cognitive Psychology* 7 (1975): 561.

saw?" and each is likely to provoke a very different answer. One famous study showed that witnesses to a staged automobile accident gave very different answers to the question of how fast the cars were going at the time of the accident, based on whether they were asked how fast the cars were going when they "smashed into each other," "collided with each other," "bumped into each other," "hit each other," and "contacted each other."[24] Biasing words are often found together with statements that have been put into questions. A question from a gun-lobby group that asks, "Do you support the right guaranteed by the Constitution of every American to purchase and bear arms to protect themselves and their loved ones from murderers and rapists?" is almost so obvious as to tempt one to give the opposite answer from that desired.

Finally, a leading question can be constructed by substituting for *a* the word *the*. By making reference to a particular entity by the use of *the* rather than *a*, a question induces the assumption that there is such an entity. For example, "Did you see the scratch on the left side of the car?" suggests that there is a scratch there, whereas "Did you see a scratch on the left side of the car?" is less suggestive. Even less suggestive is, "Did you see a scratch on the car?" Similarly, "Have you noticed the improvements in our new product?" suggests there are improvements, whereas "Have you noticed any improvements in our new product?" leaves it open to the answerer to determine whether there are improvements. Only in the second case will you find out whether the person polled really thinks there are improvements.

In general, and in any setting—whether in a courtroom, a magazine or newspaper interview, a poll or survey, or simply as a report of what someone answered—your knowledge that a leading question has been asked should make you question the credibility of the answer that is given. In terms of accuracy of response, the best kind of question to ask to obtain information is the *free report*, as opposed to the *controlled narrative*. The latter asks specifically for information, such as "Where was the blue car when you saw it?" or "What were you doing when. . .?" The free report asks questions such as, "Tell me everything you can about the accident." This allows observers to report any details they wish. Unfortunately, although it usually produces answers that are more accurate, the free report usually produces less complete answers than the controlled narrative. So the best policy is to begin with free report kinds of questions, and if answers are not received to questions one wants answered, to resort then to the controlled narrative. Only if you have carefully examined how your audience will understand and construe your questions should you attempt to develop a limited range of answers. Unfortunately, however, for large surveys this is what is required.

As we have tried to show, there are a variety of biasing factors that can enter into the questions used in a poll. This makes it particularly important, when you are presented with the results of a poll, to know what the exact questions were. If all you are told is that a certain percentage of people responded in a particular manner on a poll, but not how the questions were worded, you should be cautious

---

[24] The average respective speeds given were: 40.8, 39.3, 38.1, 34.0, and 30.8 mph. Cf. Loftus, *Eyewitness Testimony*, 96.

in interpreting the results. The questions might well have been leading, and the result that has been produced might be an artifact of the leading questions and not an indication of what the population in question really believes.

Choice of Population to Sample and Mode of Contact

As we have noted, in a poll one is likely to contact only a subset of the people in the total population of interest. This subset is commonly called the *sample*. As is pointed out in the subsequent section, one of the crucial factors in determining the accuracy of the interpretation of the poll is the raw size of the sample. The percentage of the total population sampled does not matter. As long as a sufficiently large sample is chosen, the fact that one only contacts a small percentage of the group in question does not pose a problem. What subset is chosen to be contacted, and the manner in which they are contacted, however, can significantly alter the outcome of the poll and hence its reliability.

In general, what is critical is that the sample selected for polling accurately represents the overall population. A *random* selection procedure would be most likely to generate a sample that accurately represents the general population. However, there is no *procedure* that humans can use that is totally random. The best that humans can hope to accomplish is to employ a selection procedure that does not bias the result. That is, one hopes to develop a selection procedure that is not linked to factors that might determine the answers that will be given on polling questions.

Often the selection procedure is closely linked to the mode of contact. In order to get a sample, one may go to a particular place, and try to question all who come by that place. For example, one may position oneself at the entrance to the library and question people who come into the library. Or one may find a location in a local mall, and question people as they pass that location. Unfortunately, both of these procedures may introduce biases. Not everyone is equally likely to go to the library on a particular day, nor is everyone as likely to go to the mall. If people using the library are likely to answer your questions in a different manner than those who do not use the library, than your choice of location will have biased the result. Likewise, if mall goers are likely to answer your question differently than non-mall goers, and you want your results to reflect both mall goers and non-mall goers, then you will have biased the result. Note that in deciding whether these modes of contact result in a bias, you need to consider what the general population is that you are seeking to learn about and whether the group more likely to be included in the sample is different than the group not as likely to be included. If you were primarily interested in what library users thought about a given issue, then selecting people as they entered the library would be a nonbiased procedure. (However, biases could still enter through the choice of the time during which people would be stopped.) But if you were interested in the general student population and the question asked at the library had to do with academic matters at the university, then the subgroup polled may reasonably be thought to be biased.

An extremely common mode of polling people in our society is to call them on the telephone. One might, for example, select people for a poll by opening up a telephone book and calling the last person listed on each page. By itself this procedure is not likely to produce a bias. But one should be aware of various factors that arise with this method, and consider whether they bias the outcome: Not everyone has a telephone. And some who do have telephones will have unlisted numbers. Many people will not be home when you call; those who work during the day won't be home if you call during those hours, and those who work evenings won't be home if you call during those hours. Furthermore, many people now screen their calls with answering machines and won't talk to you if you are conducting a poll. If the groups you exclude by doing a telephone poll are likely to respond differently than those whom you succeed in contacting, then a telephone poll will not give a reliable result.

One factor linked to the means of contact is the response rate to the poll. Seldom is a pollster able to get everyone to respond to a poll. (The U.S. Census Bureau comes close, but only because it is illegal to refuse to answer their questions.) Many people routinely refuse to answer questions on a telephone poll, or when approached by a pollster in a public place. Other people answer selectively, answering only those poll questions they want to answer. If someone has a strong stance on a question (e.g., they are vehemently opposed to gun control) they may be willing to answer a question on that topic, but not on others. As a result, the sample is further biased. Those who have extreme views (in either direction) are represented far more frequently in the sample than in the population and thus they make it appear that the overall population holds more extreme views than they do.

In conducting a poll there is almost always some contact between the poll giver and the recipient of the poll. (Polls given through the mail are an exception, but they have a notoriously low return rate.) The interaction between the poll giver and the person being polled can affect the answers the person gives. One reason for this is that people generally like to please other people and so try to give the response they think the person desires. Thus, what the questioner says in response to the previous answer may determine how subsequent questions are answered. Questioners who display some sympathy, agreement, or other positive disposition toward the answers they receive are very likely to provoke different successive answers than those questioners who display antagonism toward or disagreement with what they are hearing. And both of these are likely to elicit different answers from those received by the totally "neutral" questioner. "That's good. The answers you're giving are very helpful" is likely to elicit more of the same kinds of answers, whereas "If that's all you can remember, let me ask you this. . ." is likely to suggest that a change in answers is desired by the questioner. Reporters, as well as people who administer surveys, need to be especially careful about not only putting words in people's mouths, but also leading answerers to say what they think the questioner wants them to say. Obviously, some answerers are more easily led to do this than others. One U.S. Army colonel who testified in the case of General Westmoreland against CBS News offered a particularly good example of someone whose credibility was called into question by his eagerness to testify in a way he thought the questioner wanted. At one point in his testimony, Colonel Gains Hawkins concluded an answer by asking the defense attorney, "Does that (answer) get you where you need to be?"[25] Insofar as any courtroom testimony is obviously influenced by what the witness thinks a questioner wants to hear, it should be discounted. Insofar as similar factors influence people's answers to polling questions, the questioner needs to be especially careful not to influence the results. One of the best ways to overcome this when polls are being administered in person is to present the questions in writing and have the person respond in writing without human feedback.

A further factor that one must bear in mind in considering the mode of contact used in a poll is that people have a tendency to *mislead* pollsters. Not everyone takes the pollster's questions seriously and some people seem to enjoy giving bizarre or misleading answers. Sometimes people do this for mischievous reasons, other times they just do not want to admit publicly to what they are really thinking. This has turned out to be especially true in polls about people's voting intentions in contests in which the candidates are of different races. When Caucasians are polled in contests involving an African American and a Caucasian, generally the African American will do better in polls before the election than in the election itself. It seems as if many Caucasians want to appear racially unbiased by saying they will vote for the African American, but when it is time to vote, they vote for the Caucasian.

In general, there is no mode of contact that will insure both a representative sample and not bias the outcome of a poll. Rather, one must be alert to the possible factors that could influence the results and try as best as one can to counteract the influence of those factors. When you see results of polls, you should be aware of the possible pitfalls, and investigate how they might have influenced the results.

Analysis of Polling Results

We have already noted that in most instances one only polls a sample of the population in order to determine how the whole population thinks about an issue. We have already emphasized the importance of having this sample be representative. In order to determine whether the sample gives reliable information about the whole population, however, one must employ tools of statistical analysis. Statistical tools are widely distrusted. People often claim that "statistics lie" or that "you can prove anything you want to with statistics." This is simply not true. A properly done statistical analysis can be a very reliable source of information. What is true is that people can, and often do, misuse statistics. Thus, it is incumbent upon you to be aware of the major factors determining whether a statistical analysis of polling data is correct. The only way for you to fully understand the proper conduct of statistical analysis is to take a statistics course. We cannot provide such a course here; our goal is simply to provide you an intuitive understanding of what goes into a proper statistical analysis.

---

[25] Quoted in Renata Adler, "Annals of Law: Two Trials—I," *The New Yorker*, 16 June 1986, 91.

The crucial notion in statistical analysis is *statistical significance*. The first thing to note is that when one says that a result is statistically significant one is not saying that the result is important. What one is saying is that it was a result that was not likely to have occurred by chance. Unless otherwise stated, a result is claimed to be statistically significant if there is only a 5% chance that the outcome was due to chance. Properly speaking, such a result is asserted to be statistically significant *(.05)*; if a higher or lower possibility of a result occuring by chance is used, that number will replace the *.05* in the parentheses. Our interest in statistical signficance stems from the fact that if a result is very unlikely to be the result of chance, then it is very likely to reflect a real factor about the population in question, and we call the result statistically significant.

To develop your intuitions about statistical significance, think of the activity of flipping a coin. Even if the coin is "fair" (not predisposed to land more on one side than the other), if you flip it twice you will not necessarily get 1 head and 1 tail. You may get 2 heads or 2 tails. If you flip it 10 times, it becomes less likely, but still possible, that you will get all heads or all tails. However, you would not be surprised to get 6 or 7 heads or 6 or 7 tails. If you flipped the coin 100 times, you would be even less likely to get all heads or all tails, and very unlikely to get fewer than 39 heads or more than 61. In fact, the number of heads would range from 39 to 61 95% of the time when you flipped a fair coin 100 times.

So far we have assumed that we are dealing with a fair coin. Now reverse the situation and assume you do not know whether the coin is fair or biased. To tell, you engage in an exercise of flipping the coin. If you flipped it only 10 times, you would not be able to judge the coin to be biased even if you got 7 (70%) or 8 (80%) heads. But if you flipped it 100 times and got 70 or 80 heads, you would be in a good position to judge it to be biased. Less than 5% of the time when you flip a fair coin would you get a result outside of the range 39 to 61. Hence, with 95% confidence, whenever you get less than 39 or more than 61 heads you could conclude that the coin was biased. Such results are statistically significant.

Now consider what would happen if you flipped it 400 times. In that situation, 95% of the time the percentage of heads would be between 45% and 55%. If you flipped it 1,500 times, 95% of the time the percentage of heads would be between 47% and 53%. There is a clear trend here. The larger the number of flips, the smaller the range of number of heads that a fair coin would produce. With 1,500 flips, a result of 46% heads would provide good indication of a biased coin, but it would not provide such an indication with only 100 or 400 flips. With smaller numbers of flips, such a deviance from 50% could happen by chance.

In terms of coin flipping, then, a result of 46% is a statistically significant indicator of a biased coin if you have flipped a coin 1,500 times, but not a statistically significant indicator if you only flipped the coin 400 times. Let us assume that we are not dealing with a coin, but with a poll on a race between two candidates. For the purposes of our poll, we assume that everyone polled expresses their preference for one of the two candidates and answers the question truthfully. If we polled 100 people, and 55% indicated they would vote for candidate A and 45% indicated they would vote for candidate B, we would not be able to predict with great confidence who would win the election. The reason is that the result is not statistically significant: The result could have happened by chance even if the race were a dead heat or candidate B actually held a slight lead. Another way to think about it is that if we had drawn a different sample of 100 people, we might have gotten a very different result. On the other hand, if we had sampled 100 people, and 35% indicated they would vote for A, and 65% indicated they would vote for B, we would be able to predict with great confidence that B would have the support of the majority. The result would be statistically significant.

If the election were close, and we still wanted to get a reliable indication of who would win, we would need to poll more people. In the previous example, if the result of 45% for A and 55% for B were obtained with a sample size of 1,500 the result would be significant and we could reasonably infer that B was preferred. There is a general principle here: The larger the sample size, the smaller the range in which a result is likely by chance. Therefore, with a larger sample, it is less likely that a difference will be due to chance and more likely that it reflects a real difference.

Notice that we have spoken of the sample size determining whether the result is significant, but we have not referred to the percentage of people being sampled. The reason is that whether a result is statistically significant does not depend on the percentage of people sampled. A sample of 1,500 of a population of 20,000 is just as good as a sample of 1,500 out of a sample of 4 million or of 100 million. (This principle does not apply to small populations in which we might sample close to all of the group. If we poll 7 members of a 10-person committee and 6 favor a motion, we can be confident that a majority support the motion even though our sample is very small.) When you review a poll, then, you want to investigate whether the sample size was large enough that whatever differences show up in the poll are likely to be statistically significant. The range that is not statistically significant is often referred to as the *margin of error*. For most cases (exceptions arise when the distribution is very skewed or is close to one of the ends of the range) Table 11.2 can be used to determine the margin of error for polls.

If a result is outside the margin of error, then it is a statistically significant result, and is very unlikely to be due to the chance distribution of who were selected for the poll. Most responsible polls will indicate a range of error associated with their

TABLE 11.2
Margin of Error for Polls

Sample Size	Margin of Error (%)
100	11
400	5
1,500	3

poll. If not, it is useful to keep the aforementioned numbers in mind and use them to evaluate whether the results of the poll are likely to be statistically significant.

EXPERTS IN SCIENCE AND HUMAN AFFAIRS

As we have seen, we must rely on authorities because we are not in position to evaluate every piece of information for ourselves. Hence, we rely on those who know the field better than we do to tell us what is true. Nowhere is this phenomenon more prevalent than in science. Most of us live in awe of scientists. They are the paragons of people who know. To a great degree, this is due to our education. In science courses we have learned the facts. We have been taught that there is no room for opinion in science; a scientific claim either does or does not accord with the facts. In science courses we learn the body of knowledge that scientists have accumulated.

Whereas it is true that scientists often do have very important information to provide us, our awe of scientists and reverence for them as authorities is sometimes misplaced. Scientists don't just collect facts. They try to make order out of the facts. In doing this, they necessarily go beyond the evidence. They offer hypotheses. To be sure, they hope to show that their hypotheses are well supported by the evidence. But even evidence often rests on hypotheses. Most modern scientific data is produced by instruments, and frequently many hypotheses are embedded in the use of these instruments.

It is not a criticism of scientists to say that they construct and rely on hypotheses. But it is important to note that hypotheses are a form of opinion. Such hypotheses are not just *mere* opinions; they are usually reasoned opinions. But insofar as reasoning goes into the development of these hypotheses, there is a potential for error. The consequence is that scientists are *fallible*. Some of the claims that scientists make will turn out to be wrong.

One of the best ways to appreciate the fallibility of science is to examine its history. We can see how scientists have changed their minds about the truth over the course of history. One of the clearest examples of such a change of view in science comes from what is virtually the oldest science, astronomy. Although it may be difficult to appreciate today, astronomy was extremely important to our ancestors. Early humans learned that it was possible to anticipate the change of seasons based on the location of the planets among the stars. Anticipating the change of seasons was especially important for agriculture, because if crops were planted too late they wouldn't mature before they needed to be harvested, but if they were planted too early they would likely be killed by frost. Observing the location of the planets provided virtually the only way to anticipate when it was appropriate to plant crops. The word *planet* means wandering object, and the planets were observed not to move in the same manner as the stars (often referred to as the *fixed stars,* because they seemed to move together as if they were fixed to a dome). Early astronomers tried to figure out the pattern of motion of the planets and arrived at a reliable scheme. They proposed that the planets moved on orbits

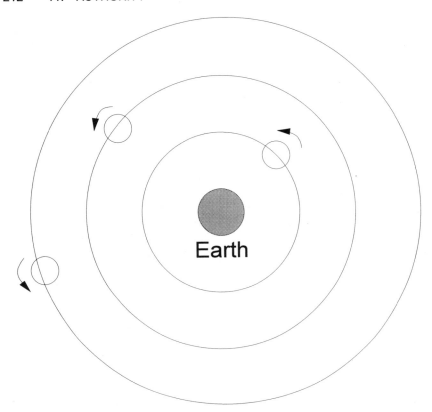

FIG. 11.1.   Ptolemaic system of astronomy. The earth is at the center of the
solar system, with the sun, moon, and planets revolving around it.

around the earth. This alone could not account for the motion, because the planets seemed at times to slow down and even move backward, and at other times to speed up as they moved amongst the fixed stars. So the astronomers proposed that the planets actually moved on circular orbits that themselves revolved around points located on orbits that went around the earth (Fig. 11.1). Using this technique, Ptolemy, a Greek astronomer working in Egypt in the 2nd century AD developed a model of planetary motion that was incredibly accurate. His theory was widely accepted for over a 1,000 years as providing the definitive astronomical theory.

In the late 15th century a scientist named Copernicus advanced an alternative conception of the movement of the planets. He proposed that instead of revolving around the earth, the planets revolve around the sun. Moreover, he construed the earth itself as a planet that revolves around the sun. By now we have all grown up learning Copernicus' astronomy, and it seems very plausible, but at first Copernicus' alternative was greeted with great skepticism. From our perspective it is worth noting how compelling Ptolemaic astronomy was. Not only did it provide quite accurate predictions of the movement of the planets, it seemed a quite plausible theory. Standing on the earth we have no sense of the earth's motion. According to Copernican astronomy, however, the earth is both rotating on its axis and traveling on its orbit at high rates of speed. The idea that the earth is moving at a high rate of speed is very counterintuitive, if not absurd. In fact, it seems easy to prove that the earth is not rotating. Hold an object in your hand and drop it. If the earth were rotating, then the object should not drop to a point directly beneath the point at which it was dropped because the earth would have turned during the object's fall. But the object falls directly beneath the point at which it was dropped. So, reasoned the defenders of Ptolemy, how could the earth be turning on its axis? In the decades after Copernicus, other scientists such as Galileo offered answers to objections such as this (the object being dropped is rotating with the earth and will continue to follow that path while it is dropping), and after a century Copernicus' theory became widely accepted.

The history of science is replete with examples of well-accepted theories coming to be replaced by alternatives. It must be emphasized that the old theories were not just silly superstitions, but powerful explanatory theories. Scientists at the time had compelling evidence for their truth. But later scientists decided they were wrong. Moreover, such dramatic changes are not just part of the ancient past in science. Only a few decades ago, the accepted theory in geology was that continents could rise and fall, but they could not move laterally. Geologists were aware of evidence that seemed to support the idea of continental drift, but the idea was rejected because there was no mechanism that could account for the movement of the continents. Around 1960 a plausible mechanism was put forward, tectonic plate theory, and geologists relatively quickly abandoned their old views and accepted the theory of continental drift. If anything, the rate of repudiation of old theories and replacement with new theories has increased in the past few years with the great increase in resources being devoted to science.

The point that we are making is that scientific theories are fallible: Theories that seem to be well-supported can and often are found to be false. There is every reason to believe that the same is true of current theories. In the future many of them will be found to be false. In the face of this, what attitude should we take toward scientists? Should we dismiss them as authorities and not pay any attention to what they have to say? That would be the recommendation of a view known as *skepticism*. A skeptic holds that unless one can be certain of something, one should just withhold belief. But skepticism is a virtually untenable position. If we ceased to rely on any of the results of science, we would soon be dead. To put the matter in perspective, we should recognize that those apparently well-supported theories of the past often provided very useful information and could be very reliable guides to action. Even today, if you study navigation you will use Ptolemaic astronomy. Why would you use a theory we know to be false? Because for the purposes of navigation it gives very reliable results and it is a much easier theory to employ than those astronomical theories that have replaced it. Similarly, even though Einstein's theories of motion have superseded Newton's, Newton's theories are sufficiently accurate at the low velocities humans are able to travel that even in space travel we use them rather than Einstein's.

In addition to recognizing that even well-supported scientific theories some-times turn out to be wrong, it is also important to realize that in many domains of science scientists disagree with each other. This disagreement is often concealed from students because textbooks cover basic areas in which, except during major upheavals of the sort described earlier, there is little disagreement. It therefore appears as if the body of scientific knowledge is established truth that everyone agrees on. But if this were the case, there would be little motivation to be a scientist. People do not go into a career in science because they want to pass on known truths. Rather, they go into science to make *discoveries*. Sometimes what scientists discover is actually a new *thing*: a new astronomical body that no one has identified before, or a new drug that no one has manufactured before. But just as often what is discovered are ideas, ideas about the laws or mechanisms that are operative in the natural world. These ideas are often referred to as *hypotheses*. When a new hypothesis is put forward, generally we cannot immediately be certain whether it is true or false. Scientists wouldn't put forward an hypothesis if they did not think it might be true. Typically, before publishing the hypothesis, the scientists will have accumulated evidence that points toward its truth. But it is important to realize that these new hypotheses are at first proposals. They have the same status as *informed opinion*.

When new hypotheses are presented, the relevant scientific community gener-ally does not simply accept them. Frequently there will be other scientists who have other ideas, other hypotheses that they are developing. Consequently, there will be a clash between scientists as they try to amass evidence and develop arguments to show that their hypothesis is the correct one. (We see how logic figures in these arguments in the next chapter.) As time passes, generally the evidence and argu-mentation on behalf of one position will become so convincing that the relevant community of scientists accepts this view and repudiates the others. Once this has happened, it is reasonable for those outside of the scientific community to accept the hypothesis as true and the scientists espousing it as authorities. This should, of course, always be done with recognition of the fallible nature of science and the possibility that the community will later change its mind. But for those who do not have the ability to conduct their own investigations, this is about as good an authority as we can have.

But we should be particularly careful with regard to those issues on which the relevant scientific community has not reached consensus. When there is active disagreement within the scientific community, this is often a sign that there are good arguments for different hypotheses. Unless we are ourselves masters of scientific inquiry, at this point we cannot conclude that one of these is true. It will not help to cite scientists who take one stand as an authority, and then accept the position they are espousing. These people may turn out to be right, but may also turn out to be wrong. What we are pointing to here is the importance of the relevant scientific community in deciding to accept scientists as authorities. The relevant scientific community will consist of those scientists who have adequate training and research experience to assess the nature of the evidence for various hypotheses. Frequently there will be a professional association representing the scientists working in a particular field of inquiry (such as the American Society for Cell Biology) and one or more journals in which scientists publish their findings (such as the *Journal of Cell Biology*). Those people who hold a PhD in the field, belong to such a society, and publish in the appropriate journals constitute the relevant scientific community. One must be careful not to assume that a paper published in a scientific journal such as the *Journal of Cell Biology* is necessarily authoritative. Even though the paper has been reviewed by other scientists in the field prior to publication, that doesn't mean the other scientists agree with its claims. It only means they find the paper sufficiently important for it to be made public. As outsiders to the field, we need to know not just whether a scientist has argued a position in a responsible journal, but whether others have accepted the position. We can tell this has happened only when other scientists begin to cite the paper in question approvingly and when the results of the paper are incorporated into textbooks. We expect individual scientists to pursue their own hypotheses; we expect the community of scientists to tell us which of those hypotheses should be believed.

We have stressed two points in our discussion of scientists as authorities. First, science is fallible. We cannot take the views of scientists as providing us with certain knowledge of the truth, but only with the most reasonable assessment possible at a time as to what is true. Second, at any given time there will be many questions on which scientists disagree. With regard to these questions, it is irresponsible to pick one scientist as an authority and simply cite what that person says as the truth. Rather, we must wait until the relevant community of scientists has reached its verdict. Then, and only then, can we rely on the hypothesis as reasonably likely to be true.

. So far we have focused on scientists, but many of the same principles extend to other domains of human affairs in which there are communities of experts. There are domains such as economics, law, ethics, literature, and the arts in which there are communities of experts. These are people who have devoted their education to mastering the field and have spent their lives working on the issues of the field. In evaluating the authority of people in these fields, we need to apply the same principles as we do with scientists. The one notable difference is that on topics in these fields there seems to be much less agreement and more controversy than in the sciences. Thus, the experts are divided on such topics as the consequences of tax cuts, the morality of abortion, the legality of the death penalty, or the definition of pornography. When we find authorities in disagreement, it does not help our argument simply to cite an authority on the side we favor. That does not build the case. It is appropriate for us to turn to the authorities to see what their arguments are. If we find their arguments convincing and want to employ them ourselves, we should cite those who originally made the argument so as to give them credit. But we should not assume that the fact that one authority took the position for which we are arguing will help to show that that position is correct.

There are, however, topics within these areas on which the authorities have reached consensus. Here we can apply the same principle as with scientists: If the experts on the subject agree, then it is reasonable to accept their position as true.

There are some prominent examples in which authorities in areas of human affairs have now reached agreement. For example, after World War II, it became an accepted principle of international law that being ordered to do something is not a sufficient defense for a soldier who commits an immoral act. In other words, it is now accepted that a soldier who is ordered to do something immoral must refuse the order. Similarly, it is now recognized that physicians and other health care workers have a moral obligation to gain informed consent from their patients before treating them. Moreover, this informed consent must be voluntary. Therefore, it is now recognized to be ethically immoral for a medical researcher to perform an experiment on someone who is not informed as to the nature of the experimental procedure and is not given the option not to participate. Finally, within fields of art and literature there is considerable consensus on identifying some of the major artists and writers of a particular genre. In these areas in which the experts agree, it is reasonable to accept the authority of the experts.

12

The Logic of Explanation

One of the distinctive features of human beings is that we seek explanations for phenomena. If there is a car accident, we want to know what caused it. If we discover that a substance often causes ill effects in humans who consume it, we want to know why it does so. When a mysterious event happens, people will often offer many suggestions as to what caused the event. Sometimes they have good evidence for their explanation, other times they are simply offering hunches. In fact, many times people become very committed to explanations that are little more than speculations. Something turns up missing from their garage, and they conclude that their neighbor, of whom they have always been suspicious, must have done it. Even in the face of contrary evidence, people hold to their pet explanations. Fortunately, logic can provide a useful tool when we want to know whether an explanation is true. Alone it cannot answer all of our questions about explanations, but it can guide us into more careful use of evidence and ultimately to settling on better explanations.

Many times a request for an explanation is a request for a cause. We want to know what factor or factors differentiated the case in which some effect happened from cases in which it failed to happen. Sometimes we can make good inferences as to the cause simply from the pattern of outcomes. In the first part of this chapter we examine the ways in which you can use logic to do this. However, to gain more confidence in assessments of causes, we often need to conduct an experiment. As we shall see later in this chapter, a very similar logic is employed in experimental situations. The quest for explanations often leads scientists to seek models, laws, or theories that characterize the general operation of parts of the natural world. Although we cannot go into detail into the process of finding and evaluating scientific models, laws, and theories, in the last part of this chapter we show how a very similar logic underlies the evaluation of putative laws and theories. Recognizing this will allow you to become a more cautious consumer of scientific claims.

FINDING CAUSES

There are many contexts in which we are interested in determining the cause of an event. Consider what you might do if the following happened to you. One evening you give a party. Approximately 25 people attend the party, at which various beverages are served. The food served includes sliced fresh vegetables, potato chips, pretzels, a cheese ball, blarney cheese, emmenthaler cheese, brie cheese, onion dip, clam dip, and lobster dip. One of the guests, David, leaves the party around 11 p.m., saying that he isn't "feeling quite well." By midnight, everyone else has left. At 8 a.m. the next day your phone rings, with the news that one of your guests, Robert, is ill. The symptoms described include vomiting, a fever, and stomach pains. An hour later another guest, Linda, calls, saying that she's experiencing vomiting, a fever, and stomach pains. At 9:30, Mark, another guest, calls saying that he's feeling the same symptoms. You become suspicious, and begin inquiring as to the health of your other guests. By noon you discover that two other guests, James and Milton, have also taken ill with the same symptoms. Suspecting that the illness has something to do with your party, you begin to wonder what it was at the party that might have poisoned your guests.

In this scenario we see one situation in which you may be led to search for causes. You want to know whether it is something that you served that caused several people to become ill. You are concerned because you realize that in some way you might be *responsible* for what has happened. Very often that is why we try to determine causes. Responsibility, and its conceptual cousins, praise or blame, attach to the people who cause things to happen (or not to happen), and so we are often interested, in both legal and nonlegal situations, in finding out who or what caused the event in question to occur.

But you might be searching for the cause simply because you want to know. Your guests were your friends, after all, and you're not afraid of being sued or accused or being held to blame. You might just be interested in finding out what caused the unfortunate events. The desire to know about causes is surely a large part of humankind's general desire to know—to know simply for the sake of knowing, and for no other reason. What caused Achilles to sulk? What caused the Spaniards to lose the battle? What caused the disappearance of the Anasazi Indians? What caused Beethoven's deafness? These are all questions to which answers are sought chiefly for the sake of knowledge itself.

A final reason for asking what caused something is to try to gain some control over what happened. "Should I ever give a party again," you may be thinking, "how can I avoid a repeat of this culinary disaster?" We often want to prevent undesirable events from recurring, and we often want to be able to repeat desirable ones. We wonder what caused our daylilies to bloom so profusely this year, in hopes that whatever it was is in our control and we can cause them to bloom so well again next year. The desire to repeat past events or to prevent them from recurring is perhaps the principal force behind science, and so the seeking of causes is one of the scientist's chief aims. But, as we have seen, causes are also of interest to lawyers, judges, historians, and anyone interested in knowledge for its own sake.

Having considered the reasons, we might be interested in knowing the cause of an event. Let us consider what is meant in calling an event, C, the cause of another event, E, the effect. We start with the simplest case, one in which one event is taken to be the cause of another event (e.g., the eating of one food is taken to be the cause of the illness of the various people at the party). More complex situations are possible (e.g., it was eating a combination of two foods that made people sick, or some people were made sick by one food, others by another), but we overlook these for now. Taking just the simple case, there has been enormous discussion over the past 300 years as to what is meant by saying C causes E, and our goal is not to resolve that long controversy. Instead we focus on what are generally accepted aspects of the analysis of causation. When you, or a scientist, or a judge, ask about what the cause of something is, the following are common threads: You are seeking an event that happened prior to the event you are trying to explain, which, had it not happened (and everything else had stayed the same), the event itself would not have happened. A further component of a cause is that it be something that, if it had happened in cases in which the effect was not brought about, it would have led to the occurrence of that effect. That is, the search for a cause is a search for

1. another event, C,
2. that is prior to E, the event to be explained,
3. which is such that if C had not occurred, E would not have occurred, all other things being equal, and
4. such that if C had occurred in other similar situations, E would have occurred.

The first two conditions are fairly obvious, but are clearly not sufficient to make C the cause of E. One of the events that happened prior to the reunification of Germany in 1990 was the U.S. moonwalk in 1969, but no one thinks that the U.S. moonwalk was the cause of the reunification of Germany. What is crucial in making a prior event the cause of something else are Conditions 3 and 4. These are meant to establish the relation between C and E. Condition 3 claims that C was necessary for E (had C not occurred, E would not have occurred), whereas 4 claims that C is sufficient for E (had C occurred in cases where it did not, E would have been brought about). (If you do not remember the technical construal of the terms *necessary* and *sufficient*, review the discussion in chapter 3.)

Before we proceed, we should make clear that Conditions 1–4 are not redundant. Take the sickness resulting from your party. If we ask, what event prior to the sickness is such that if it had not occurred, the sickness would not have occurred, then there is literally no end of answers that can be given. If the guests had not received an invitation, then they would not have come to the party, and they would not have taken ill. Likewise, if they had not been born, then they would not have come to the party, and would not have taken ill. And if their parents, and their grandparents, and so on, had not been born, then they would not have come to the party, and would not have taken ill. So there are many events in the world that satisfy Conditions 1 through 3. But when we ask what caused the guests to take ill, we won't count most of these events as answers. Robert's receiving an invitation is not going to be counted as a cause of his having taken ill at the party, although his receiving an invitation is (1) an event that was (2) prior to his having taken ill, and (3) if he had not received an invitation, he could not have taken ill at the party.

What condition 4 requires us to do is identify, among the candidates that meet Conditions 1–3, those that, when they occur, are themselves not sufficient to bring about the effect. Granted that if Robert had not received an invitation, he would not have gotten sick at the party, it still is the case that receiving the invitation was not followed, in most cases, by people getting sick. Elsa and Richard and Jerry, for example, all received invitations, and all attended the party, but they didn't get sick. So what we need to do is to remove invitation getting from the list of possible causes. What Condition 4 requires us to do is seek factors that, when added to conditions that might prevail elsewhere, produce the effect in situations in which the effect would not otherwise occur.

As we shall see, Conditions 3 and 4 are the basis for the logical arguments we use in identifying causes. We turn now to three different tactics that are useful in identifying causes.

The Method of Difference

Let us develop the party scenario a bit. You are on the phone with one of the people who got sick, Alex. Because you did not get sick, you begin to review what each of you ate at the party. You assume that anything both of you ate did not cause the illness because you did not get sick. And of course anything both of you did not eat could not have caused the illness because Alex did not eat it but still got sick. So you look for differences in what you ate. Your comparison might lead you to develop Table 12.1 (where No and Yes indicate that the food was not or was eaten, and in the case of the effect, whether sickness occurred).

There is only one difference in what Alex and you ate. *If* it was true that the cause of the illness lay in the foods they ate (a very big "if"), then it appears that the cause of Alex's illness must be the clam dip. This is the only difference between his case and yours. Because there is only one difference in cause, and a difference in effect, the additional factor in Alex's case seems like a likely candidate for causing the illness.

Although this one comparison leads you to focus on the clam dip, it is hardly sufficient to be certain that it is the clam dip. Alex's memory might be faulty, and there might be other things he ate that you did not. Furthermore, the assumption that it was one of the foods eaten at the party that caused the illness might be faulty. Finally, the actual culprit might have been something you in fact ate, but you might have immunity to the disease agent that was in that food. What you might do at this point is to contact other individuals to determine whether a similar pattern can be found in them. Thus, you might develop Table 12.2 for two others, Erik and Alice.

As the comparison between you and Alex, Erik's and Alice's cases are identical, with two exceptions: One became ill and the other didn't, and one ate the clam dip and the other didn't. Again, the clam dip appears to be suspicious. The case against it is beginning to mount.

TABLE 12.1
Matrix for Method of Difference

Possible Causes

	Fresh Vegetables	Potato Chips	Pretzels	Cheese Ball	Blarney Cheese	Emmenthaler	Brie Cheese	Onion Dip	Clam Dip	Lobster Dip	*Effect*
You	no	yes	yes	yes	no	yes	no	yes	no	no	no
Alex	no	yes	yes	yes	no	yes	no	yes	yes	no	yes

TABLE 12.2
Matrix for Method of Difference

Possible Causes

	Fresh Vegetables	Potato Chips	Pretzels	Cheese Ball	Blarney Cheese	Emmenthaler	Brie Cheese	Onion Dip	Clam Dip	Lobster Dip	*Effect*
Erik	yes	no	no	no	yes	no	yes	no	yes	no	yes
Alice	yes	no	no	no	yes	no	yes	no	no	no	no

The method whereby these results were obtained is called the *method of difference*. It is called this because it suggests that whenever two causal situations differ in only one detail, and the presence of that possible cause is matched with the presence of the effect, and the absence with the absence of the effect, then the detail that alone makes the two situations differ is very likely to be the cause. Rarely do real-life causal situations present data as neat as those in Tables 12.1 and 12.2. When they do, however, the method of difference can be used to help determine the cause.

Let us take a careful examination of the logic underlying this method. Consider again Conditions 3 and 4 we established earlier. For C to be the cause, it must be the case that:

3. If C had not occurred, E would not have occurred, all other things being equal, and
4. If C had occurred in other similar situations, E would have occurred.

One thing to note about these conditionals is that the antecedent proposes something that did not occur. Hence, we speak of these conditionals as *contrary to fact conditionals*. We cannot ever find situations that will show us that these conditionals are, in fact, true or false. But if the only difference between Alex and you is that he ate the clam dip and you did not, then you have reason to think that *if you had eaten the clam dip, you would have gotten sick* and *if Alex had not eaten the clam dip, he would not have gotten sick.*

We have this confidence because we are assuming the following two conditionals:

> If the clam dip were the cause, then if what Alex ate and I ate differed only in the clam dip, he would have gotten sick but I wouldn't.
> If the clam dip were not the cause, then if what Alex ate and I ate differed only in the clam dip, either we would both have gotten sick or neither would.

Depending on the outcome, we now have two possible modus tollens arguments we can make. If, as we assumed in Table 12.1, Alex got sick and you didn't, you can reason using the second of the aforementioned premises (why can't you use the first?):

> If the clam dip were not the cause, then if what Alex ate and I ate differed only in the clam dip, either we would both have gotten sick or neither would.
> What Alex and I ate differed only in the clam dip and it is not the case that either we both got sick or neither did.
> ∴ The clam dip is the cause of the illness.

(This is a somewhat more complex form than we have used previously, but it is rather easy to see that it is a version of modus tollens. The consequent of the conditional in the first premise is itself a conditional. A conditional is false whenever its antecedent is true and its consequent false. That is precisely what the second premise asserts. Hence, the second premise denies the consequent of the main conditional in the first premise.) Had it turned out that neither of you got sick (or that both of you got sick), you would have eliminated the clam dip using the following argument:

> If the clam dip were the cause, then if what Alex ate and I ate differed only in the clam dip, he would have gotten sick but I wouldn't.
> What Alex and I ate differed only in the clam dip and it is not the case that he got sick but I didn't.
> ∴ The clam dip is not the cause of the illness.***

An argument that something is not a cause is always subject to an important qualification. One thing may in fact be the cause of something else, and not clearly manifest itself. The previous argument is valid, but the first premise must always be accepted only in a very guarded fashion. Something could be the cause of an effect, but a difference not be observed because of intervening factors. For example, someone might have eaten the clam dip and not have gotten sick because they had built up immunity. If this were the case, then the first premise would not be true, and the argument would not be sound. A similar qualification applies to all arguments in this chapter that purport to show that one thing is not the cause of another. All of these conclusions might better be qualified as "X has not been demonstrated to be the cause of Y." To emphasize this, we put three asterisks by all of these conclusions.

There are numerous weaknesses in the method of difference. First, it requires you to be able to match cases perfectly, but rarely in real life do we find such perfect pairings as we showed earlier. Second, you must be absolutely certain that the possible causes you list are the only possible causes. Adding another possible cause is likely to introduce another difference. When this happens, the method of difference cannot be used to detect the cause, because it depends on there being only one difference present. In a situation in which more than one difference exists, all you can say is that one or more of the differences is likely to be the cause of the event. Third, with small numbers, we cannot have much confidence in the result. The reason has to do with the plausibility of the first premise. Particularly in the case of the argument claiming the clam dip is the cause, the premise is only somewhat likely to be true. Even if the clam dip were not the cause and you and Alex ate only the same foods, there are numerous other things that could cause Alex to get sick but not you. For example, he may have eaten something for lunch that you didn't, or he may have come into contact with someone carrying a virus. If 10 other party-goers were just like Alex and you in having eaten the three dips, and the 6 of them who ate clam dip, say, were the same as those who got sick, whereas the 4 who didn't did not get sick, then the premise for the argument would be much stronger, and hence the argument would support a stronger conclusion than the one outlined in Table 12.1. Such a situation, however, is even rarer still in real life. Rarely do 10 people wind up having eaten exactly the same things at a party except for one thing, and in general it is exceptional to find a large number of people differing in one respect only.

This does not mean that the method of difference is not useful, but it does mean that its usefulness is limited. Generally, it is useful as a means of identifying possible candidates for further examination, but not sufficiently strong to give us great confidence that the identified candidate really is the cause. We turn now to a method that is more generally useful because it does not require that the individuals being compared turn out identical in all characteristics except for the possible cause.

The Methods of Direct and Inverse Agreement

Even when no two people perfectly match, there are ways of identifying potential causes. If you were particularly diligent, you might have collected data on all of the people attending the party who got sick, determining each food that they had tried. On the basis of this, you might have generated Table 12.3.

Table 12.3 points us to two possible causes of the illness: the onion dip and the clam dip. It is important to see why it does so. It does so by eliminating eight of the possible causes. Recall that Condition 3 stated if C had not occurred, E would not have occurred, all other things being equal. From this condition we can infer the following conditional premise:

> If C were the cause of E, then it would be present in all cases in which the effect occurred.

The fact that eight of the possible causes were not present in all of the cases in which the effect occurred allows us to argue by modus tollens that each of these is not the cause. Using the fresh vegetables as one example, the argument would appear as follows:

> If the fresh vegetables were the cause of the illness, then they would have been eaten by all of the people who got sick.
> The fresh vegetables were not eaten by all of the people who got sick.
> ∴ The fresh vegetables were not the cause of the illness.***

The name for this first matrix derives from that given to it by its "discoverer," the 19th-century philosopher, logician, and economist, John Stuart Mill. It is called the *method of direct agreement*. One way to remember this name is to realize that the columns you are interested in locating when you use this method are those that *directly agree* with the results listed in the effect column.

The direct method of agreement only allows us to determine that Condition 3 seems to be satisfied by two candidates: the clam dip and the lobster dip. As we

TABLE 12.3
Matrix for Direct Method of Agreement

| | Possible Causes | | | | | | | | | | |
	Fresh Vegetables	Potato Chips	Pretzels	Cheese Ball	Blarney Cheese	Emmenthaler	Brie Cheese	Onion Dip	Clam Dip	Lobster Dip	Effect
David	yes	no	no	yes	yes	no	no	yes	yes	no	yes
Robert	no	yes	no	no	no	no	yes	yes	yes	no	yes
Linda	no	no	no	no	yes	no	yes	yes	yes	yes	yes
Mark	no	yes	no	no	no	no	no	yes	yes	yes	yes
James	no	yes	no	yes	yes	no	no	yes	yes	yes	yes
Milton	yes	yes	no	yes	no	no	yes	yes	yes	no	yes

TABLE 12.4
Matrix for the Inverse Method of Agreement

| | Possible Causes | | | | | | | | | | |
	Fresh Vegetables	Potato Chips	Pretzels	Cheese Ball	Blarney Cheese	Emmenthaler	Brie Cheese	Onion Dip	Clam Dip	Lobster Dip	Effect
You	yes	no	no	no	yes	yes	no	yes	no	yes	no
Alice	no	yes	yes	yes	no	yes	no	no	no	yes	no
Ralph	yes	no	yes	no	no	yes	no	yes	no	yes	no
Nick	yes	yes	yes	yes	yes	no	no	yes	no	yes	no
Omar	no	yes	yes	yes	yes	no	yes	yes	no	yes	no
Cynthia	no	yes	yes	yes	no	yes	no	yes	no	yes	no

noted earlier, this is not sufficient to determine that either of these dips was the cause of the illness. Accepting the invitation to the party, being born, and innumerable other factors would have sufficed to pass this condition. So we need also to check on Condition 4. To do this, we need to construct another matrix, this time considering those individuals who did not get sick. This may also help us to eliminate one of the two dips that are still candidate causes. If anyone who did not get sick ate one of these dips, then it can be eliminated as a cause, because it was not sufficient to bring about the effect in similar conditions (that is, it failed Condition 4). To find out whether any of the possible causes were not followed by the effect, you need to interview some of the people who did *not* get sick, to find out what they ate. Suppose that such an investigation were to produce Table 12.4.

When we examine Table 12.4, we are looking for instances in which the food was eaten. Any food that at least one of the people listed in Table 12.4 did eat can be eliminated, because that person did not get sick. Hence, the food was not sufficient to produce the illness. This matrix reveals that the fresh vegetables were eaten by you, Ralph, and Nick. Yet none of you got sick. Therefore you can eliminate the vegetables (once again) as causes. Similarly, the other foods that were eliminated in the first matrix are eliminated here as well. As for the two that were not eliminated in the first matrix, and that therefore remained as possible causes, the onion dip was eaten by several of the people who did not get sick. Therefore it too can be eliminated as a possible cause. Because the clam dip was not eaten by anyone who did not get sick, it remains as the only possible cause of the sickness.

Let us consider once again the logic of this inference. Recall that Condition 4 stated that if C had occurred in other similar situations, E would have occurred. From this we can infer the premise:

> If C were the cause of E, then C would not be present in cases in which the effect did not occur.

The fact that nine of the foods were eaten by people who did not get sick allows us to use modus tollens to show that they are not the cause. Using the case of the onion dip, which was still a candidate cause after we used the direct method of agreement, we generate the following argument for eliminating it:

> If the onion dip was the cause of the illness, then the onion dip would not have been eaten by any of the people who did not develop the illness.
> The onion dip was eaten by people who did not develop the illness.
> ∴ The onion dip was not the cause of the illness.***

We call this second method the *method of inverse agreement*. It too displays the agreement of possible causes with the effect, but we call it the inverse method because we are now looking at cases in which the effect *did not occur*.

In this case, by using Tables 12.3 and 12.4, we have been able to isolate a likely cause for the illness at the party. We should stress that the direct method of agreement and the inverse method of agreement must be used together. Alone, each only accomplishes part of the task. We have already shown that for the direct method of agreement, but a similar consideration will show why the inverse method of agreement is not alone sufficient. With the inverse method of agreement, we are looking for factors that were not present in cases in which the effect fails to appear. Consider some other things that might not have been present in the cases of the people who did not get sick. It may be the case that none of them was born in Alaska or that none of them owned a Toyota car. In this case, none of these factors could have been eliminated by the method of inverse agreement. In general, therefore, these two methods should be used together, and we should speak of the methods of direct and inverse agreement as one means to establishing causes.

It is important to realize that not all uses of the methods of direct and inverse agreement will yield equally strong results. Consequently, the conclusions you reach in using these methods will be of various "strengths." Sometimes you can conclude only that something is "possibly" the cause of something else, other times that it is "quite likely" that one thing is the cause of another. The reason for this is that the methods of direct and inverse agreement can only rule out possible causes. You began by listing all the possible causes you could think of across the top row, and all the occurrences down the far left column. From there you tried to eliminate possible causes until, if you are lucky, only one remained. Thus, you are implicitly reasoning using an alternative syllogism:

> Either the fresh vegetables or the potato chips or. . .or the clam dip or the lobster dip was the cause of the illness.
> The fresh vegetables were not the cause.
> The potato chips were not the cause.
> .
> .
> .
> The lobster dip was not the cause.
> ∴ The clam dip was the cause.

As we have learned, however, for this argument to be sound, the first premise must be true. You must have listed all of the causes. Unfortunately, this is seldom something you can be sure that you have done. The strength of your argument is only as strong as the likelihood that you have included all of the causes and that only one factor was the cause.

Whereas we can never be certain of the truth of the alternative premise, in some cases the premise will have more plausibility than in others. Suppose that in our original example only three people had taken ill after the party. In this case, the method of direct agreement would only have listed three occurrences. Suppose also that these three people consumed only one food in common, say the clam dip. In this case the conclusion that the clam dip was the cause of their illness would have to be hedged quite severely, because it is possible that they have some other factor in common that doesn't relate to the party. Perhaps each of them, without knowing it, ate at the same restaurant before coming to the party, or they shopped at the same grocery, and bought (and ate) the same brand of cottage cheese. Either of these factors could be the real cause of their illness, and the clam dip only a coincidence. Obviously, as the number of people involved grows, the chances that they all shared another unknown common factor will decrease. And because the problem here arises because eating at the same restaurant and shopping at the same grocery were not listed among the possible causes, the possibility of not listing the real cause will decrease the larger the number of possible causes you begin with. In general, then, the larger the number of occurrences and possible causes that have been taken into account, the stronger the conclusion that is warranted when using these methods, and vice versa. Because no matter how large the number of occurrences, it is always conceivable (although sometimes only barely) that there could be a common factor that could be causing the effect other than the one that the methods of agreement point to, these methods never license one to infer that A is necessarily the cause of B. They do, however, allow one to infer from among the list of conclusions ranging from "There is some possibility that A is the cause of B" to "It is extremely likely that A is the cause of B."

The Method of Concomitant Variation

So far we have considered cases of causes and effects that either do or do not occur. Sometimes, however, events can occur in degrees. For example, the temperature in a room can vary over a wide range, the distance a baseball is hit varies, and the length of time it takes a student to do an assignment in a course varies. When one is dealing with an effect that appears at different times in different degrees, a powerful technique is to seek as a cause a factor that varies proportionately with the effect. For example, if you notice that the light in a given room is sometimes brighter and sometimes darker, and you notice that the setting on a rheostat in the room seems to vary with the degree of light, then the inference that the setting of

TABLE 12.5
Matrix for Method of Concomitant Variation

| | | | | Possible Necessary and Sufficient Causes | | | | |
	A	B	C	D	E	F	G	Effect
1	0	0	2	1	1	4	1	1
2	0	2	0	5	1	1	2	2
3	5	1	0	0	1	3	3	3
4	0	0	0	2	1	2	4	4
5	3	0	1	0	1	5	5	5
6	5	0	3	0	0	0	0	0
7	0	4	1	2	0	0	0	0
8	5	0	0	3	0	0	0	0
9	0	3	2	0	0	0	0	0
10	1	4	0	1	0	0	0	0

a

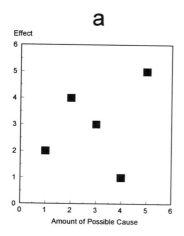

b

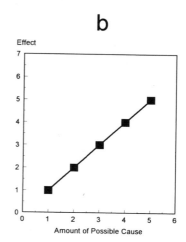

FIG. 12.1.   (a) Graph of relation between Possible Cause F and effect, which shows no correlation. (b) Graph of relation of Possible Cause G and effect, which shows high correlation.

the rheostat is causing the amount of light in the room is a reasonable hypothesis. When you do so, you are using the *method of concomitant variation.*

The method of concomitant variation is actually a generalization of the methods of direct and inverse agreement. As when we employed those methods, we set up Table 12.5 (here we combine the two tables used in the methods of direct and inverse agreement by including in one table both the cases in which the effect occurred and those in which it did not). To see how the method of concomitant variation is used, consider Table 12.5 in which the numbers in each row indicate the degree to which the possible cause or the effect identified at the top of each column is present.

If we only considered the presence or absence of an effect, and used the methods of direct and inverse agreement, E, F, and G would all be candidate causes. But the method of concomitant variation allows us to choose between these. Notice that only one of the these three possible causes seems to vary in some regular way with the effect. The amount of E remains the same in each of the first five occurrences, even though the effect varies in amount. The amounts of Possible Causes F and G both vary with the amount of the effect, but only G varies with the amount of the effect in any regular way. This points to G as the most likely cause.

Concomitant variation does not require that there be a perfect numerical correspondence between the degree of the cause and the degree of the effect. What is required is that there be a detectable regularity in the relationship. One of the best ways of determining whether there is such a relationship is to graph the relationship. In Fig. 12.1 the amount of the potential cause is graphed on the *x*-axis and the corresponding value for the effect is plotted against the y-axis. The left-hand graph shows the relationship between Possible Cause F and the effect, and the right-hand plot shows the relationship between Possible Cause G and the effect. The fact that the points on the left-hand graph are scattered whereas those on the right-hand graph lie on a line indicates that a causal relationship may exist between G and the effect, but is unlikely to exist between F and the effect. In this case all of the points lie on the line, and the line is a straight line with a slope of 1.

However, this is not the only possible regular relationship. The relation could remain linear (which means that one can draw a straight line between the points) and yet the slope could be considerably different from 1. Figures 12.2a and 12.2b show such different linear relations. The relations need not be linear, however, for there to be a causal relation. The relationship could also fit various curves, such as those shown in Figs. 12.2c and 12.2d. Finally, it is often the case that there is some "noise" in the relationship. That is, the points might lie close to the curve, but show some scatter, as in Fig. 12.2e. All of the relations plotted in Fig. 12.2, however, fit the criterion for concomitant variation and may be indicative of a causal relation.

One further point should be taken into account when considering the values of causes and effect. Many phenomena in nature exhibit what are known as *threshold effects*. Threshold effects exist whenever a certain range of values for a cause fails to change the value of the effect, but higher or lower ranges do. For example, if

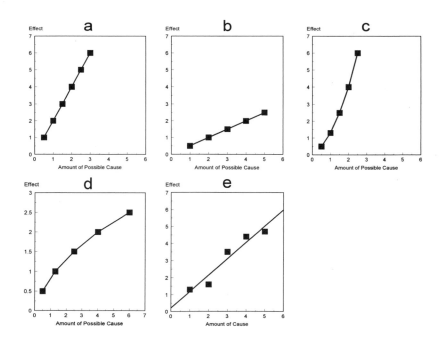

FIG. 12.2.   Graphs of regular relationships for concomitant variation.

you were plotting the causal relation between the amount of pain relief in a person and the amount of aspirin, you might well expect that for very small quantities that differ from each other only minutely, there will be no noticeable effect. A typical tablet of aspirin contains about 5 grains of analgesic. But the difference between 1, 2, 3, 4, and 5 milligrains will be insignificant, when measured against the amount of pain relief, because one will be detectable at such low levels. It is only when a certain threshold is reached that you can even begin to detect any pain relief, and then it is likely to vary regularly with the amount of aspirin administered. On the other end of the scale, however, there would probably be no difference in effect between 50,000, 60,000, and 70,000 grains, because the patient would be either comatose or dead. Arsenic is a good example of a drug with exactly this kind of tendency. At low levels, it is used to treat various medical problems, but at higher levels it is deadly. Threshold effects must always be watched out for when using the method of concomitant variation, because the lack of any variation in the cause may only be a result of your observing the cause below a threshold level. Noting the values for the cause at a different level may reveal a ratio between a varying cause and a varying effect.

As with the method of difference and the methods of direct and inverse agreement, using concomitant variation in arguments to establish causation requires setting up appropriate premises. The arguments will have very much the same form as before. If, as in the case of F, you know that the possible cause did not vary concomitantly with the effect, then you will use the following form to argue against F being the cause:

> If F were the cause of the effect, then it would vary concomitantly with the effect.
> F does not vary concomitantly with the effect.
> ∴ F was not the cause of the effect.***

On the other hand, if concomitant variation is found for G when it would be surprising for it to occur if G were not the cause, then you will use this form:

> If G were not the cause of the effect, then it would not vary concomitantly with the effect.
> G does vary concomitantly with the effect.
> ∴ G is the cause of the effect.

Some Limitations of These Methods of Finding Causes

In discussing these three methods we noted some potential weaknesses with each. Overall, the main weakness is that in each case we relied on a conditional premise that, although somewhat plausible, was far from certain. Thus, at best the methods provided us more or less reason to suspect that something was in fact the cause. We need to keep this qualification clearly in focus when using these methods in finding causes. As we discuss later, experimental methods provide us a way of further increasing our confidence that one factor really is the cause of another, but even then we will have to hedge our conclusion. However, there are some other limitations of these methods that we now note.

First, in order to use any of the methods, you have to identify all the possible causes. These are the factors that we list across the top row of our various tables. But the methods themselves offer absolutely no help in selecting the possible causes of an effect. Your success in guessing at possible causes will depend on the background knowledge and experience you bring to the analysis. In the party case you were relying on the background information that if several people get sick at a party it was probably due to something they ate at the party, not things like the heating system in the home where the party was held or the flowers planted outside the front door. If you have no idea of what the possible cause or causes of an event are, and cannot even guess what some might be, the methods are useless. But even when you can suggest some possible causes, there may still be problems. Four problems in particular are worth discussing: the problems of common cause, no cause, too many causes, and false cause.

The problem of *common cause* occurs when the methods lead you to conclude that Event A (e.g., vision problems) is the cause of Effect B (e.g., a migraine headache), but in fact both A and B are the effects of some other cause. Suppose you notice that the rise in stock prices last year was followed by an increase in the amount of sales in your business. Wondering whether the first is a cause of the second in general, you check back for several years and find that usually a rise in stock prices is followed by an increase in retail sales, and a failure of retail sales to increase is preceded by a failure of stock prices to rise. Although this fits the patterns of the methods of direct and inverse agreement, it may be that both the rise in stock prices and increase in sales are due to a further factor. You should look for a common factor that may have caused both events to occur before you conclude that the first event was the likely cause of the second. In this case, it may be that a decrease in the prime lending rate accounted for both the increase in stock prices and in retail sales.

A second difficulty that can arise in using the methods we have discussed is that of *no cause*. Despite your best efforts to list all possible causes, it may be that no factor among those listed occurs each time the effect does. In this situation, there are two ways out of the difficulty: look for a further cause, or eliminate one or more of the occurrences. The first solution is the most obvious. Your failure to find a cause may just be a result of the fact that these methods do not tell you where to look for possible causes. Perhaps asking someone who is more experienced in the area you are studying will suggest more possible causes, and perhaps one of these will appear every time the effect does, but not when the effect doesn't. The second solution to the difficulty may appear at first sight to be a form of cheating. Many elementary chemistry students are familiar with a procedure they can use when their experiment produces, say, too much of a compound for the weights of the constituent elements—throw the excess down the sink until you reach the right amount of the compound you were supposed to be producing. Eliminating one or more of the occurrences from your matrix may sound very much like doing this, and it *is* a form of cheating, unless you have some independent reason for doing so. Sometimes, however, a case that seems at first to be like others is actually different and has a different cause. In such instances, that case should be ignored. Suppose that in Table 12.3 Milton did not have the clam dip, yet he became ill. Because excluding him from the matrix would lead you to conclude that the clam dip was quite likely the cause of the illness suffered by the guests, you would do well to investigate his case a little more closely. It would be cheating just to overlook his case, but if you could find something different about his case, then you would have grounds for treating him separately. Suppose that after investigation you talk to his wife, who remembers that he is allergic to brie cheese and always gets ill when he eats it. This will allow you to eliminate him from the matrix, and thus to conclude that the clam dip was the likely cause. Notice, however, that it is only because you have an *independent* reason for eliminating him from the list that this is a legitimate solution to the problem of no cause.

The opposite of the difficulty of no cause occurs when the methods leave us with *too many causes*. When you had finished using Table 12.3, you were left with two possible causes of the illnesses: the clam dip or the onion dip. To eliminate one of them, you then used the method of inverse agreement, which showed that the onion dip could not be a sufficient cause of the illnesses. Suppose, however, that after using the method of inverse agreement, you still had two possible causes. In that case, there are three ways of responding to the difficulty. You can either (a) claim that one or both is the cause, without saying which, (b) search for a common cause, or (c) eliminate a possible cause. The first solution is the easiest, and often the most honest, but usually the least satisfying. You simply state what the matrices show: that one or both of the possible causes are the real cause or causes, but that you don't know which. Medical diagnoses commonly end this way, with the doctor being able to rule out several possible causes as the real ones, but unable to decide which of two or more remaining possible causes are the real one or ones. The second option is to try to find a common cause of the two (or more) causes. Whereas earlier you saw the problem that results from failing to recognize a common cause, and jumping to a causal conclusion too soon, now a common cause may be a *solution* to the problem. In this case you may discover that both dips were made from the same contaminated sour cream. In this case the sour cream becomes the cause of the illness. The last way of solving the problem is to eliminate a possible cause, and there are two ways of doing this. One can continue to search for more occurrences, in hopes of finding another one such that one of the causes still remaining does not occur when the effect occurs, thereby eliminating that cause as a real one, or one can search for independent reasons to eliminate one of the causes altogether. Again, medical diagnosis is an area where this often occurs. After investigating the matter with the methods of agreement, one is left with giardia and *e. coli* as the possible causes of the gastrointestinal distress presented by the patient. Further checking reveals however that the patient originally contracted the illness in Georgia, and that giardia is seldom a problem south of the Mason-Dixon line. This leaves *e. coli* as the likely cause. Again, the warning to be followed when using this method of resolving the problem of too many causes is that you must have *independent reasons* for rejecting one of the causes as possible. Otherwise you can be accused of doctoring the evidence to fit the conclusion.

The last problem, that of *false cause,* arises when something does satisfy the conditions set forth in our methods, but when it is not in fact the cause. An old story that logicians like to tell helps to illustrate this: It seems a man was trying to find the cause of his headache and sickness that occurred each morning. He listed what he had consumed the night before in the following way: Monday—scotch and water, Tuesday—bourbon and water, Wednesday—gin and water, Thursday—vodka and water, Friday—brandy and water. Using the methods of direct and inverse agreement, he concluded that water was the cause of his illness. His mistake lies of course in not recognizing the other common factor—alcohol—in all his drinks. Here again the problem lies in the way in which the possible causes were identified. By differentiating the causes too finely (in this case, by type of alcohol, rather than as alcoholic beverages), the true cause was missed. What this shows is the importance of judicious use of background knowledge when using the methods we have outlined.

Contributory Causes

In our discussion so far we have assumed that one factor was *the cause* of an effect, that it occurred in all instances in which the effect occurred, and was always followed by the effect. That is, we assumed that the cause was necessary and sufficient to bring about the effect. In real life, however, causal factors seldom work this way. A factor may increase the likelihood of the effect occurring, but neither be present in all cases in which the effect occurs, nor sufficient in itself to produce the effect. A very prominent example is smoking. When people say smoking causes lung cancer, they neither intend to say that all cases of lung cancer originate with smoking, nor that smoking always results in lung cancer. It is well known that people develop lung cancer who have never smoked, and that some smokers never develop lung cancer. When it is said that smoking causes lung cancer, therefore, what is being claimed is that smoking increases one's risk for developing lung cancer. In other words, when we compare those who smoke with those who are otherwise similar who do not smoke, we find a higher incidence of lung cancer among those who smoke.

When people in ordinary life worry about causes, they are often worried about contributory causes. When people are concerned about unprotected promiscuous sex as a cause for AIDS, they are not concerned about whether it is necessary and sufficient for developing AIDS, but only that engaging in unprotected promiscuous sex is likely to raise one's chances of getting AIDS. It need not even raise the risk to a high number for the cause to be important to us. It is certainly not the case that even half of the time that people engage in unprotected promiscuous sex that they develop AIDS. An incidence rate of 1% or 5% would be sufficiently high to make unprotected promiscuous sex an important causal factor in contracting AIDS, one that most people would want to know about. The same holds for a variety of other causes: drunk driving as a cause of traffic accidents, careless use of fireplaces as a cause of house fires, and so on.

Unfortunately, without modification the methods we have developed so far will not work to identify contributory causes. If we tried to use the method of direct and inverse agreement to find a common factor among people who developed lung cancer that was absent in those who did not, we would discover that smoking turned up only occasionally among those who developed lung cancer, and would not be absent in all of those who did not develop lung cancer. But it is worth noting a principle underlying all of the methods we used, for this will enable us to generalize the methods to cases of contributory causes. In all of the cases we considered, what was important was that the occurrence of the cause was *correlated* with the occurrence of the effect. In fact, with necessary and sufficient causes, the correlation was perfect (1.0) because every time the cause happened, the effect followed, and every instance of the effect was preceded by the cause. However, correlations of less than 1.0 can be informative of contributory causes.

How high a correlation is needed is a bit challenging to determine. To determine whether the correlation between Event 1 and Event 2 is sufficiently high to conclude that Event 1 is a contributory case of Event 2 requires use of statistical measures, and you would need to take a course in statistics to learn how to make such judgments with precision. However, the basic idea is relatively straightforward. Let us imagine that a certain effect (severe body rust on a car after 5 years) occurs with a frequency of 10% in the general population. We then consider the frequency of body rust on cars painted with a certain brand of paint. Looking at a sample of say 100 such cars, we discover that the frequency of severe body rust after 5 years is 60%. Looking at another sample of 100 similar cars (this qualification is discussed later) painted with another brand of paint, we discover that the incidence of severe body rust was only 8%. There is a major difference in the frequency of severe body rust between the cars painted with the two brands of paint. Severe rusting appears to be highly correlated with being painted with a certain brand of paint. Provided that the paint is the major factor that differs between the two groups of cars (an important qualification), we can infer that the brand of paint was likely to be a contributory cause for the body rust on the cars.

In the case we just considered, we considered 100 cars painted with the paint in question, and another 100 painted with another paint. In order to determine whether the difference in frequency of rusting can be attributed to the paint, we need to know whether the difference is one that could happen by chance. Some difference in frequency of rusting would be expected by chance. If 11% of the cars painted with one brand of paint rusted, against 8% for those painted with another brand, and we only looked at 100 cars of each brand, that result could have happened by chance. On the other hand, a difference between 60% and 8% is not likely to occur by chance.

The crucial idea here is that the difference in frequency of the effect between two groups must be statistically significant for us to conclude that what differentiated the two groups is causally responsible for the differences in frequency of effects. A statistically significant difference is one that is very unlikely to have occurred by chance. (Usually we accept a correlation as showing cause if the potential for that difference to occur by chance was less than 5%. In such cases we would say that the difference was significant at the .05 level. In other cases we might demand an even lower potential for the result to have happened by chance.) As we learned in the previous chapter, when we considered the reliability of polling data, whether a result is statistically significant depends on the sample size that was considered. With a larger sample size, a smaller difference in frequencies will be statistically significant. (With a sample size of 5,000, the difference between an 11% and an 8% frequency in an effect will be statistically significant.) Although you will need to take a course in statistics to be able to determine whether a result is statistically significant, you should be aware of the following principles and employ them in your evaluation of causal reasoning:

1. If a difference between two populations is said to be statistically significant, then it is unlikely to have been produced by chance.
2. With a small sample size it takes a large difference to be statistically significant; with a larger sample, smaller differences may be statistically significant.
3. Even if a difference is said to be statistically significant, it need not be important.

The last point is to remind us that some causal factors are not important enough to worry about. There are various things that we do in our lives that expose us to radiation (walk outside, fly in airplanes, walk near television sets). This radiation may be a causal factor for some kinds of cancer, but unless we do these things frequently enough, they will not raise our risk of cancer sufficiently for us to worry about them. Hence, although they are causes of cancer, they are not important causes.

When we set up the examination of the two groups of cars mentioned earlier, we noted as a qualification that the two groups of cars had to be otherwise similar. The reason for this is that if there were differences between the two groups, these differences could account for the different outcomes in the two groups. For example, if the group showing severe body rust after 5 years were from climates in which there is extensive ice and snow, and heavy use of salt to clear roads, whereas the group not showing rust were from warm dry climates in which salt was not used, then we would not be able to determine whether the rust was from the paint, the climate and salt, or a combination of these factors. Thus, it is important to compare groups that are as similar as possible except for the potential causal factor.

Let us consider now the logic of the arguments that are used in determining whether or not something is a contributory cause. As in previous cases, we start with two premises:

If X is a contributory cause for Y, then the frequency of Y in the population
    in which X is present will be statistically significantly higher than in the
    population in which X is not present.
If X is not a contributory cause for Y, then the frequency of Y in the
    population in which X is present will not be statistically significantly
    higher than in the population in which X is not present.

If you set up your comparison carefully, these conditionals will be true. There are
at least two things you must attend to so as to insure the plausibility of these
conditionals. First, you must insure that X is the only factor that varies significantly
between the two populations. Second, you must make sure the two populations are
large enough that it is likely that statistically significant results will emerge. You
will determine how large a population you must use by the size of the effect you
expect to find. If the effect is expected to be large (e.g., a drug is expected to produce
hair growth in 50% of bald men), then you can use relatively small populations and
still have true premises. If the effect is expected to be small (e.g., a drug is expected
to reduce the rate of incidence of a disease that is already rare), then the populations
will have to be large. (When the Salk vaccine was tested for polio, it was recognized
that the number of incidents of polio was already small, on the order of a few per
thousand. Cutting this in half, however, would be a major accomplishment. To
detect an effect of this small size, however, required a sample population of over
1 million subjects.)

If these conditions are met, then the conditional premises will likely be true.
Then, depending on the outcome, you can use the appropriate premise to argue that
X was or was not the contributory cause of Y by modus tollens. For example, in
the rust example, we would end up with the following argument:

If brand A paint is not the contributory cause of extensive rust after 5 years,
    then the frequency of extensive rust will not be statistically significantly
    higher among cars painted with brand A than those painted with another
    brand.
The frequency of extensive rust is statistically significantly higher among
    cars painted with brand A than those painted with another brand.
∴ Brand A paint is the contributory cause of extensive rust after 5 years.

If no statistically significant difference were found, the other premise would have
been invoked to argue (again, by modus tollens) that brand A was *not* the contributory cause of the extensive rust. (As we noted earlier, this conclusion would have
to be qualified so as to state that brand A had not been demonstrated to be the cause
of the extensive rust.)

What we have done in arguing for contributory causes is to relax the considerations used in the methods considered earlier so as to require only a correlation
between the cause and effect. You may have heard in the course of your studies
that correlation is not the same as causation. This is indeed true. Two things can be

correlated without either one of them being the cause of the other. One of the frequent reasons for things to be correlated without being causally linked is that both are in fact the result of a *common cause*. Thus, just as with the methods for determining necessary and sufficient causes, we must always question whether the correlation observed might be the result of a common cause. Another frequent reason factors may be correlated without being causally linked is that the factor on which we are focusing may itself be correlated with the true cause without them being causally linked (much as the water was correlated with the various alcoholic beverages in our previous example). We need also to recognize that the other limitations we noted also carry over to cases in which we are trying to find a contributory cause. Namely, our investigation may reveal *no cause* or *too many causes*. For example, our attempts to correlate an effect with a cause may reveal no statistically significant correlations. This may be because we have failed to identify the true cause, or because we may have clustered together effects that have very different causal origins. Another reason for failure to find a cause that we have already noted is that we may have used too small of a population for the effect to show up. On the other hand, we may end up with too many causes: Too many different factors might be correlated with the effect. Here, as in our previous discussion, this may be due to a common factor underlying our different causes. Sometimes, however, finding multiple causes is appropriate. Because the causes we are considering are only contributory, not necessary and sufficient, it is possible for several factors to all contribute to the effect, and hence for all of them to correlate with the effect.

INVESTIGATING CAUSES EXPERIMENTALLY

In addition to the limitations already noted, the methods we have examined so far can only be employed when we confront multiple examples of the same effect (e.g., when many people get sick at the same party). In such instances they provide us useful clues as to what might be the cause of the effect in question. But in many situations, we don't have such luxury. If you got sick one day and had go to the health center for treatment, you would not be pleased to be informed "We must wait until some others show up with the same symptoms so we can use the methods of direct and inverse agreement to determine the cause of your ailment." You expect the health workers to find out what is wrong with you and to do so now.

Sometimes in such cases health care workers already have a good deal of information about what is likely to cause symptoms such as those you are exhibiting. This information may be based in part on previous uses of the methods of direct and inverse agreement or statistical measures to detect contributory causes. That is, when people in the past presented with symptoms such as you are exhibiting, researchers sought a common factor that was present in all of those who exhibited the particular set of symptoms, and not found in those who do not manifest the symptoms. If so, they may then be in a position to respond to your symptoms by identifying a potential cause.

Sometimes, however, the effects in which people are interested are new effects or ones that have not been noted before. In these instances, there aren't any comparison cases. One must figure out from the individual case what is causing the effect. To take a related kind of example, imagine that your car begins to make a screeching noise even while idling. You take it to a trusted mechanic who gives you the bad news "Gee, I have never seen this before. Let me do some poking around." What the mechanic is likely to do is open the hood, listen first to see the source of the noise can be determined, and then start to "tinker." That is, the mechanic will begin to adjust different components (change the tension on the belts, etc.) to see if the noise can be stopped. If one of the manipulations the mechanic makes solves the problem, you will be told that the problem is solved. If you asked what the problem was, the mechanic will identify the part just manipulated, thereby stopping the noise.

Your mechanic will be exhibiting a very common kind of reasoning that is used in identifying causes. The mechanic will change one thing (adjust a belt, replace a part), and see if that solves the problem. If not, the mechanic will decide that this was not the cause of the problem. The reasoning will go like this:

> If the problem was that the fan belt was too loose, then tightening the fan belt should solve the problem.
> Tightening the fan belt did not solve the problem.
> ∴ The problem was not that the fan belt was too loose.***

When at last the mechanic changes something that solves the problem, the mechanic will also use a logical argument to conclude what the cause had been. However, the mechanic cannot start with the same premise as in the previous argument, because that cannot produce a valid argument:

> If the problem was that the speedometer cable needed lubrication, then lubricating the speedometer cable should solve the problem.
> Lubricating the speedometer cable did solve the problem.
> ∴ The problem was that the speedometer cable needed lubrication.

This argument, unfortunately, has the form affirming the consequent. Rather, one must develop a different argument:

> If the problem was not that the speedometer cable needed lubrication, then lubricating the speedometer cable should not solve the problem.
> Lubricating the speedometer cable did solve the problem.
> ∴ The problem was that the speedometer cable needed lubrication.

Detecting a cause through such experimental manipulation, therefore, depends on the truth of the following two conditional premises:

If X was the cause of Y, then changing X will bring about a change in Y.
If X was not the cause of Y, then changing X will not bring about a change
  in Y.

One generally needs some background knowledge to determine whether these
principles are true. For example, one needs to know how much tightening of the
fan belt would be sufficient to stop the noise if the problem was that the fan belt
was too loose. One could tighten it, but not enough, or one could tighten it, but too
much. In this case, the fan belt still would be the problem, and we wouldn't know
it. Thus, even when a mechanic is just "poking around," typically a great deal of
knowledge is guiding this search. What is of interest to us, however, is the strategy
of reasoning that is involved. Even if the mechanic did not present them explicitly,
the reasoning employed two modus tollens arguments, one of which was used to
rule out factors that were not the cause, and one of which was used to identify the
cause. We see further use of these two argument structures in what follows.

   This example provides us an introduction to the experimental investigation of
causes. What makes an experimental investigation different from the methods we
introduced in the first part of this chapter is that in experimental investigation one
is explicitly making changes in order to determine whether something is the cause.
This is important because, if we are careful to introduce only one change at a time
(this is a very important qualification) and by means of it are able to effect another
change, then we can be confident that the factor we have changed is indeed a cause
of the effect we have produced. (Note we said *a cause*. This qualification is needed
since there may be different factors that could produce the effect. To determine
whether the factor we altered experimentally was indeed the causal factor in a
natural situation requires further inquiry. We might, for example, discover in the
laboratory that a particular chemical produces dandruff in humans, but it might be
a different factor than the one that is at work in people who develop dandruff in the
real world.)

   Generally one conducts an experiment by altering what one thinks might be a
causal factor in an individual and determining what effect is produced. One of the
most crucial factors in setting up an experimental investigation is to insure that the
factor we are altering (usually called the *independent variable*, because it is a factor
we are able to alter independently) is the only factor that is varied. It is for this
reason that it is important to employ a *control*. This involves working with two
entities (or the same entity at different times), changing the putative cause in only
one of them, and seeing whether the effect occurs only in that situation. It is partly
for this reason (and partly because they are often dealing with contributory causes,
not necessary and sufficient causes) that scientists tend to work with populations
and not single cases of experimental subjects and controls. The logic underlying
the use of populations is that if changing the independent variable in several
individuals produced the effect (also known as the *dependent variable*, because it
is thought to depend on the independent variable) in all of them, whereas the effect
never occurred in the controls, then the alteration in the independent variable is
likely to be the only common factor that differentiates the experimental group from

the control group. To insure that the independent variable is the only factor that changed between the experimental and control groups, one must verify that the two groups that one starts with are as similar as possible. A common technique is to start with one population, and randomly assign members of it to the control and experimental populations.

The strategy that is used in an experiment can be seen by taking a case of a new drug (call it *Alpha*) that is thought by the manufacturer to be a cure for the dermatitis brought on by exposure to poison ivy. To set up this experiment, the experimenter will need first to decide who to experiment on. Laboratory animals could be used—rats, say—but then the results would have to be extrapolated to the case of humans. Because the skin of humans is known to be quite different from that of animals, this extrapolation will be difficult to carry out, so the experimenter may well decide to use human subjects. (Generally, however, before a substance is administered to humans, it will be administered to animals to test whether there appear to be any harmful consequences of taking the substance.) The experimenter could use paid volunteer subjects, but this might be quite expensive to carry out using a large number of subjects, because being exposed to the poison with no guarantee of a quick cure would cause the fee paid to the subjects to be high. So perhaps the easiest method to use would be to select subjects who have already contracted the dermatitis, and have come to a doctor for treatment. This will bias the study to some degree, because the subjects presenting themselves for treatment will probably be suffering from fairly acute cases. But if Alpha cures severe cases, then there will be time perhaps in the future to study its effects on milder cases. (Before any such experiment would be carried out on humans, various procedures would have to be followed to insure that the experiment did not violate ethical norms. For example, the subjects would have to be informed as to the nature of the experiment, and would have to elect to participate in the experiment voluntarily. Typically, committees at hospitals and universities, known as *institutional review boards*, review any experimental protocol using humans or animals before an experiment can proceed.)

The study must have some limits as to the number of patients studied (it cannot examine every poison ivy patient in the world, and furthermore it is not necessary to do so), so the patients examined will constitute what is called a *sample population*. Out of this sample population, two classes of patients will be selected. One half of the group will constitute the experimental group and will be administered Alpha; and the other half will constitute the control group and will not receive Alpha. Receiving or not receiving Alpha will thus constitute the independent variable in our experiment. (The control group will likely be given what is considered at the time the *standard* treatment for poison ivy, but for our purposes we assume that they will receive no treatment.) Both groups will be told not to take any other medicine for their dermatitis than what is administered in the experiment, or any other related drugs (such as cortisones).

If, in this experiment, the control group does not improve and the experimental group does, or the experimental group improves more rapidly or to a greater degree than the control group, then it becomes reasonable to infer that Alpha was the cause of the cure in the experimental group. The reasoning depends on the following two premises:

> If Alpha is not a successful treatment for poison ivy, then it should not be the case that a significantly larger percentage of those in the experimental group should improve than in the control group.
> If Alpha is a successful treatment for poison ivy, then a significantly larger percentage of those in the experimental group should improve than in the control group.

The main reason for believing these premises to be true is that the subjects have been assigned to the two groups randomly. Thus receiving or not receiving Alpha should be the only factor that differentiates the two groups. Provided we choose an adequate size group on which to experiment, give an adequate dose of the drug, and wait a sufficient period for the drug to show its efficacy (all crucial assumptions), if the drug is effective, it should generate a statistically significant difference between the two groups.

Depending on whether there turned out to be a significant difference between the experimental group and the control group, the experimenter would use either the first conditional (when there is a difference between the two groups) or the second conditional (when there is no difference) to reason by modus tollens to the appropriate conclusion. In the case we just considered, in which there was a difference between the two populations, the argument would look like this:

> If Alpha is not a successful treatment for poison ivy, then it should not be the case that a significantly larger percentage of those in the experimental group should improve than of those in the control group.
> A significantly larger percentage of those in the experimental group improved than of those in the control group.
> ∴ Alpha is a successful treatment for poison ivy.

If the results had turned out negative, then the other premise would have been used to argue that Alpha was not a successful treatment for poison ivy.

To fully appreciate the complexities of designing good scientific experiments you would need to take a course in research methodology. However, in completing this discussion of experimentally determining causes, there are some considerations that we should emphasize. These are factors you should attend to whenever you are presented with the results of an experiment and want to know whether the causal claim based on the experiment is justified.

First, it is necessary that the independent variable you have tested is the only difference between the experimental and control groups. If other factors also differentiate between the experimental and control groups, they can *confound* the result. One cannot be sure whether the result is due to the independent variable, or one of these confounding factors. For example, if the experimental group were to wash the site of poison ivy-induced dermatitis more frequently than the control group, that could introduce what is called a confound. This might happen if Alpha were a cream, and the directions for use required the person to wash the site of dermatitis prior to administration. One way to control for this would be to require the control group to also put on a cream that is similar to the experimental cream except lacking the active drug. Then both groups would employ the same procedure and avoid a confound. An additional potential confound is simply the knowledge that one is in the experimental rather than the control group. This can result in what is known as the *placebo effect*. A placebo is a medically inert substance, such as a sugar pill, that is administered to a patient. Often, simply thinking that they are being treated for their medical problem will cause the patients to be cured, even though no medicine is administered. For this reason, it is important that patients be "blind" as to whether they are receiving the real medicine or the placebo. Moreover, the mere knowledge of who is in the experimental and control group can influence how the experimenter judges a subject's outcome. For example, the experimenter may be inclined to see greater improvement in the dermatitis in the experimental group than in the control group. Thus, it is also important that at the time of treatment the experimenter be "blind" as to whether the real drug is being used. Thus in experimenting with human subjects, it is always important to construct *double-blind experiments*, in which neither the experimenter nor the subject knows whether the real substance or a placebo is being administered. In experiments with animals it is often not important whether the animal knows, but it is still important that the experimenter not know. These are called *single-blind experiments*. In all of these cases, the goal is to remove any factor that can differentiate the experimental and control group other than the independent variable.

Second, as we have already noted, it will almost always be necessary to rely on the statistically significant differences in the dependent variable in the experimental and control populations. If our sample size is large enough to insure that all effects are due to the manipulation of the independent variable, it will hardly ever be the case that *all* members of the control group fail to experience the effect that is being tested, and that *all* members of the experimental group experience the effect. Nature seldom presents itself to the experimenter in such neat ways, and it is very likely that the experiment has been "rigged" if such results do ever occur. (One famous study linking IQ with race was first called into question just because the results were too "neat." As it turned out, most of the data were entirely fictitious.) Earlier in the chapter we stressed some of the important features of the notion of statistical significance. In particular, we emphasized that with small populations, only very large effects will be statistically significant. To detect small effects we must use relatively large samples so that the differences between the experimental and control populations will have a chance to be statistically significant. One thing to be on careful guard for in experiments claiming that a factor is not a cause of an effect is whether a large enough sample was used. Sometimes with a small sample one may discover a difference in the dependent variable between the experimental and control population, but not a difference that is statistically significant. In such cases one should not conclude that there is no causal relation, but rather that *if there is a causal relation, it is too small to show up with this size experiment*. The proper response at this point is to repeat the experiment on a larger population to see if that produces statistically significant results.

Finally, it is necessary to insure that the sample population is representative of the whole population. Because the experimenters are trying to generalize about the effects of the new drug on *anyone*, they need to be certain that the experimental group is not unusual. For example, it might be that the poison exuded by the poison ivy plants in the area where the experiment is being conducted is less virulent than that exuded by poison ivy plants in other parts of the country or the world. In that case, all the experiment would show is that the new drug was highly effective against poison ivy in that part of the country, and not that it was highly effective against poison ivy generally. Detecting bias relative to sample populations is not always an easy or obvious matter, but it is one for which an experimenter always needs to be on guard.

TESTING LAWS, MODELS, AND THEORIES

So far in this chapter we have focused on finding causes. That is indeed one of the major ways we as humans have to explain phenomena. Moreover, it is extremely useful: Once we have identified causes, we can often alter outcomes by changing these causes. If we learn that a particular paint causes cars to rust extensively after 5 years, we can use a different brand of paint until the formula of the first brand is changed. If we learn that a drug is useful in overcoming the dermatitis of poison ivy, we can use that drug if we develop poison ivy. But sometimes scientists seek more than simple knowledge of causes. They seek the basic laws of nature: regularities that apply widely in nature. Knowing these gives even more power because we can apply such knowledge in the many varied contexts in which it is pertinent. Such general principles that identify regularities are known as scientific laws.

Two examples of such scientific laws are found in the work of Isaac Newton. One of these laws (the force law) establishes that the force an object exerts on another equals the mass of an object times its acceleration:

$$F = ma$$

Another of these laws (the law of universal gravitation) establishes the attractive force between two bodies. It holds that any two bodies attract each other with a force that is proportional to the product of their masses divided by the square of the distance between them:

$$F = (m_1 \times m_2)/r^2$$

In this brief discussion we are not able to enter into the process by which Newton discovered these basic laws. We do want to indicate, however, the sort of process by which Newton and others could evaluate them. What is crucial to evaluating such laws is to be able to make predictions from them. What we want to know is what we should expect to happen in the universe if a law were true. Newton himself applied these laws to a wide range of phenomena, both terrestrial and astronomical. To illustrate Newton's reasoning, we use an astronomical case. Prior to Newton's research, Kepler had determined with great precision the orbits of the various planets. Contrary to most expectations at the time, Kepler showed that these orbits were elliptical, not circular. Rather than being at the center of the orbits, Kepler showed that the Sun was at one of the foci of the orbits. What Newton did was to show that such elliptical orbits are what one should expect from his law of universal gravitation. That is, he provided a logical derivation from his law to Kepler's orbits. In a sense, what Newton did was predict, using his law of universal gravitation, the orbits that Kepler had discovered. It is the truth of such predictions that allow us to judge the truth of laws.

The logic of using predictions to evaluate laws follows much the same pattern as we have already seen with causes. We start with two conditional relations:

> If the putative law were not approximately true, then we would not expect this prediction to be true.
>
> If the putative law were approximately true, then we would expect this prediction to be true.

In order for the outcome of a prediction to provide us useful information about a law, it is necessary for both of these conditionals to be true. That is, we need to make a prediction that would accord with our putative law, and we would not make otherwise. In Newton's own case, it might appear as if the first conditional is not satisfied. Because Kepler had already worked out the orbits of the planets, these are the orbits we would predict regardless of Newton's law of universal gravitation. But there is a sense in which the conditional is true. Prior to Newton's work, no one had any idea as to why Kepler's orbits were correct. They had been empirically verified, but there was no *explanation* of them. Hence, at the time it was surprising to find a law that could predict them. So, in an attenuated sense, Newton was able to gain support for his law of universal gravitation given that it led him to predict the very orbits of the planets that Kepler had discovered. In this case his reasoning went as follows:

> If the law of universal gravitation is not approximately true, then the planets should not have the orbits Kepler discovered.
>
> The planets do have the orbits Kepler discovered.
> _____
> ∴ The law of universal gravitation is approximately true.

The evidence from Kepler's orbits was *contaminated* by the fact that these orbits were already known, and Newton might have used this information in developing his laws. This would contaminate the result because it would then seem that the laws were designed just to explain known data, and it is often thought that this is less impressive than offering new predictions based on putative laws and having them turn out to be true. In Newton's case, however, many such predictions were also possible, and most of them have turned out to be true. Just to take one example, shortly after Newton published his result, an astronomer named Edmond Halley applied Newton's law to a comet he had discovered. He showed that the comet should be traveling on an orbit that would bring it close to earth every 75 years. He therefore calculated back from the time he saw the comet in 1682 and "predicted" that there should have been a comet observed regularly every 75 years. Investigating astronomical records he ascertained that this prediction was true. Because without Newton's laws it would not have seemed likely that comets would have appeared on the schedule Halley developed, he already seemed to have an impressive confirmation of Newton's theory. But he also made a prediction into the future: He predicted the return of the comet in December 1758. This was indeed a risky prediction because, without Newton's law, there was no reason to predict such a comet. Hence, the following two conditionals were true:

> If Newton's law of universal gravitation was not approximately true, then there should be no comet appearing in December 1758.
>
> If Newton's law of universal gravitation was approximately true, then a comet should appear in December 1758.

By 1758 Halley was dead, but the comet he had found appeared right on schedule. The following argument was very compelling:

> If Newton's law of universal gravitation was not approximately true, then there should be no comet appearing in December 1758.
> A comet did appear in December 1758.
> ∴ Newton's law of universal gravitation was approximately true.

The comet became known as Halley's Comet and Halley's correct prediction provided one of the main sources of evidence as to the correctness of Newton's theory.

As we have indicated with demonstrations of causal claims, there is a great deal more to be mastered in order to develop good demonstrations of scientific laws. But the general strategy underlying the demonstration of scientific laws, theories, and models is clear. The task the scientist faces is to predict results based on the law, theory, or model that would not be predicted otherwise. Then, if the prediction fails, modus tollens can be used to show that the law, theory, or model is false. But if the prediction turns out to be correct, we can also use modus tollens, but with an alternative first premise, to show that the law, theory, or model is approximately true. When investigating reports of scientific claims, you should pay special attention to determining whether the two conditions we have identified are met. In particular, make sure that the following condition is satisfied:

> If the law were not approximately true, then the prediction would not turn out to be true.

If it is not, then there is no way that the experimental investigation can offer logical support for the law.

13

Arguing from Analogy

One of the tasks to which we made reference in the previous chapter, but for which we provided little guidance, was *proposing* an explanation. The logical arguments we developed there were useful primarily in selecting between possible causal factors or in showing that proposed explanations were or were not satisfactory. Before these techniques are useful, however, one must come up with possible explanations. One of the most useful tools for doing so is *analogy*. In analogy one compares one entity or group of entities with others and argues that as a result of the similarities the new item or group exhibits with these other items, the item of interest will also behave like them in a certain, but previously unknown, respect. This chapter explores the logic of this reasoning.

DEMONSTRATING SIMILARITIES

The ability to develop and use analogies rests on the ability to identify similarities between objects. Comparing (and contrasting) objects and events is something that we all do every day of our lives, often without realizing it. Our everyday language is filled with *similes* and *metaphors*, which compare one object to another. The finish on a grand piano is as smooth as satin. The road was as crooked as a dog's hind leg, and driving on it was like riding a rollercoaster. Poems and songs are especially abundant with such figures of speech. His love is like a red, red rose, says the poet, and some children promise to be a sunbeam for Jesus. A hymn even compares life in general to a railroad:

> Life is like a mountain railroad, with an engineer that's brave
> We must make the run successful, from the cradle to the grave
> Watch the curves, the fills, the tunnels; never falter never quail;
> Keep your hand upon the throttle, and your eye upon the rail.

The ability and the need to find similarities between and among different objects is apparently a universal one among humans. Even the person who has little use for poetry is apt, on occasion, to say that a certain brand of beer tastes like mud, or that a certain car engine sounded like a washing machine, or that it's all downhill once a certain point in a day's events has been reached. The universality of comparison is also reflected in the most basic forms of our language. Without the ability to compare, we would not be able to use any class words, such as *tree*, *table*, *piano*, or *car*. The very ability to have the concept of *tree* requires that we see various objects—an elm, a cedar, a beech, and a sycamore, for instance—as being similar. If we did not see a sycamore and a cedar as more like each other than a sycamore and a Chevrolet, we would not be able to discriminate between trees and cars.

Imagine a language for people who did not have the ability to compare different objects, and you'll see how basic this ability is to us, and how requisite to our language it is. People who could not compare objects would have a language in which all the nouns were proper nouns. Unable to see a particular elm as similar to a pine, they could not use the word *tree*, which in our language is used to refer to different but similar kinds of objects. Nor, for that matter, could they even use our word *pine*, for this word implies that there are some similarities between two different trees (no two pine trees are ever *exactly* the same) that warrant calling them both pines. Instead of saying, "Please pass the butter," they would have to say something like "Please pass me Fred," where *Fred* denoted the particular stick of butter in front of them. At the next meal, they would have to say "Please pass me Alice" when they wanted some more butter, because to say *butter* would mean they had been able to detect some similarities between two sticks of butter. In short, the inability to detect similarities would make their ways of conceiving and talking about the world radically different from ours.

An important logical lesson follows: As basic as *comparison* is, it is no more basic, and indeed goes hand in glove (speaking of the inevitability of metaphor!) with the ability to *contrast*. No two objects are ever exactly the same. If they were, we would not have two objects, but only one. Even two brand new chairs, straight off the production line, are not exactly the same. One had to come off the production line before the other, and this fact about its history makes it different from the other. When the two chairs are placed in a room, one of them must be in a different position in space from the other. Without this difference, they would occupy the same space, and we would then not be able to distinguish them. This principle—that no two things are ever exactly the same—means that when we notice the relevant similarities between two objects and classify them as oaks, at the same time we discount some differences. The fact that one is 52 feet tall, and the other only 28, or that one is to the left of the other, or that one has a name carved in its bark, we regard as irrelevant to their being oaks. For other purposes, of course, those differences might play an important role. The difference between a tall and a short oak might make quite a difference in which we harvest now and we allow to stand. So although there *are* differences between any two objects, it is important that for certain purposes we be able to overlook them.

Having noted that no two things are completely alike (and noting also that no two things are totally different), we can draw our first crucial lesson: When claiming that things are similar, it is necessary to specify the respects in which they are similar. It is not sufficient to claim "Items A and B are similar." You are similar to the moon in weighing more than 10 lbs, in being in the vicinity of the earth, and in containing carbon, but these similarities are not generally speaking important or notable ones.

Our second crucial lesson is closely related: In comparing items, what we focus on are features or characteristics that the items share. We also want to note characteristics on which the items differ. In identifying these characteristics, however, we must have some focus. If we just started listing characteristics on which two items were similar or different, we could quickly end up with a very long and varied list. When comparing people, for example, the list might start as follows: height, weight, eye color, grades on calculus exams, knowledge of German, knowledge of Greek, knowledge of Mandarin, grade school attended, number of different teachers during first grade, age of first kiss, speed in the 100 yd dash, size of ankle, and so on. A likely reaction when reviewing the previous list of items is: "Come on, why are we interested in size of ankle? That's not relevant!" What this comment reveals is that in comparing two or more items in terms of their features or characteristics, we must have some criteria for determining *relevance* of characteristics. This indicates that we always develop a comparison for a purpose.

Let us imagine that you want to compare two cities. What might be your purpose for doing this? It might be that you are interested in taking a trip or it might be that you are thinking about moving there. But these are not the only purposes you might be considering. You might be writing a novel, and considering a place to set the plot. Or you might be looking for a place to test market a product. Each of these purposes is likely to make different features relevant to your comparison. If you are considering moving to a place, then the cost of living and the availability of housing might be particularly relevant. If you are only considering a visit, then these are much less relevant, and you might be far more interested in the cultural events occurring in the city and the cost of hotel rooms. If, on the other hand, you were not going to the city at all, but considering it as a place to situate the plot of your novel, you might be far more interested in the popular image of the city and the common stereotypes of the people living there. Finally, if you are considering the city as a test market, you are likely concerned with such factors as how well your competitors are represented there and how representative the consumers of the city are to those elsewhere.

What you must do, then, in developing a comparison, is to identify features or characteristics the items being compared might or might not share that are relevant to your objectives. The second concern is that you be *complete* in identifying relevant characteristics. Failure to identify relevant characteristics can radically skew your comparison. Here it is important to keep your focus on the purpose of your comparison and determine what features are relevant to being similar or different for your purposes. If you are comparing two cities with respect to how economical it is to live there, then some of the factors you will not want to overlook are the cost of transportation, the cost of housing, and the cost of food. A further factor in considering the features or characteristics on which you are going to compare items is whether the items you identify *overlap* each other. You should strive to minimize features that are subfeatures of another feature you have already identified. For example, if you are comparing cities in terms of cost of transportation, you should not list as a separate factor the cost of a bus ticket. It may be important for you to consider bus transportation independently of other modes of transportation, but then you should also consider the other pertinent modes of transportation separately.

The concern for lack of overlap interacts with another concern: How much should you *lump* characteristics together, and how much should you *split* them into different categories? We could lump all modes of transportation together, or split the criterion by kinds of transportation. There is no one answer to this question that applies to all comparisons. It will depend on your purposes how finely or coarsely you will need to identify features or characteristics for comparison. But you should strive to use the same *grain* of features for all the characteristics on which you make your comparison. If you are going to split transportation costs into costs for different modes of transportation, then you will probably want to do the same for other costs such as costs of food. Otherwise you run the risk of making two items seem far more similar to each other than they are. Insofar as you focus on how they are alike in the myriad of fine-grained features on one dimension and downplay the differences on other dimensions, your comparison may be misleading.

ANALOGIES

There are many reasons why you might be interested in comparing items. For example, you might be interested in comparing items so as to evaluate them (e.g., which would be the better city for me to move to?). We discussed this sort of comparison in chapter 6. Our concern now is with comparison between items so as to draw analogies between them. An analogy tries to establish that one item will show a particular feature because other items, which are similar to it, show that feature. The following scenarios exhibit this form of reasoning:

> Laura's car develops a strange noise in the engine. Her friend Maria asks her what kind of car she owns. It turns out they both own the same kind of car, even the same model, but Maria's is 3 years older than Laura's. Maria recalls that hers developed the same kind of noise at about the same mileage as Laura's, and she had to replace the rod bearings, at some expense. As a result of their conversation, Laura concludes that her problem is probably with the rod bearings.

> Kate, a college sophomore, wonders whether to take English literature or Introductory Ethics as a humanities elective next year. Tom suggests the English course, because he enjoyed it when he took it, and made an "A" in it. Carlos recommends the philosophy course, because he enjoyed it when he took it at another university, although he only made a "B" in it. Regarding her tastes as more like Carlos' than Tom's, Kate decides to take the philosophy course.

Anabelle notices some mealy bugs on the beans in her vegetable garden. She has part of a can of Sevin dust left over from when she dusted the roses in her flower garden. The Sevin seemed to eliminate the Japanese beetle problem there, so she concludes that it will probably work on the mealy bugs, and uses it.

The general plot of each scenario is this: A person faces a situation in which a question (Laura, in the first scenario), a decision (Kate, in the second), or an action (Anabelle, in the third) presents itself. The person who wants to find the answer, make the decision, or take an action looks to past experience—either someone else's, or (as in the case of Anabelle) her own—as a guide to what to do. Because the past situation seems fairly similar to her present one, she concludes that the outcome of her present situation will be similar to the outcome of that past situation. It is this element of similarity—similarity of situations and of their outcomes—that makes these cases logically interesting. Because the situations and outcomes are similar, or analogous, to one another, we refer to arguments based on analogous situations as *arguments from analogy*.

Using the language that we have already developed to describe comparisons and contrasts, we can describe the basic logical structure of any argument from analogy in the following way: One or more items are claimed to be similar to an item in question with respect to certain characteristics. The first set of items are claimed to have a further characteristic, which the item in question is not known to possess. Because all of the other items possess this one characteristic, it is inferred that the item in question will possess the characteristic that it was not known to possess. A useful way of representing the information that goes into an analogy is to develop a matrix (Table 13.1). In Table 13.1 we identify the features or characteristics on which we are comparing the items on the left, and the items to be compared across the top. We then determine whether the items being compared are alike or different in each of the features under consideration. The item we are interested in is shown in the right-most column, and the feature or characteristic of interest is shown on the bottom row.

Notice that in this general matrix form, all of the items being compared to Item X possess Characteristic N. Because it is this characteristic that is in question in

TABLE 13.1
General Matrix for Analogy

Purpose: To Determine Whether Item X Has Characteristic N	Item A	Item B	Item C	Item D	Item X
Characteristic 1	possesses	possesses	possesses	possesses	possesses
Characteristic 2	possesses	possesses	possesses	possesses	possesses
Characteristic 3	lacks	lacks	lacks	lacks	lacks
Characteristic 4	possesses	possesses	possesses	possesses	possesses
Characteristic N	possesses	possesses	possesses	possesses	?

TABLE 13.2
Matrix for Analogy—Cars

Purpose: To Determine Whether the Rod Bearing In Laura's Car Needs Repair	Maria's Car	Laura's Car
Kind of car	Chevette	Chevette
Mileage when noise began	61,000	60,000
Age of car when problem began	6 years	3 years
Kind of noise	low-pitched throbbing sound	low-pitched throbbing sound
Problem with car	Rod bearings needed replacing	?

the case of item X, we fill in the blank at that point with a question mark. The strength of the analogy depends very much on all the items other than X having Characteristic N. If we find, when we compare the items, that one of them does not possess Characteristic N, we need to note that fact, because it will have to be included elsewhere. Notice also that the purpose of the analogy is stated in the upper left corner of the matrix. The purpose of all arguments from analogy will always have the same format: To determine whether the item in question has the characteristic in question.

Two factors are crucial for making an argument from analogy. First, the set of characteristics considered and listed in the left-hand column must be as complete a list as possible of the features that are relevant to the question of whether the item of interest is likely to have Characteristic N. Second, the items being compared must be comparable in terms of whether or not they possess these characteristics. In the previous example, Items A, B, C, D, and X were presented as being exactly comparable with respect to Characteristics 1–4. However, such a perfect match may not always occur. What is critical is that there be a basic similarity between X and those items known to have N.

To see the matrix at work, let us apply it to the first example of an analogical argument we looked at in this section. Regarding Laura's and Maria's cars as the relevant items, and the problem behind the noise as the characteristic in question, we can see that the basic argument can be displayed (Table 13.2).

In the left-hand column of Table 13.2 we have identified all of the factors mentioned in the original example. The matrix makes it clear that the two cars are similar in a number of respects, although there is a significant difference between them: Maria's car was 3 years older than Laura's. We have listed a question mark by *Problem with car* for Laura's car. Now the question arises: Are we justified in inferring from the similarities between Maria's and Laura's car that the problem with Laura's car is that the rod bearings in her car need replacing?

To help us in addressing this question, let us begin by noting what structure an argument for this conclusion would have. What is most reasonable is to construct a modus ponens argument in which the similarities and differences between Maria's and Laura's cars are identified in the antecedent, and the consequent claims that they will be alike in terms of the problem:

> If Laura's car is like Maria's in being a Chevette, having approximately 60,000 miles, and having developed a low-pitched throbbing sound and the problem with Maria's car was that her rod bearings needed replacing, then the cause of the problem with Laura's car is that her rod bearings need replacing.
> Laura's car is like Maria's in being a Chevette.
> Laura's car is like Maria's in having approximately 60,000 miles.
> Laura's car is like Maria's in having developed a low-pitched throbbing sound.
> <u>The problem with Maria's car was that her rod bearings needed replacing.</u>
> ∴ The cause of the problem with Laura's car is that her rod bearings need replacing.

As it stands, there are at least two serious problems with this argument. First, our matrix revealed a difference between the two cars: Their age at the time the noise developed. This could be relevant, so we need to take note of it. If we do not think this difference will undercut our conclusion, then we need to accommodate the difference through the use of an *even if* clause in the first premise. Second, no matter how many relevant similarities we identify between two items, we can never establish that the two are certain to be alike in the additional characteristic on which we are focusing. Hence, we must qualify our conclusion. Thus, we should amend the argument as follows:

> If Laura's car is like Maria's in being a Chevette, having approximately 60,000 miles, and having developed a low-pitched throbbing sound and the problem with Maria's car was that her rod bearings needed replacing, then even if Laura's car is 3 years older than Maria's was, it is likely that the cause of the problem with Laura's car is that her rod bearings need replacing.
> Laura's car is like Maria's in being a Chevette.
> Laura's car is like Maria's in having approximately 60,000 miles.
> Laura's car is like Maria's in having developed a low-pitched throbbing sound.
> <u>The problem with Maria's car was that her rod bearings needed replacing.</u>
> ∴ It is likely that the cause of the problem with Laura's car is that her rod bearings need replacing.

The previous argument exhibits the form arguments from analogy will typically take. Because the form is certainly valid, the question in evaluating this form is whether the premises are true. The premise of greatest concern is the conditional premise (we call it the *analogical premise*). What we must ask is whether the similarities (and differences) listed are such that if they exist, then the items are likely to be similar in the additional respect. Because the word *likely* allows for gradations in degree, what we need to ask is how likely is it that, as a result of their demonstrated similarities, the items will be alike in the new respect? The following items are factors that affect the truth of this premise:

Elements of a Strong Analogy

Large number of items being compared
Large number of comparison characteristics
Comparison characteristics highly relevant
Small number of items showing contrasts
Small number of characteristics on which there are contrasts
Contrast characteristics not highly relevant

Let us examine each of these requirements in turn. It is easy to see why a large number of comparison items will strengthen an analogy. Suppose that Laura, in our original example, had been told by Pete, Janice, and Phyllis that they all had Chevettes with the same problem. The more items that possess the characteristics, the larger the *base* on which the inference is being made. In general, all other things being equal, a larger number of comparison items will make the analogical premise more likely to be true, and hence strengthen the analogical argument.

Similarly, the more characteristics each of the items share with the item in question, the more likely it will be that the analogical premise is true, and the stronger the analogy will be. That is, if in addition to having almost the same number of miles as Laura's car, Maria's, Pete's, Janice's, and Phyllis' also have used the same oil, and have had the oil changed just as often as Laura's car, these factors will strengthen the analogy.

In addition to a large *number* of comparison items and characteristics, however, a strong analogy will also have highly *relevant* characteristics on which a comparison is being made. Because the goal is to show that the item under consideration will be alike with respect to a particular characteristic, large numbers of similar characteristics mean nothing if the characteristics are not relevant to that item. If everyone's car happened to be blue, for example, adding that characteristic would not strengthen the analogy, because it is not (presumably) relevant to the sound that Laura's car is making. On the other hand, having had the oil changed just as often may very well relate to engine noise. If included, it will strengthen the analogical premise, and hence the analogy.

Whether, and to what extent, a characteristic is relevant to an analogy, is often a judgment that requires background information. When such information is lacking, it is hard to tell whether to include a characteristic. For example, suppose we find that Laura's car, as well as everyone else's, happened to be produced on a Monday. Is that relevant to the analogy, and does it strengthen the conclusion that Laura's car has bad rod bearings? Well, it *could* be that the manufacturer got its rod bearings from supplier A on Mondays, and from different suppliers on the other days of the week. If supplier A, but not the others, was producing defective products, the car's having been produced on Monday would make a difference in the problems it had.

A special additional rule in assessing the strength of analogies needs to be noted. When one doesn't know the nature of a characteristic of the item in question, then one needs as much diversity as possible in that characteristic of the items being compared to it. For example, the kind of car Laura owns is highly relevant to the nature of the noise she hears it making. But if we don't know the kind of car she owns, then the other cars we would want to compare to it should be diverse (i.e., they should include Chevrolets, Fords, etc.). Of course if we know that Laura's car is a Chevette, then comparing Chevrolets, Fords, and other kinds of cars to it will be weaker than comparing just Chevettes.

We have spoken so far of the similarities between the items being compared in an analogical argument. Any two or more items being compared will also have some differences, however, so we must identify them and determine how they affect the truth of the analogical premise. In order for that premise to remain plausible, both the items and characteristics must exhibit only a small number of highly relevant contrasts. If in Laura's case, for example, it emerged that in addition to Maria, Laura knew several other people who had Chevettes that developed a similar noise, but the problem turned out not to be rod bearings, then the analogical premise will be less likely to be true. Similarly, even if they all had rod bearing problems, if Maria's car and the other cars all had automatic transmissions, whereas Laura's did not, then that contrast would weaken the analogy.

Table 13.3 is a complete analogical matrix illustrating these points. It permits a fairly strong analogy. On the basis of it, one could conclude that Fred is quite likely to enjoy rafting the Ocoee River.

TABLE 13.3
Matrix for Analogy — Fred's Rafting

Purpose: To Determine Whether Fred Will Enjoy the Ocoee	Allen	Barbara	Carol	Daniel	Edith	Fred
Knows how to swim	yes	yes	yes	yes	yes	yes
Enjoys mountain scenery	yes	yes	yes	yes	yes	yes
Enjoys outdoor activities	yes	yes	yes	yes	yes	yes
Enjoys exciting activities	yes	yes	yes	yes	yes	yes
Minds getting cold or wet	no	no	no	no	no	no
Is overly fussy about his or her appearance	no	no	no	no	no	no
Is physically active	yes	yes	yes	yes	yes	yes
Enjoys rafting the Nantahala	yes	yes	yes	yes	yes	yes
Minds a 6-hr round trip drive	no	yes	no	yes	no	no
Has paddled a canoe before	often	never	expert	never	never	once
Enjoys rafting the Ocoee	yes	yes	yes	yes	yes	?

Consider what the argument will look like:

> If Fred is like Allen, Barbara, Carol, Daniel, and Edith in knowing how to swim, enjoying mountain scenery, outdoor activities, and exciting activities, not minding getting cold or wet and not being overly fussy about appearance, being physically active, and enjoying rafting the Nantahala, and Allen, Barbara, Carol, Daniel and Edith all enjoy rafting the Ocoee, then, even if there are some differences between Fred and the others in terms of whether they mind a 6-hr round trip and how expert they are with canoes, it is very likely that Fred will enjoy rafting the Ocoee.
> All know how to swim.
> All enjoy mountain scenery.
> All enjoy outdoor activities.
> All enjoy exciting activities.
> None mind getting cold or wet.
> None are overly fussy about appearance.
> All are physically active.
> All enjoy rafting the Nantahala.
> <u>Allen, Barbara Carol, Daniel, and Edith all enjoy rafting the Ocoee.</u>
> ∴ It is very likely that Fred will enjoy rafting the Ocoee.

To see that this argument is a good one, consider the first premise. The truth of this premise depends on the factors we noted earlier. First, Fred is being compared to a relatively large number of other individuals. Of course if there were others who were like these individuals in all of these traits but who did not like rafting the Ocoee, they would have to be noted. But presumably none were identified. The individuals are also being compared on a significant number of characteristics, all of which are clearly relevant to whether a person will like rafting on a particular mountain river. Third, there are some differences, but it is plausible to claim that they are not relevant. To support the claim that they are not relevant, you would need to develop a supporting argument in which you would show that the differences with respect to minding a long trip don't matter because Fred himself doesn't mind and the differences with respect to experience in canoes don't matter because even those with less experience have still liked rafting the Ocoee. Thus, the first premise is a strong one, and thus this analogy is strong.

Table 13.4, however, would not support a strong analogy. In this case, Harry is only being compared to one other person, and they are similar only on two characteristics that are relevant to the question of whether they would enjoy rafting the Ocoee. On the other hand, there are significant differences between Harry and George, and these are all highly relevant to the question of whether a person is likely to enjoy rafting the Ocoee. Table 13.4 would not support even a very weak claim that Harry would enjoy the Ocoee.

The matrices that we have learned how to construct in this section provide a beginning for a written argument from analogy. When we need to construct our own arguments from analogy, constructing matrices for them can serve two

TABLE 13.4
Matrix for Analogy — Harry's Rafting

Purpose: To Determine Whether Harry Will Enjoy Rafting the Ocoee	George	Harry
Knows how to swim	yes	yes
Enjoys mountain scenery	yes	yes
Enjoys outdoor activities	yes	no
Enjoys exciting activities	yes	no
Minds getting cold and wet	no	yes
Enjoys rafting the Ocoee	yes	?

purposes. First, they will help to ensure that the analogies we construct are as strong as possible. They will force us to see the purpose of the analogy, and what its items and characteristics are. Often they will also help us to think of comparisons to add among characteristics. Second, when we need to argue for the analogy in prose, they will provide a guide for our written argument. As we did in some of the previous examples, you can use the matrix to construct the main modus ponens argument through which you will present the analogy. After you have constructed this argument, you will need to proceed as we did with earlier demonstration arguments: Examine each premise and determine whether it needs a supporting argument. If it does, develop that argument and build a logical diagram to show the relation of the supporting argument to the main argument.

Sometimes it will even be helpful to include your matrix in your written argument. If you do so, you will have to explain to your reader how to interpret the matrix. But that may be worth it, because the matrix will provide a powerful organizing device. Writing out the argument becomes simply the task of "talking the reader through" the matrix—showing why each of the points of similarity is relevant, showing that the items really are similar on each of these characteristics, and so on.

CRITIQUING ANALOGIES

In addition to the fallacies discussed in chapter 8, there are a number of fallacies that are peculiar to analogical arguments. Most of these can be detected by developing a matrix for the analogy. Then you will be able to note whether in the analogy you are considering, say, too few items were compared, or too few characteristics were used, or the characteristics that were compared were not really relevant to the argument. What you cannot directly see, however, is the *absence* of relevant contrasts. As good critics, we will need to develop these ourselves. Very few people, in using an argument from analogy, ever stress the large number of contrasts that would weaken their argument. It is therefore our job to do this—to imagine relevant characteristics not considered by the person originally offering the argument, but that when taken into account weaken the argument.

We briefly discuss three fallacies that occur rather often with analogies and for which you should be on the lookout. The first of these is the *fallacy of asserted analogy*. This involves arguing that one item will share a property possessed by another when no characteristics are offered to support the claim that the two items are similar. Someone might argue, for example, "Charging students tuition in public colleges is as objectionable as charging people for withdrawing books from a public library." It is clear that what are being compared are public libraries and public colleges, and the claim is that insofar as they are similar, it is objectionable to charge for public colleges because we do not charge for public libraries. But the claim that public colleges and public libraries are similar has not been made by showing any characteristics they share. No doubt you can think of some. For example, both are supported by the government. The problem, however, is that you can equally easily think of relevant differences. For example, although books do decay with use, they can be checked out over and over again many times without having to be replaced. On the other hand, once a course has been taken by a student, the commodity is expended. For another student to take a course, a new course must be taught. It is the responsibility of the author of the analogy to show that the items being compared do show relevant similarities, and in the case of asserted analogies, this responsibility has not been discharged.

Sometimes an author will advance similarities, but they bear no relevance to the characteristic that the analogy is trying to establish. This is the *fallacy of irrelevant analogy*. If, for example, one were to compare two brands of television sets in terms of their features, showing that both had remote control, cable hook-ups, and so on, and then argued that therefore they are likely to produce the same quality picture, one would commit the fallacy of irrelevant analogy. In general, it is the duty of the person making the analogy to show the relevance of the characteristics on which items are being compared. Failure to do so runs the risk that the reader won't appreciate the relevance, and will suspect an irrelevant analogy.

Finally, in presenting an analogy one may identify similar characteristics and they may be relevant characteristics, but one may still commit the *fallacy of weak analogy*. This happens when there are insufficient characteristics in common, or when there are overriding differences. One might argue, for example, that because we paid for rights to the Panama Canal, just as we paid for rights to Texas and Alaska, we should never have surrendered the Canal. But this overlooks a fundamental difference: Our payments for Texas and for Alaska were purchases, whereas our payment for the Panama Canal was for a lease. With leased property, one only acquires rights to the property for a specified period of time. This difference overrides the cited similarity between the Panama Canal and Texas and Alaska, thus rendering this a weak analogy.

EXAMPLE OF ARGUMENT FROM ANALOGY

Arguments from analogy are very common. One of the best-known examples of such an argument is the argument for the existence of God known as the argument from design. The strategy is to compare the world to other objects exhibiting complex order, and then to point out that these objects all have designers and would not have simply appeared by chance. The conclusion then is that the world too must have a designer. One rendition of this argument is found in the writings of the Scottish philosopher David Hume:

> Look around the world. Contemplate the whole and every part of it. You will find it to be nothing but one great machine, subdivided into an infinite number of lesser machines, which again admit of subdivisions to a degree beyond what human senses can trace and explain. All these various machines, and even their most minute parts, are adjusted to each other with an accuracy, which ravishes into admiration all men who have ever contemplated them. The curious adapting of means to ends, throughout all nature, resembles exactly, though it much exceeds, the productions of human contrivance, human design, human thought, wisdom, intelligence. Since therefore the effects resemble each other, we are led to infer, by all the rules of analogy, that the causes also resemble; that the author of nature is somewhat similar to the mind of man; though possessed of much larger faculties, proportioned to the grandeur of the work, which he has executed. By this argument *a posteriori* and by this argument alone, we do prove at once the existence of a Deity, and his similarity to human mind and intelligence. (Hume, *Dialogues Concerning Natural Religion*, Part II)

One of the important points to remember in dealing with arguments from analogy is that the conclusion of such arguments can never be more than that the result is probable or likely. Moreover, one must make sure that the comparison really does support the conclusion one wants to defend. Otherwise, the analogy can be taken over for the opposite purpose. This is what Hume in fact did in his attempt to defend skepticism about religion. Among his strategies for drawing different conclusions from the analogy was to focus on the imperfections and miseries in the world and then raise the question of whether the responsibility for these rests also with the designer:

> This is not, by any means, what we expect from infinite power, infinite wisdom, and infinite goodness. Why is there any misery at all in the world? Not by chance surely. From some cause then. Is it from the intention of the Deity? But he is perfectly benevolent. Is it contrary to his intention? But he is almighty. Nothing can shake the solidity of this reasoning, so short, so clear, so decisive. . . (*Dialogues*, Part X)

A further strategy was to ask us to attend more carefully to the way in which human designers develop their designs. This leads, in Hume's hands, to a very sacrilegious conception of deity.

> If we survey a ship, what an exalted idea must we form of the ingenuity of the carpenter, who framed so complicated, useful, and beautiful a machine? And what surprise must we entertain, when we find him a stupid mechanic, who imitated others, and copied an art, which, through a long succession of ages, after multiplied trials, mistakes, corrections, deliberations, and controversies, had been gradually improving? Many worlds might have been botched and bungled, throughout an eternity, ere

this system was struck out: Much labour lost: Many fruitless trials made: And a slow, but continued improvement carried on during infinite ages in the art of world-making.

A great number of men join in building a house or ship, in rearing a city, in framing a commonwealth: Why not several Deities combine in contriving and framing a world? This is only so much greater similarity to human affairs. By sharing the work among several, we may so much farther limit the attributes of each, and get rid of that extensive power and knowledge, which must be supposed in one Deity. . .And if such foolish, such vicious creatures as man can yet often unite in framing and executing one plan; how much more those Deities or Dæmons, whom we may suppose several degrees more perfect?. . .

[A person who adopts the analogy] is able, perhaps to assert, or conjecture, that the universe, sometime, arose from something like design: But beyond that position he cannot ascertain one single circumstance, and is left afterwards to fix every point of his theology, by the utmost license of fancy and hypothesis. This world, for aught he knows, is very faulty and imperfect, compared to a superior standard; and it was only the first rude essay of some infant Deity, who afterwards abandoned it, ashamed of his lame performance; it is the work only of some dependent, inferior Deity; and is the object of derision to his superiors; it is the production of old age and dotage in some superannuated Deity; and ever since his death, has run on at adventures, from the first impulse and active force, which it received from him. (*Dialogues*, Part X)

As this example suggests, arguments from analogy are both very useful and quite risky. You need to be very careful to have developed sufficient relevant similarities in putting forward your analogy, and to have considered any potential differences that might undercut the analogy. Recognizing these liabilities, however, we should still recognize the usefulness of analogical arguments. They are one of our most useful tools for discovering new phenomena.

Subject Index